Dual Disorders
Essentials for Assessment and Treatment

THE HAWORTH PRESS
New, Recent, and Forthcoming Titles
of Related Interest

Pain and Its Relief Without Addiction: Clinical Issues in the Use of Opioids and Other Analgesics by Barry Stimmel

Drug Abuse and Social Policy in America: The War That Must Be Won by Barry Stimmel

Group Psychotherapy with Addicted Populations: An Integration of Twelve-Step and Psychodynamic Theory, Second Edition by Philip J. Flores

Women and Substance Abuse: Gender Transparency edited by Sally J. Stevens and Harry K. Wexler

Addiction Intervention: Strategies to Motivate Treatment-Seeking Behavior edited by Robert K. White and Deborah George Wright

Hidden Addictions: A Pastoral Response to the Abuse of Legal Drugs by Bridget Clare McKeever

Drugs, the Brain, and Behavior: The Pharmacology of Abuse and Dependency by John Brick and Carlton K. Erickson

Social Services in Latino Communities: Research and Strategies edited by Melvin Delgado

The Integration of Pharmacological and Nonpharmacological Treatments in Drug/Alcohol Addictions edited by Norman S. Miller and Barry Stimmel

Chemical Dependency Treatment: Innovative Group Approaches edited by L. Donald McVinney

Dual Disorders
Essentials for Assessment and Treatment

David F. O'Connell, PhD

The Haworth Press
New York • London

The Haworth Press, Inc., 10 Alice Street, Binghamton, NY 13904-1580

Cover design by Monica L. Seifert.

Library of Congress Cataloging-in-Publication Data

O'Connell, David F.
    Dual disorders: essentials for assessment and treatment / David F. O'Connell.
       p.   cm.
    Includes bibliographical references and index.
    ISBN 0-7890-0401-1 (alk. paper).
    1. Dual diagnosis. I. Title
RC564.68.028 1997
616.89–dc21   97-10777
                                                    CIP

CONTENTS

ABOUT THE AUTHOR

David F. O'Connell, PhD, is Clinical Director of Adult and Adolescent Services at the Carow Foundation, one of the nation's leading addictions treatment facilities. A licensed psychologist with seventeen years' experience in psychodiagnostics, psychotherapy, training, college teaching, and consulting, he holds a diplomate with the American Academy of Psychologists Treating Addiction and is listed in the National Register of Health Service Providers in Psychology. Dr. O'Connell is an instructor in the College of Health and Human Development at the Pennsylvania State University and in the Addictions Studies program at Alvernia College in Reading, Pennsylvania. He is a member of the American Psychological Association, the Pennsylvania Psychological Association, and the Berks Area Psychological Society. Dr. O'Connell serves on the editorial board of the *Journal of Adolescent Chemical Dependency*; on the board of the Institute for Science, Technology, and Public Policy; and on the medical staff of three hospitals in Reading, Pennsylvania. He is the author or editor of three books on addictions treatment including *Managing the Dually Diagnosed Patient: Current Issues and Clinical Approaches* (The Haworth Press, Inc., 1990) and *Self-Recovery* (The Haworth Press, Inc., 1994), and has contributed numerous articles to professional journals including *Alcoholism Treatment Quarterly, Journal of Chemical Dependency Treatment,* and *Journal of College Student Personnel* (all published by The Haworth Press, Inc.).

Dr. O'Connell developed and implemented the first on-campus alcohol intervention group at Kutztown University of Pennsylvania and the first peer-counseling group for college students at Alvernia College. He was also the coordinator and developer of the Impaired Physicians Program for the Caron Foundation and a professional trainer for the Health and Education Council in Baltimore, Maryland. Dr. O'Connell has been a consultant to several large addictions treatment organizations including Recovery Centers of America, Addiction Recovery Corporation, and the Caron Foundation and to industry on employee wellness, job stress, and addiction policies and procedures. He has provided training to corporations including Dupont, AT&T, Western Electric, and Gilbert Associates.

Preface

The treatment of patients with coexisting psychiatric and addictive disorders demands a greater understanding of psychiatric conditions, better assessment skills, and more sophisticated psychotherapeutic and clinical management skills than the addictions therapist usually needs. Patients with dual disorders are prone to relapse to both kinds of disorder and generally show atypical and complicated clinical courses in treatment. Yet the impact of a psychiatric disorder on the treatment of the patient's addictive disorder is definite and predictable, as is the addiction's impact on treatment of the psychiatric disorder.

Fortunately, over the past decade, researchers and clinicians have given increased attention to the problem of dual diagnosis. A number of useful texts have emerged to assist addictions therapists with the clinical management of dually diagnosed patients. This book is such an offering. It grew out of my experience as a practitioner and consultant in the addictions field for over eighteen years. Through my daily involvement in case consultations, psychological evaluations, treatment planning sessions, and the clinical supervision of addictions therapists, I confronted a recurring pattern of questions about understanding and managing patients with dual disorders. This book is a formal response to those questions. My intent is to help addictions counselors better comprehend their patients' problems and offer them practical suggestions in the day-to-day clinical management of dually diagnosed patients.

After I was licensed as a psychologist and in the years after graduate school and internships, I found that there was a lot I did not know about treating my patients. I had had excellent supervision in course work and good continuing education. However, there were still many gaps in my knowledge. To fill those gaps, I sought out those rare books that offer specific guidelines and practical tips in the assessment and treatment of psychiatric disorders. I found them invaluable in my professional preparation as a psychologist. My hope is that the present volume will be such a book for others.

Acknowledgments

I wish to thank Eileen Kastura and Barbara Rankin for their assistance in the preparation of the manuscript. I would also like to thank Janet Gray for her editorial work.

A special acknowledgment goes to Barbara Reeve, MD, who gave me valuable input on both the content and structure of this book. Dr. Reeve contributed extensively to the chapters on cognitive disorders and sexual abuse and to the appendix on psychiatric medications. Dr. Reeve's extensive experience as a psychiatrist treating patients with dual disorders, as well as her background as a researcher, were invaluable to me in writing this book.

Chapter 1

Overview

Over the past decade, addictions counselors have increasingly been involved in the treatment of chemically dependent patients who present with one or more coexisting psychiatric disorders, a condition known as *dual diagnosis*, *dual disorders*, or *comorbidity*. The presence of such disorders renders the clinical management and treatment of these patients eventful and often difficult. Clearly, specialized knowledge and skills well beyond the basic treatment approach to primary addictive disorders are vital if an addictions therapist is to successfully manage these cases.

To meet this need, there has been a growing trend in the training of addictions counselors to include courses and workshops on topics such as psychopathology, psychiatric assessment and management, and psychotherapy. A number of publications have emerged as professional resources for treating dual disorders. (See the list of suggested readings in the reference section at the end of the book.) The present book is one such offering. It is intended for the *addictions counselor* responsible for the care of such patients. The information and guidelines contained in it are fundamental to the sound treatment of patients with dual disorders. The guiding assumption of this book is that any addictions therapist, regardless of professional training and experience, can master the basic information and approaches needed to effectively manage the dually diagnosed patient.

Although the concurrence of addiction and psychiatric illness in some patients has been recognized for many years, these individuals have been inadequately served by the traditional healthcare delivery system. Teague, Schwab, and Drake (1990) and Caragonne and Emery (1987) discuss the mental health perspective on dual diagnosis, and Gottheil, McLellan, and Druley (1978); Todd (1980); Woody et al. (1984); and Perkins, Simpson, and Tsuang (1986) give the addictions treatment perspective. Neither perspective provides definitive answers to the clinical dilemmas that arise with dually disordered patients. Furthermore, these two views, with divergent service delivery systems and seemingly contradictory treatment goals, seem actually to have *added* to the plight of individuals with dual diagnoses.

The solution is in joining these two perspectives to create a fresh, new approach. This is not as easy as it may appear. We each come to this work with our own orientations and experiences. The distinction some authors have drawn between the *craft* model and the *scientific-professional* model helps to sketch out the differences in orientation that affect this field. The craft model, referring to the traditional addictions counseling training, relies heavily on personal experience and on-the-job apprentice-style supervision. The scientific-professional model, referring to the training of psychologists and psychiatrists, emphasizes classroom teaching of "facts" (Penick et al., 1990; Kalb and Propper, 1976). Each of these approaches has limitations with regard to dually diagnosed clients, but addictions counselors and other healthcare professionals can serve the needs of this population by joining and struggling together.

This chapter presents a survey of concerns involved in the treatment process with dually disordered patients, as well as suggestions about how to address these concerns.

FIRST STEPS

Learn About the Disorder

How should a counselor proceed when assigned a dually disordered patient? Learning about the psychiatric disorder is the obvious first step, but many clinicians do not take the time to find out about their patient's "other" disease. This book is designed as a first source in the information-gathering process. Other books to consider include the *Diagnostic and Statistical Manual of Mental Disorders* or DSM-IV (APA, 1994) and *Managing the Dually Diag-*

nosed Patient: Current Issues and Clinical Approaches (O'Connell, 1990). (See also suggested readings.)

If a psychiatrist or psychologist is available as a consultant to the program, the counselor is strongly urged to use this consultant fully. Ask questions such as: What should I avoid doing with this patient? How do I discuss the psychiatric disorder with the patient? Is my patient in any physical danger due to the psychiatric disorder? If so, what should I do? Is the patient on medication? If so, what are the side effects, if any? How does the psychiatric disorder affect the addiction and vice versa?

In dealing with consultants, be direct and thorough in your questions. Keep in mind that patients are individuals and vary considerably in how they function. All patients with borderline personality disorder, for example, will exhibit common symptoms. However, from patient to patient there will be many differences in the nature and expression of these symptoms. For this reason, knowing the symptoms of the psychiatric disorder is not enough; learn how the psychiatric disorder specifically manifests itself in your patient.

My experience has been that understanding the psychiatric disorder allays much of the counselors anxiety and confusion. Psychiatric problems are, after all, human problems. For the most part they are not so mysterious. Addictions counselors are understanding and empathic about the problems of the addict. It is not a big step to extend this empathy and understanding to the dually diagnosed addict.

Assess the Patient Carefully

Most dually diagnosed patients come into the addictions counselor's care after a psychiatric or psychological evaluation. They also need a careful, thorough chemical-dependency evaluation. In many cases the psychiatrist or psychologist has not done this evaluation. Just as addictions counselors may not be attentive to the symptoms of psychiatric disorders, mental health professionals are often unaware of the nature of addictive diseases. Many dually diagnosed patients entering chemical-dependency treatment facilities are misdiagnosed. Typically, symptoms of the addictive disorder are mistaken for signs of another psychiatric disorder. Addictions counselors can be of enormous help here. Through a careful chemical-dependency assessment and observation of the patient in treatment, counselors can help correct a misdiagnosis.

Even when the psychiatric diagnosis is accurate, a thorough chemical-dependency evaluation helps the counselor to understand the impact of the psychiatric disorders on the nature and course of the addictive disease, and thus to plan treatment and follow-up.

Learn What to Avoid in Treatment

"What should I avoid with the patient?" is a question counselors frequently ask and is an important one to address. Like physicians, we should take seriously the Hippocratic exhortation to do no harm. One example of common techniques that may be counterindicated for a dually diagnosed patient is the expression of anger. Borderline personality patients typically show extremes in rage that manifest deep, pervasive psychological problems. Techniques to stimulate the expression of anger, while often appropriate for a highly functioning or an emotionally inhibited patient, may create more problems for the borderline patient. Another example involves taking interpersonal risks. Urging a schizoid patient who has deep interpersonal problems to engage in a high-risk encounter in group therapy can so heighten the patient's anxiety that he/she will leave treatment. Further, prompting a schizophrenic addict to discuss his/her hallucinations in group treatment can have a destabilizing effect on the patient and alienate other group members.

As is obvious from this discussion, avoiding interventions that may be appropriate for primary addicts is an important consideration in the treatment of the dually diagnosed patient. Experience shows that, in many cases, it is what the counselor does *not* do in treatment that makes for success. We know that any psychotherapeutic technique has both general and specific effects. Addictions therapy is a very powerful health-promoting treatment that can have a curative impact on the patient's psychiatric disorder as well as the addictive disease. In many cases, all the counselor has to do is to avoid certain high-risk interventions and simply allow the growth-enhancing aspects of therapy to have their effect.

Learn Appropriate Treatment Strategies

There are certain approaches that the addictions counselor *can* use in treatment to promote sobriety in the dual patient. This book discusses a number of these approaches for each psychiatric disorder considered. To become highly effective in dealing with these types of patients, however, the addictions counselor may have to obtain additional training and stretch professionally. Cognitive-behavioral therapy has proven very effective in treating depression, anxiety, and a number of other psychiatric disorders. Many publications are available on this type of therapy and training in its practice is widely offered (see Appendix A). A counselor who pursues such training makes a quantum leap in his/her ability to treat dual patients.

OTHER CONSIDERATIONS

Continuing Care

Like addiction, many psychiatric disorders are life-long, chronic illnesses. Dual patients are generally at a high risk for relapse to active addiction. These patients need continuing care beyond standard aftercare counseling and AA (Alcoholics Anonymouse) or NA (Narcotics Anonymous) involvement. Counselors need to identify mental health professionals and addictions counselors qualified to provide follow-up care for the dual patient and should become thoroughly familiar with appropriate resources in their geographical area.

Role of Medication

Pharmacotherapy, the use of medication to treat psychiatric symptoms, is indicated for many psychiatric disorders. Many in the field of addictions treatment have problems accepting this fact. However, there is substantial clinical and experimental research to validate the effectiveness of psychotropic medications in treating dually diagnosed addicts. It is true that many addicts have been overmedicated or inappropriately medicated by well-meaning but ill-informed physicians and psychiatrists. These cases have led many addictions counselors to condemn the legitimate use of psychoactive medications and to regard psychiatrists with suspicion.

However, the misuse of psychoactive medications is becoming less frequent as psychiatrists learn more about the nature and course of addictions and the use of appropriate medication for the dually diagnosed addict.

My position on medications is that they have a definite place in the total plan of care for the dually diagnosed addict, and with some disorders, are essential. They should be used conservatively and sparingly. Medication should be monitored closely and discontinued as early as accepted clinical guidelines allow. These are good practices for any patient being managed on psychotropic medication, but they are especially important for the addict, since the chance of relapse and its associated problems is very high.

In many psychiatric disorders, such as schizophrenia and bipolar disorder, there is no valid reason to avoid the use of psychotropic medications. Without them, the patient could hardly function, much less benefit from chemical-dependency treatment. In other disorders, such as certain types of depression and some of the personality disorders, the decision to use medication is not clear-cut and depends on many factors, including the quality of psychotherapeutic care available as well as the patient's medical condition, level of functioning, and ability to comply with treatment. Fortunately, great strides are being made both in understanding the neurophysiology of many mental disorders and in the development of effective medications with less serious side effects and lower addictive potential. As these medications become available, the dually diagnosed addict will benefit from their use.

Therapists should become thoroughly familiar with the medications that their patients are receiving. Both the counselor and the client should know what medications are being given, the dosage, the intended benefits, the likely side effects, and what behavioral or dietary restrictions apply. Appendix B discusses psychiatric drugs and their effects, but the best source of information is the prescribing physician.

Psychiatric and Psychological Reports

In many cases, the only information a new therapist will have on a patient is a psychiatric or psychological report from the patient's therapist or previous hospitalization. The psychiatrist or psychologist who consults for the drug treatment program can decipher and explain these often cryptic reports. If possible, the addictions counselor should also contact the psychiatrist or psychologist who performed the evaluation to get a more thorough understanding of the patient's condition.

Counselors often complain about psychiatric and psychological reports. Typical complaints are that the conclusions are too general, that the report is not thorough enough, that it is full of jargon, and that it lacks specific recommendations. If there are several reports on a patient, they often indicate different diagnoses and conflicting opinions about the patient's functioning.

In reading psychiatric or psychological reports, counselors should be aware of the following:

1. Psychologists and psychiatrists often avoid including information that they think may be damaging to the patient. Therefore, some information may be deliberately left out of the report.
2. Reports vary depending on the intended recipient. Routine reports generally do not convey as specific information as reports designed to address particular problems such as suicide potential. A report from one mental health professional to another may contain much more psychiatric or psychological nomenclature than one directed to an employer, spouse, or other nonprofessional.
3. Most psychiatric and psychological reports are cautiously worded. A number of parties, including the courts, the school system, insurance companies, and utilization review committees, may use the report. Therefore, examiners take care to be as objective as possible, often leaving out "softer" data and clinical "hunches."
4. Despite the effort to present findings objectively, the assessment of a patients' ability to function will vary somewhat depending on the reason for evaluation. For example, if the patient is to be hospitalized, the admitting doctor needs to make a strong case that the patients' functioning is impaired. A neuropsychological report for the victim of a car accident may go into great detail on the patient's diminished functioning. Few reports are without bias, and none is completely objective.

There is also much variation in the quality of psychiatric and psychological reports. A good report is clear, jargon is minimal, and recommendations are concrete and useful. However, counselors should keep in mind that the arts of diagnosis, in particular, and patient evaluation, in general, are highly subjective processes. Mental dysfunction is not as readily identified or explained as physical disease. The human mind and personality may be unfathomable; at best, they are difficult to understand. The counselor should be aware of the huge task the psychiatrist or psychologist has in diagnosis and assessment. With such an awareness, the variation among assessments and the sometimes vague nature of reports can perhaps be more readily understood.

The following are areas of information on a patient to which addictions counselors should pay special attention when reviewing a psychiatric or psychological report. Counselors can use this information to maximize the effectiveness of their clinical interventions.

Impulse Control

It is important for the counselor to be aware of the patient's tendency to act on feelings, thoughts, or impulses. This is especially true if the patient has a history of suicide attempts or impulses or a history of aggression. Patients with tenuous control over aggressive impulses toward themselves or others need special care. They are generally inappropriate for traditional inpatient addiction facilities that do not have a psychiatric component. Patients who have fairly good control over aggressive impulses except under extreme stress can be treated in addictions facilities, but clinicians should be aware of their limitations, especially in therapy situations involving confrontation or the release of anger.

Level of Functioning

Many dually diagnosed patients function adequately from day to day but, when faced with extreme stress, decompensate and become symptomatic. They may become depressed, withdrawn, agitated, anxious, hysterical, or even overtly psychotic. The stress of interpersonal encounter and the internal pressure experienced in addictions therapy can lead to regression during treatment.

The counselor should pay close attention to the information in the psychiatric or psychological report on the patient's level of functioning. This includes how well they manage their impulses, emotions, and interpersonal relationships; how effective they are at getting their needs met; how effectively they deal with daily life; and how successful they are at handling stress.

Awareness of the patient's level of functioning in these areas, and particularly of his/her limitations, can guide the clinician in planning therapeutic interventions that avoid decompensation and keep the patient stable. In some cases, the information on level of functioning may indicate adjunctive treatments to assist the patient in developing coping skills such as communication and problem solving.

Affective Expression

Most psychiatric disorders involve some type of disturbance in the patient's emotional life. Depending on the disorder, the patient may show constricted affect (a limited range of feelings), flat affect (a zombie-like emotional expression seen frequently in schizophrenic disorders), or isolated affect (feelings split off from thoughts, seen frequently in very intellectually defended patients). A disturbance in the regulation or control of affect (often seen in manic-depressive illness and cognitive disorders) may be present, as well as a number of other types of disturbance in emotional functioning.

The more familiar the counselor is with the patient's style of emotional expression, the better position he/she is in to make appropriate interventions in the therapeutic process. Traditional chemical dependency treatment focuses heavily on identifying and expressing feeling states and reducing defenses that prohibit their expression. A dual diagnosis, however, often complicates this approach. Some patients are not able to change much in their style of emotional expression, particularly in a short-term inpatient stay. Some patients may respond better to a cognitive approach to treatment which focuses on thoughts rather than emotions.

Personality tests can describe a patient's typical mode of emotional expression and style of interpersonal relating. With this data, counselors can gear their psychotherapeutic interventions in ways that a particular patient can understand and accept. A psychological report that includes projective and personality testing often provides in-depth, detailed information on the patient's emotional expression, conflicts, and defenses, and is a good source of direction in formulating a treatment plan.

Cognitive Functioning

Most addiction programs place considerable emphasis on patient education in such forms as lectures, films, and writing and reading assignments. Therefore it is important that the clinician have a good understanding of the patient's level of intelligence and any intellectual limitations, such as learning disorders, the patient might have. This is especially important for older addicts, in whom severe long-term chemical dependency may have resulted in cognitive limitations. Most psychological reports and many psychiatric reports include a section on the patient's intellectual functioning. In treatment planning for cognitively limited individuals, it is important to avoid overwhelming them with facts and figures, medical information, and the like. Concepts that require a capacity for abstract thinking, such as surrender, spiritual awakening, and psychological defenses, may be beyond their comprehension. Having a clear idea of the patient's cognitive capabilities can help the counselor and the patient avoid unnecessary frustration and can lead to the development of a more effective treatment plan.

Perceptual Functioning

Almost all patients suffering from perceptual disturbances—for example, schizophrenic and schizotypal patients—are receiving antipsychotic medication to control these symptoms when they enter an addictions-treatment program. Even with such medications, however, many patients still experience perceptual disturbances such as delusions, hallucinations, and bizarre physical sensations (discussed more fully in Chapter 5). These disturbances can affect their ability to engage in and profit from addictions treatment.

Counselors should be aware of the nature and frequency of the patient's perceptual disturbances. Such awareness can increase empathy for the patient's plight and guide the clinician's therapeutic interventions in group and individual sessions. Patients suffering from auditory hallucinations, for example, may seem preoccupied, absent-minded, or inattentive. Knowledge of the patient's perceptual functioning gleaned from the psychiatric or psychological report can help the counselor tactfully question the individual and sensitively probe for the possibility of internal distractions.

Reevaluation

In many cases, a patient is admitted to an addictions program with a provisional diagnosis. This means that at the time of the psychiatric or psychological evaluation, the examiner either did not have the appropriate information or did not have enough information to make a more certain assessment. For example, a patient may be provisionally diagnosed as having a cognitive disorder pending the availability of laboratory and neuropsychological test results to corroborate the diagnosis. In such a case, the patient may need to be reevaluated sometime after the original evaluation. The counselor should keep a close watch on provisionally diagnosed patients and should refer them for reevaluation if their clinical picture changes.

Any patient may experience symptoms or run into problems that merit reevaluation by the psychiatrist or psychologist. With the dually disordered patient, any significant change in the patient's functioning should be considered a sign that a new evaluation may be needed.

Discussing the Diagnosis with Patients

The patient has the right to information about his/her psychiatric condition. The counselors sharing pertinent medical and psychological information can enhance the patients compliance with treatment and reduce anxiety and confusion about his/her status. Discussing the diagnosis also helps offset a sense of alienation or "differentness" that the patient may experience in the treatment community, particularly if he/she is receiving psychotropic medication.

I favor a frank, open discussion of the psychiatric disorder in an individual counseling session early in treatment. The counselor should explain the diagnosis and the impact the condition may have on the patient's rehabilitation. The counselor may omit from the discussion any information from the psychiatric or psychological report that he/she feels is inappropriate to share with the patient. Methods for addressing the psychiatric dysfunction can be identified and shared with the patient in individualized treatment planning.

If a psychiatric or psychological consultant is available and the counselor does not feel comfortable discussing psychiatric diagnoses, he/she can refer the patient for an informational counseling session with the mental health professional. This is particularly appropriate if the patient is receiving psychotropic medication and has questions about its effects.

Counselors should maintain an optimistic, concerned tone during the informational session. The message to be conveyed is that even with his/her special treatment needs, the patient can look forward to sobriety if he/she works with a program and attempts to get the most out of treatment. Information on relapse-prevention counseling and aftercare recommendations such as psychotherapy can also be dispensed at this time.

Avoid Undermining Treatment

The treatment of the dually diagnosed patient depends upon mental health and addictions professionals sharing the task of creating a unified approach. Experience has shown that counselors can unwittingly undermine the treatment of the dually diagnosed patient out of distrust of mental health consultants, particularly if the patient is receiving psychotropic medication. Although conditions are rapidly changing, psychotherapy and pharmacotherapy are still bad words in many circles, and some counselors only reluctantly accept the consultant's advice and guidance. As a rule, counselors should separate their personal feelings about medications and psychiatric or psychological treatment from the best interests of the patient. In cases where an addictions counselor has reservations about treatment suggestions from a mental health professional, however, I encourage a direct, frank discussion of feelings and issues between the counselor and the professional. If the counselor feels that a patient is being mismanaged, he/she should air those concerns with supervisors as well as the attending psychiatrist or psychologist.

AA or NA Involvement

As much as any other addict, the dually diagnosed patient needs the benefits of involvement with self-help groups. The author believes that AA, NA, and other self-help groups provide the best method of addictions treatment. The dually diagnosed patient, however, may have difficulty with AA or NA due to internal or interpersonal problems associated with his/her psychiatric disorder. For example, a personality disordered patient may have problems with trust and intimacy and consequently have difficulty opening up in large groups. Anxiety-disordered patients may have great difficulty with groups and shy away from the intensity of twelve-step involvement. I recommend that the addictions counselor sit down with dually diagnosed patients and openly discuss their fears of AA involvement. Accompanying the patient to AA meetings is often helpful if the counselor can do so. A sensitive sponsor can also make the difference between a successful and an unsuccessful engagement with the AA program.

The importance of a positive initial experience with a self-help group for the dually disordered patient cannot be overemphasized. Unfortunately, some AA members alienate a patient who is attending psychotherapy or receiving psychotropic medication. I know of several patients who had such negative experiences in their first AA or NA meeting that they never returned or returned only after a long delay. I recommend that the dually disordered patient attend AA or NA groups that are stable, heterogeneous (have alcoholics and addicts present), and have a reputation for openness and hospitality toward new members (for example, "double trouble" groups).

Preparing patients for their first AA or NA experience can be useful. Explain what they are likely to encounter, predict for them that all members may not be equally understanding of their special problems, and encourage them to seek out those who do seem to understand. Also, as the patient engages with the self-help group, time is well spent in helping him/her put the experience into perspective.

Supervision

Since treating the dually disordered addict requires special sensitivity, the addictions counselor needs to receive close supervision from clinical supervisors and from a psychiatrist or psychologist if one is available. Supervision is important not only for the clinical management of the patient, but also to provide the counselor with emotional support. Dealing with an unfamiliar situation and spending more time with a patient can push the limits of a counselor's skill and raise conflicting feelings about one's own competency. For all of these reasons, the addictions counselor needs to secure additional professional and emotional support when treating dually disordered patients.

Other Considerations

In this era of managed care, with restrictions on services and decreased length of stays in treatment programs, it is more important than ever for addictions counselors to become skilled diagnosticians and therapists. Chemically dependent patients represent a diagnostically diverse, clinically heterogeneous group with significant comorbidity for both psychiatric and physical disorders. With proper training, education, and supervision, addictions therapists can become competent in handling most of the clinical management problems that arise with this population. In many cases, well-trained addictions therapists can skillfully treat the psychiatric disorder and substance-abuse disorder concurrently. To do this, they must acquire formal training and supervision in psychotherapeutic approaches to psychiatric disorders. Competence in the brief therapies is particularly needed, and training in cognitive behavioral therapy in particular provides an invaluable set of skills for the assessment, clinical management, and treatment of dual disorders. Cognitive therapy is relatively easily learned, well researched, and well received by patients, and has proven effective in the treatment of a wide variety of disorders, including depression, eating disorders, anxiety disorders, and personality disorders. It has also emerged as a viable primary treatment for substance dependence (O'Connell and Patterson, 1996). It can be an important adjunct to traditional twelve-step addictions approaches. Moreover, cognitive behavioral therapy demystifies the psychotherapeutic process, recasting the patient's symptoms and problems into manageable, treatable forms. Many of the treatment guidelines offered in this book are informed by cognitive behavioral therapy. (Appendix A discusses the use of this approach in the treatment of depression and suggests several references for learning more about cognitive behavioral therapy.)

The days are apparently over when the addictions therapist was an insular specialist focusing exclusively on the assessment and treatment of addictive disorders. A growing body of knowledge on the neurobiology of mental and addictive disorders, research suggesting shared etiologies and complex interrelationships among many mental and addictive disorders, and more sophisticated models of psychopathology, all indicate the need for clinicians to have a broad, holistic understanding of the nature of addictive diseases. In addition, research on the outcome and efficacy of psychotherapy and addictions treatment points to the need for more refined, specific therapeutic interventions. This need, in turn, demands greater clinical sophistication on the part of the therapist. The financial realities of the current treatment marketplace, with its focus on time-limited treatments and measurable outcomes, reinforce the importance of flexible, adaptable, broadly trained treatment providers. I hope addictions therapists will find this book a useful preparation for meeting the growing challenges of delivering quality addictions treatment.

Chapter 2

Assessment

Psychodiagnosis is a complex process performed by psychiatrists and psychologists. It requires many years of education and experience and relies heavily on finely honed assessment skills. Addictions counselors are not expected to be psychodiagnosticians, but solid preparation in patient assessment can increase their understanding of patients' functioning and help them make appropriate and timely referrals to mental health professionals. Armed with awareness of the signs and symptoms of mental illnesses, the addictions clinician can tailor treatment to the patient's needs and ensure that the patient receives a thorough psychiatric or psychological evaluation when needed. Outpatient counselors especially need to be skilled at identifying patients with dual disorders, because outpatient addictions treatment is the first contact many patients have with a professional counselor and they may have had no previous psychodiagnostic evaluation.

This chapter has three sections, the first of which addresses the elements of the mental status examination and provides questions that addictions counselors can ask themselves when evaluating a patient. The second section discusses some common symptoms, and the third section considers screening tests that can supplement the counselor's subjective evaluation.

THE MENTAL STATUS EXAMINATION

Increasingly, addictions counselors are called on to conduct a mental status examination as a component of patient assessment. Even if the counselor is not responsible for a *formal* mental status examination, having the elements of the exam in mind is useful in organizing an assessment of the patient's functioning and clearly communicating the results to other helping professionals. The following discussion uses some psychiatric terms, but it is more important to be able to describe behaviors accurately than it is to know the jargon. To illustrate, which of the following statements provides more useful information: "She heard voices saying, 'Jump from the Lee Street bridge'" or "The patient experienced auditory command hallucinations leading to suicidal impulses"? Reassessing the patients mental state periodically is important too. As a mental state changes with detoxification and withdrawal, previously masked symptoms may become evident.

Yager (1989) offers a complete discussion in a chapter titled "Clinical Manifestations of Psychiatric Disorders." A brief outline of the relevant areas of psychological functioning follows.

Affect

Affect is the patient's emotional expression. It may remain stable throughout the interview, but more than likely it will change as the patient describes his/her feelings and responds to the counselor's questions.

The following are important to consider:

- Is this patient's affect consistent with his/her thinking? (For example, the patient appears sad and tearful when relating information on the death of a loved one.)
- Does this patient show a broad or a very narrow range of feelings? Does his/her affect change rapidly (lability)?
- Does this patient have difficulty controlling affect? (For example, does he/she exhibit uncontrollable crying, anger, or fear?)
- What quality is there about this patient's affect? Is it flat (no feeling) or blunted (diminished feeling)? Are the patient's emotional responses disproportionate to the questions asked? (For example, the patient gets uncontrollably angry in response to a nonthreatening question.)

Mood

Mood is the dominant feeling the patient presents. Mood is longer lasting and more stable than affect. The relationship between affect and mood is often described by the following analogy: affect is like the weather (changeable) and mood is like the climate (not so changeable). Be aware of these factors:

- What is the patient's mood? Is he/she depressed, anxious, angry, tearful, fearful, aloof, excited, alienated?
- Does this patient have any problem with the control of moods?
- Does he/she have a history of depressed mood? If so, how long does this mood last? Does he/she have a history of excited mood (mania)?
- Is the patient's mood appropriate given the circumstances of his/her life (for example, angry due to having been arrested, depressed about the loss of a job) or does it seem unrelated to his/her situation?

Impulse Life

Impulses are drives such as sexual or aggressive urges. Impulse life involves how the patient controls his/her drives. States of intoxication and other psychiatric symptoms (such as delusions) influence this control; however, impulse life merits separate attention.

- Can this patient control him/herself when angry or is he/she at the mercy of hostile impulses?
- When sexually aroused, can this patient control him/herself and act appropriately?
- Can this patient delay gratification of impulses? (Can he/she save money, engage in education, perform tedious work?)
- Is this patient violent, homicidal, suicidal?
- When threatened, does this patient flee or confront life's problems?
- Does he/she show an understanding of the distinctions among feeling, thought, and action?

Thinking

In many mental disorders the patient shows abnormalities of thinking. These can range from various subtle disorders—such as mild slips of memory early in an organic syndrome or odd speech in schizotypal disorder—to gross disturbances such as those evident in chronic schizophrenia and bipolar disorder. By paying close attention to the patient's thinking and speech, the addictions counselor may detect abnormalities that warrant a full evaluation.

- Does this patient eventually get to the point when responding to a question, or does he/she ramble and lose track of his/her thinking (become circumstantial or tangential)?
- Is it hard to follow the logic of this patient's responses to questions? Is it confusing, totally disconnected, or disjointed?
- Does this patient have problems completing thoughts (blocking)? Are there long silences in the middle of thoughts?
- Does this patient keep saying the same thing over and over in response to different questions (perseveration)?

Content of Thought

It is important to focus on *what* the patient talks about along with *how* the patient thinks. Some questions to ask are:

- Is this patient preoccupied with any particular concern (such as his/her health or other aspects of his/her life)?
- What are the patient's fears? Are they severe? Irrational?
- Does this patient have recurring homicidal or suicidal ideas, or other thoughts of self-harm?
- Does this patient have bizarre thoughts?
- Does this patient show paranoid thinking? (For example, "The CIA is plotting to murder me.")

Perception

Perception is the patient's awareness of his/her environment and internal state. A variety of disorders can lead to a disturbance in the patient's perception; the most serious perceptual disturbances are associated with psychosis. It is important to actively inquire about these symptoms, as the patient may not volunteer such complaints.

- Does the patient report hearing voices, seeing things, or feeling things that the counselor cannot detect or understand?
- Does the patient complain that he/she feels like a stranger to him/herself (depersonalization) or that the environment looks strange or unfamiliar (derealization)?

Intelligence

It is important to have an understanding of the patient's capacity for processing information. Patients who show borderline intelligence or mild mental retardation can have great difficulty in treatment programs, especially those that emphasize education, lectures, and other high-level communication. Ask yourself:

- Can this patient understand my questions?
- Does he/she show common sense?
- Does this patient have enough common everyday knowledge to deal with day-to-day living?
- Does this patient have a good vocabulary? (Vocabulary is the best general measure of intelligence.)
- Is this patient able to see similarities and relationships (abstract thinking)?

Memory

A disturbance in memory may be a sign of a cognitive disorder or may be secondary to other symptoms (such as poor attention span). Determine the following during a conversational interview:

- Can this patient remember such basic information as his/her birthday, social security number, and phone number?
- Does this patient seem excessively forgetful and apologetic about his/her poor memory?
- Can this patient remember prior events of the day (such as what he/she ate for breakfast)?

Consciousness and Orientation

A disturbance in consciousness almost always indicates a cognitive condition such as delirium, dementia, or intoxication. Again, these factors can be assessed during conversation:

- Does the patient know where he/she is and what the time and date are?
- Does the patient look drowsy?
- Is the patient coherent?
- Is the patient alert and aware of his/her surroundings?

Addiction can lead to a variety of symptoms that may mimic serious psychiatric conditions. A systematic and routine assessment of symptoms can help the counselor decide when a psychiatric or psychological consultation is needed. The result can be peace of mind for both the counselor and the patient.

SYMPTOMS AND SITUATIONS

The following situations and symptom groupings occur often enough in the addictions treatment setting to warrant special consideration.

The Potential for Violence

The patient expressing suicidal or other violent thoughts should be assessed by a professional who has the authority to detain the patient if this appears indicated. However, there are some guidelines to help the counselor make thoughtful decisions about the potential for suicidal or other violent acts. Keep in mind that the most experienced authorities acknowledge that it is impossible to predict violence, so if in doubt, err on the side of caution (Kreitman, 1986; Patterson et al., 1983).

Acute Intoxication

An intoxicated individual expressing violent intent should not be dismissed. The state of intoxication impairs judgment and reduces impulse control. The patient should be held in a safe environment until the acute intoxication passes and he/she can be more completely evaluated.

Poor Reality Testing

When an individual is experiencing hallucinations or delusions (regardless of origin), his/her reality testing is limited and consequently impulse control may be impaired.

History of Violence

A prior history of violent actions directed toward self or others has been found to be positively associated with future violence.

Situational Factors

It is important to understand the patient's stressors and supports when deciding how much professional intervention may be needed to provide for safety. Get permission from your patient to talk with family members or others who will be involved in helping to ensure safety.

Medical Emergencies

Delirium is a life-threatening alteration in mental functioning resulting from injury or metabolic insult to the central nervous system. (Delirium is discussed further in Chapter 6.) Due to the potential for irreversible consequences, the ability to identify delirium is absolutely essential in the addictions treatment setting. Benzodiazepine and alcohol withdrawal (delirium tremens) are the most frequently encountered causes of delirium.

Prompt and thorough medical evaluation should be conducted if delirium is suspected. Elevated pulse, blood pressure, and temperature, together with sweating, tremor, and agitation, are the physical signs of severe withdrawal. Confusion or disorientation and especially a *fluctuating* or changing mental status are also indicators of delirium. Perceptual distortions, illusions, or hallucinations (especially visual or tactile) may also be present. Any disorientation or changing mental status, whether or not accompanied by physiologic signs of withdrawal, needs immediate medical assessment (Behnke, 1976).

Isolation or Social Withdrawal

Withdrawal from interpersonal interactions can be a factor in many different illnesses, including delusional disorder, schizophrenia, anxiety disorders, mood disorders, and personality disorders. In many cases, isolation or avoidance may be the first or only observable sign of the psychiatric illness.

If these behaviors are stable and unchanging over time, they may represent personality traits that need to be addressed in the treatment process. If, after becoming engaged in treatment, an individual is observed to become withdrawn, further assessment is needed to determine whether anxiety, depression, or a psychotic process is emerging. Not all behavioral changes during treatment are due to chemical withdrawal or treatment resistance (denial). When behavioral symptoms impede addictions treatment, it is important to discuss this with the patient. The patient's control over the behaviors varies depending on the cause; however, a direct discussion will help the counselor and the patient determine whether further evaluation is needed and develop a strategy for progressing in treatment.

Distortion of Perceptions or Thoughts

Distortions of perception (hallucinations) may involve the auditory, visual, or tactile senses and may occur in numerous conditions, including intoxication, withdrawal, schizophrenia, bipolar illness, and major depression. Visual and tactile hallucinations most often indicate an organic or cognitive condition (for example, the snakes on the wall or the crawling skin in delirium tremens). Auditory hallucinations are often associated with nonorganic psychiatric illnesses. One notable exception is the common experience of hearing one's name called during chemical withdrawal. The best way to find out whether a patient is hallucinating and in what way is to ask the patient. Any report of hallucinations should be referred for complete evaluation.

Disordered thoughts take many forms, including thought insertion, thought withdrawal, and false beliefs or delusions. Again,
when these symptoms occur, they require a complete psychiatric
evaluation. Delusions are quite resistant to logic, and little can be
gained by trying to talk someone out of a delusional belief.

Poor Memory, Limited Attention Span, Poor Concentration

The ability to learn is fundamental to addictions treatment and
recovery. While full cognitive functioning is not essential for successful treatment, a patient's limitations need to be identified early
in treatment if he/she is to effectively learn the concepts and skills
of recovery. If a patient's symptoms seem to impair normal conversation or seem likely to impede the process of addictions treatment, complete evaluation is needed (Tarter and Edwards, 1987).

TESTS AND QUESTIONNAIRES

There are a number of tests, inventories, and questionnaires that
counselors can use to evaluate troublesome symptoms and to help
him/her know when to suspect a psychiatric disorder that needs
further evaluation. Interpretation of these tests is straightforward
and does not require an in-depth knowledge of psychodynamics,
psychopathology, or statistics. If administered early in treatment,
these tests may reflect the effects of toxicity or withdrawal. However, as the time since last drug use increases, the likelihood
decreases that symptoms are due solely to the effects of toxicity or
withdrawal. The counselor may wish to use these scales early in
treatment and repeat them periodically as treatment progresses to
provide an objective record of which symptoms persist and which
resolve with abstinence.

The regular use of these instruments by addictions counselors
can greatly enhance the effectiveness of the assessment process.

Beck Depression Inventory

This is a twenty-one-item multiple-choice self-report inventory
that measures clinical symptoms of depression. The patient is

instructed to complete the test based on his/her feelings at the time of the test administration. The test takes approximately ten minutes to complete. The counselor simply adds up the number of items circled by the patient and arrives at a total score. High scores indicate the presence of depression, and the patient should be referred for further evaluation. The test does not differentiate among the many types of depression (endogenous, reactive, situational) or affective disorders (bipolar, unipolar, dysthymic), but it is quite effective at differentiating depressed from nondepressed patients. This test is available from: Beck Institute, GSB Building, Suite 700, One Belmont Ave., Bala Cynwyd, PA 19004-1610. Information on this test can also be obtained from: The Center for Cognitive Therapy, Room 602, 133 South 36th Street, Philadelphia, Pennsylvania 19104.

Beck Anxiety Inventory

This test is a list of symptoms of anxiety. The patient circles answers that indicate how frequently he/she experiences these symptoms. A score is obtained by adding the frequency scores of all symptoms. High scores indicate the possible presence of an anxiety disorder. The test does not differentiate amongst the many types of anxiety (panic disorder, generalized anxiety disorder, PTSD, phobia), but rather identifies the patient with severe or frequent symptoms of anxiety. This test is a companion to the Beck Depression Inventory and is available through the same source.

Dissociative Experiences Scale (DES)

This is a twenty-eight-question self-administered scale that can be used to screen for dissociative symptoms linked with some anxiety disorders and dissociative disorders. The scale and scoring technique can be found in Bernstein and Putnam (1986). A score of 30 or more indicates a need for further evaluation with an appropriate specialist.

Shippley Institute of Living Scale

This is a brief (twenty-minute) screening test for cognitive damage. It consists of two subtests, Vocabulary and Abstraction. The test is based on the clinical finding that in mild to moderate cognitive disorders, the capacity for abstract thinking declines markedly while vocabulary levels remain relatively intact. Comparing the results of these two subtests yields a ratio or quotient. Low scores (80 and below) indicate strong suspicion of brain damage, but very low scores may be due to low IQ, poor reading, or poor test-taking skills. The test does not differentiate amongst the many types of cognitive disorders. A neuropsychological or neurological examination is required for a specific diagnosis. For addicts and alcoholics suffering from organicity due to substance abuse or other conditions, this test can provide a good initial evaluation and a rationale for referral for more comprehensive evaluation. As discussed in Chapter 6, early detection and treatment of dementia and amnestic disorder are keys to successful treatment. This test is available from: Western Psychological Services, 12031 Wilshire Boulevard, Los Angeles, California 90025. It is reproduced in its entirety in Pollack (1942).

Mini-Mental State (MMS)

Developed by Folstein, Folstein, and McHugh (1975), this test is designed as a quick evaluation of cognitive functioning and has been found to differentiate cognitively impaired from nonimpaired patients. It takes about ten minutes to administer. The test contains items that assess orientation, registration of information, attention, calculation, recall, and some aspects of receptive and expressive language functions. A perfect score is 30. A score of below 20 points most likely indicates cognitive impairment, and patients achieving this score should be referred for a more comprehensive evaluation.

Diagnostic Survey for Eating Disorders (DSED)

This is a multi-item survey that focuses on aspects, signs, and symptoms of anorexia nervosa and bulimia. Divided into twelve sections, it provides information on demographic factors, weight history, body image, dieting, binge eating, purging, exercise, sexual functioning, menstruation, medical and psychiatric history, life

FIGURE 2.1. Mini-Mental State

Patient _____

Examiner _____

Date _____

MINI-MENTAL STATE

Score   Orientation

( )   What is the (year) (season) (month) (date) (day)? (5 points)

( )   Where are we? (state) (county) (town) (hospital) (floor) (5 points)

Registration

( )   Name 3 objects: one second to say each. Then ask the patient
to repeat all three after you have said them.
1 point for each correct. Then repeat them
until he/she learns them. Count trials and record.
_____ (3 points)

Attention and Calculation

( )   Serial seven's. 1 point for each correct. Stop at five answers. *Or* spell
"world" backward. (Number correct equals letters before first
mistake—i.e., d l o r w = two correct). (5 points)

Recall

( )   Ask for the objects above. 1 point for each correct. (3 points)

Language Tests

( )   Name—pencil, watch (2 points)

( )   Repeat— no ifs, ands, or buts (1 point)

( )   Follow a three-stage command: "Take the paper in your right hand,
fold it in half, and put it on the
floor." (3 points)

Score

Read and obey the following:

( )   CLOSE YOUR EYES. (1 point)

( )   Write a sentence spontaneously below. (1 point)

( )   Copy design below. (1 point)

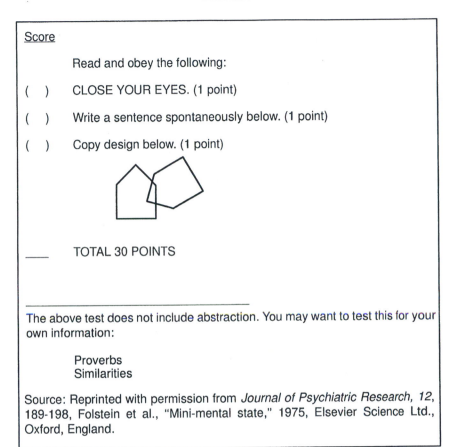

____   TOTAL 30 POINTS

The above test does not include abstraction. You may want to test this for your own information:

Proverbs
Similarities

Source: Reprinted with permission from *Journal of Psychiatric Research, 12,* 189-198, Folstein et al., "Mini-mental state," 1975, Elsevier Science Ltd., Oxford, England.

---

adjustment, and family history. It can be used as a self-report instrument or administered as part of a structured interview. The DSED is not a scaled, standardized instrument; rather, it is designed as a standardized format for collecting important patient information to aid in assessment, treatment, and communication among the treatment team. Craig Johnson, PhD, at the Institute of Psychiatry Eating Disorder Program of Northwestern University Medical School, developed this instrument. It is reproduced in its entirety in Garner and Garfinkel (1985, pp. 34-49).

These tests, consistently applied, can help counselors heighten their awareness of the signs and symptoms of psychiatric disorders and thus improve the quality and appropriateness of care given to the dually disordered patient.

CONCLUSION

When evaluating and treating dually diagnosed patients, a comprehensive mental status assessment is as important as a detailed drug history. In early recovery, all chemically dependent patients are expected to experience some change in mental state. The routine assessment and recording of mental status will facilitate the identification and referral of patients who have psychiatric illness along with their addictions.

Chapter 3

Mood Disorders

Mood (affective) disorders are a class of illnesses characterized chiefly by a disturbance in mood. They are very common psychological illnesses. Over one hundred million people have been stricken with a mood disorder, and about one in ten persons will be diagnosed as having a clinically significant depression at least once in their lifetimes.

Addictions program personnel are frequently faced with trying to sort out symptoms of mood disorders, especially depression, from the symptoms of addiction and withdrawal. This often occurs when a patient insists, for example, "If I wasn't depressed, I wouldn't drink." If a firm diagnosis has not been established, the patient should be evaluated by a psychologist or psychiatrist experienced in dual disorders. However, the counselor and patient should keep in mind that, except in the most severe cases, mood disorders cannot be definitively diagnosed while the patient is still experiencing the effects of substance abuse or withdrawal. Therefore abstinence from alcohol and drugs is the first order of business for the diagnostic and treatment processes.

The mood disorders are classified as *depressive disorders*, including *major depression* and *dysthymic disorder*, and *bipolar disorders*, including *bipolar disorder I and II* and *cyclothymic disorder*. The formal, detailed diagnostic criteria for each of these disorders may be found in DSM-IV (APA, 1994). This chapter addresses the clinical features and treatment issues that are important for the addiction counselor to know.

DEPRESSIVE DISORDERS

Major Depression

The symptoms of depression are often present in alcoholics and addicts when they enter treatment. Mayfield (1985) describes four subgroups of patients who present as acutely depressed alcoholics: (1) the "depressive syndrome of chronic intoxication," which disappears with abstinence; (2) situational depression in response to drinking or drug-related problems, which resolves as the crisis resolves; (3) "characterological depression," a longstanding, persistent depression independent of drinking behavior and usually unresponsive to antidepressant medications; and (4) major depression independent of the drinking and in need of antidepressant medication. Symptoms of depression are also a prominent feature of the "crash" from cocaine dependence and other stimulant abuse. These symptoms resolve spontaneously, usually within two weeks of abstinence.

In recovery, an unidentified or untreated major depression may lead to early relapse. A depression that develops during a period of sobriety can also lead to relapse. It is well documented that depressed alcoholics are more likely than other patients to attempt suicide. The following case example illustrates the complications that untreated depression can add to addictions treatment.

Case A

> One year after first entering treatment for alcoholism, a thirty-five-year-old small business owner was admitted to his third rehab program following a five-day binge and a suicide attempt. He had been able to stay sober for six months following his first rehab program and for three months after his second by attending three to five AA meetings per week and a weekly early recovery group for men. He had not yet been able to ask anyone to be his sponsor because he did not believe anyone would want to be his sponsor. Other symptoms of depression, including low energy, a sense of hopelessness, inability to take in positive feedback, and an intermittent sense of doom, had persisted throughout the year.
>
> Complete addiction, psychiatric, and family histories were taken, and major depression was diagnosed. It was learned that antidepressant medications were recommended following a psychiatric consultation during his previous treatment. The patient refused, convinced that all he needed to do was to work with a "more serious program."

He was started on antidepressant medication and his mood remained somewhat depressed for the first two weeks, but he gradually became able to believe the positive feedback and to feel better about himself. By the time of his discharge, he had been able to get an AA sponsor, his energy had increased, and he experienced a hopefulness he had not previously known.

In this case, untreated depression impeded the patient's recovery efforts and kept him from hearing the message of hope. Appropriate treatment of his depression made it possible for him to follow through with recovery tasks, apply recovery tools, and experience positive results.

Patients with major depression show a number of symptoms indicating disturbances in cognitive, affective, and psychological functioning. Many depressed patients entering chemical-dependency treatment have had previous psychotherapy or hospitalization for their depression. Many if not most of these patients have been treated at some time with an antidepressant medication, and a significant number are taking an antidepressant when they enter chemical dependency treatment. Occasionally the chemical dependency therapist encounters an alcoholic or an addict with an undiagnosed depression who shows a number of the symptoms discussed in this section. Patients receiving antidepressant medication, however, may show few or none of the symptoms discussed below, especially if they have responded well to their medication and to psychotherapeutic intervention.

Depression, like alcoholism, tends to run in families, and a history of familial depression may predispose an individual to develop a depressive illness. Further, based on studies of alcoholism and depression in families, Winokur and Coryell (1991) hypothesize a "depressive spectrum disease" expressed as alcoholism in some individuals and major depression in others.

Major depressive episodes uncomplicated by chemical use generally have a rate of onset of about six to nine weeks. They affect men and women of all ages. Depression is about twice as common in women as it is in men. Most patients seek treatment after enduring depressive symptoms for five or six months. They grow increasingly concerned about their physical and mental health and come to treatment following a severe breakdown in their capacity to cope with day-to-day living. The use of alcohol or drugs can significantly alter this sequence. Many patients with major depression have a history of mild depressive symptoms persisting over a period of a few months to a few years. Others have had a significant period of anxiety preceding their first depressive episode.

Long before the depression becomes evident, many depressed patients show personality characteristics that experts believe render them highly vulnerable to a depressive illness. Some of these characteristics are: (1) lack of energy and drive, (2) insecurity, (3) unassertiveness, (4) strong dependency, (5) introversion, and (6) a tendency to break down under stress. When a depressive episode finally develops, these traits tend to persist and become more pronounced (Paykel, 1982).

Symptoms of Depression

The most common symptoms of depression are depressed or sad mood, loss of interest in living, and anxiety. In severe depression, feelings of guilt and suicidal thoughts accompany depressed mood. The next most commonly reported symptoms are difficulty falling asleep or early morning waking, loss of appetite, and fatigue or a lack of energy. In mild forms of depression, as in beginning stages of a severe depression, the patient may complain of numb feelings or a total loss of the ability to feel. These symptoms can be distressing to the patient but are rarely incapacitating. Many patients can ignore these symptoms while engaged in work, family, and social interaction.

Mood. The sadness or depressed mood reported by clinically depressed patients differs markedly from the everyday experience of sadness or grief and from the sense of loss that often accompanies recovery. Many depressed patients can distinguish their depressive feelings from other feelings of sadness that they have experienced. When depression becomes severe, however, the depressive illness overshadows all emotions, and the patient cannot feel or express subtle states of mood and feeling. Severely depressed patients often describe their depressed moods with distinctive images, such as a "black shroud," "black mist," or "living in a dark cage." Descriptions like these suggest the pervasiveness of the depressed mood.

In the beginning stages of depression, many patients are prone to crying spells, which may occur for no apparent reason. As the depression progresses, the bouts of tears increase. In late stages, however, the patient regularly complains of an inability to cry at all.

Thinking. Many depressed patients show distortion in their judgment of themselves and their environment, evidenced by their tendency to be unnecessarily pessimistic. Internally they feel helpless, ineffectual, and worthless. They tend to hold an irrationally grim view of their life and work. Many become convinced that they have never had anything to contribute to others. They see no hope for the future and do not respond to encouragement. Many depressed patients are so filled with guilt and self-blame that others view them as illogical. As the depressed patient's thinking becomes more gloomy and distorted, he/she begins to withdraw from life. The depressed patient generally shuns interpersonal relationships and becomes increasingly solitary. Hobbies and activities that once interested the patient lose their attraction. The patient comes to view life's struggles as a useless waste of time. These patients tend to drift toward simple, uncomplicated lives and keep work and social involvement to a minimum.

Distinguishing the faulty thinking in depression from the shame, guilt, and isolation of active addiction (Bean-Bayog, 1986) is often impossible. However, it may be unnecessary to make this distinction to provide effective early treatment, as the same therapeutic techniques can be useful regardless of the etiology of the symptoms. If faulty thinking persists well into sobriety, a concurrent depression or other mental disorder should be considered.

The disturbances in cognition characteristic of depression have led a number of researchers and clinicians to focus on faulty thinking in treating these disorders. Cognitive therapies have proven very effective, especially in conjunction with psychotropic medication, in the treatment of depression. (Suggestions for treatment by cognitive techniques are included later in this chapter and in Appendix A.)

Physical Symptoms. Many of the physical symptoms of depression are similar to those of addiction. However, certain patterns exist in depression that can help to distinguish between major depression and the organic depression of addiction. Severely depressed patients show a pronounced physical and mental slowing known as *psychomotor retardation*. These patients move slowly, as if they are carrying a hundred-pound weight on their shoulders, and maintain a drooping or unanimated facial expression. Such patients complain that they feel exhausted all the time and that sleep provides no relief. They also complain of slow thinking, difficulty carrying out decisions, and mental confusion. They may speak in a monotone. They keep conversation with others to a minimum.

Depressed patients often report sleep disturbances. The most common is the inability to fall asleep. Less common is the complaint of early morning awakening, usually in more severe depressions. Patients may also have their sleep interrupted by crying spells and terrible nightmares. Many depressed patients complain of extreme fatigue upon rising in the morning. Depressive symptoms generally are more severe in the morning hours. Appetite may also be disturbed, with either a decrease or increase in food consumption and an accompanying weight loss or gain.

Depressed patients regularly report a disturbance in their sexual drive early in the depressed cycle. The most common complaint is the loss of interest in sexual intercourse. Some men complain of the inability to obtain an erection or the inability to ejaculate.

Some depressed patients report the presence of significant anxiety or agitation. The former is reflected in complaints of tension and inability to relax. The latter is seen as restlessness that can range from excessive pacing to a variety of fidgety behaviors, such as hand-wringing, pulling at one's clothing, or rubbing one's body parts.

A number of depressed patients complain of vague but persistent bodily aches and pains, and many spend much time going to general practitioners for treatment. Many patients become convinced that their depression is really a physical illness. Depressed patients generally show an overconcern with health problems and make frequent physical complaints.

As the foregoing discussion implies, depression is a complex psychobiological illness. Like addiction, it is a disease that affects all spheres of the patient's functioning—cognitive, social, psychological, emotional, and spiritual. The competent clinician will be alert to its symptoms and therefore understanding when working with the depressed addict. When mood symptoms occur concurrently with addiction, withdrawal and early recovery can be especially difficult, as illustrated by the following case.

Case B

At the insistence of her family, a forty-five-year-old homemaker and mother was referred by her family physician for inpatient detoxification and treatment of benzodiazepine dependence. Since the birth of her first child twenty years earlier, countless psychiatrists and other physicians had treated her for a variety of mood and anxiety disorders, including major depression, bipolar disorder, and panic disorder. She had also undergone numerous surgeries for back and abdominal pain. Ten years before this admission, the patient decided to stop drinking because her family convinced her that she had a "drinking problem"; however, she never attended twelve-step meetings or used other recovery supports.

On admission, the patient was slow with rambling speech, disorganized, and at times disoriented (for example, she was unable to locate her room on the hall). A complete physical examination revealed no physical condition other than benzodiazepine dependence that could account for her variety of physical and emotional symptoms, despite her insistence that "there must be something wrong with me." She was placed on a phenobarbital detox regimen to provide a smooth and safe withdrawal from the high doses of benzodiazepine she was consuming. During the four weeks of her detoxification, she showed significant mood lability, including extreme agitation, tearfulness, and isolation, as well as panic symptoms. She developed a severe tremor of her head and neck and was further evaluated neurologically. Throughout this period, she attended addiction program activities, including addiction education, group therapy, and twelve-step meetings. Even though she and many of her doctors had been convinced that she had a severe mental illness or a rare physical disease, through the support of her peers she became motivated to suspend all psychotropic medication until her symptoms could be fully assessed.

Despite her numerous and distressing mood, anxiety, and physical symptoms, the patient was able to find enough hope, encouragement, and acceptance within the recovery program to tolerate these symptoms long enough for a definitive diagnosis to be reached. By the end of her six-week hospitalization, the patient had been totally drug-free for two weeks. Her tremor had resolved, she had self-diagnosed alcohol and benzodiazepine dependence, and had developed coping skills and social supports that enabled her to tolerate residual anxiety and mood symptoms.

The patient continued to experience severe mood swings for many months after being discharged. However, she was able to work at an effective recovery program and to return to work for the first time in many years. Before entering the program, she agreed with her psychiatrist, based on her history, family history, and current symptoms, that she probably had a bipolar illness and could benefit from mood stabilizers. Afterward, however, she was so pleased with her newfound freedom from chemicals that they decided to use medication only if her symptoms became so severe as to interfere significantly with her ability to function.

This case illustrates many of the complexities of assessing and treating mood disorders coexisting with addiction. Most important, it illustrates the need for both the individual in treatment and the treatment team to be patient and open-minded.

Dysthymic Disorder

Dysthymia refers to a type of depression that is less severe but more prolonged than a major depressive illness. It is characterized by depressed mood for most of the day, more days than not, lasting two or more years (APA, 1994). Dysthymic disorder may be punctuated by episodes of major depression, sometimes called "double depression." A number of the symptoms described in the previous section on major depression may be present in dysthymic disorder. Generally, however, these symptoms are not as severe. While low self-esteem may be present, severe self-blame and guilt are absent. The delusional beliefs or hallucinations sometimes found in severe depression are absent in dysthymic disorder, and risk of suicide is lower. Patients with this diagnosis are not usually treated with anti-depressant medications, although they can be useful (Howland, 1991). Some of the cognitive therapy techniques used to treat depression can be quite effective with dysthymic disorder. Many of the tools of recovery from addiction, such as the serenity prayer and daily meditation and affirmations, can also be useful.

Treatment Considerations

Many patients with depression receive psychotherapy or medication from a psychiatrist or psychologist. The addition of treatment for addictions can support and enhance this ongoing treatment. A supportive approach to counseling drawn from interpersonal schools of psychotherapy can be combined with cognitive therapy techniques to tailor addictions counseling to the special needs of the individual with depression.

One of the best choices of counseling approach with a depressed patient is cognitive therapy. This type of therapy has proven very successful in the treatment of addiction as well as depression (Beck et al., 1993). The goal of cognitive therapy is to develop better coping strategies by uncovering dysfunctional, distorted (or nega-tive) thinking and supplanting it with more adaptive, rational think-ing. Appendix A presents a detailed discussion of the characteristics of the thinking of depressed persons and techniques of cognitive intervention.

Medications used to treat depression are beneficial in controlling the most severe, disabling, and life-threatening symptoms. Lack of energy or initiative, poor concentration, psychomotor slowing, and suicidal or delusional thoughts can cause extreme dysfunction in daily living and can impede an individual's efforts to make use of addictions treatment. Medication can ameliorate the severity of these symptoms, making it possible for the individual to carry out his/her obligations and put into practice the teachings of addictions treatment. Patients should be helped to identify their "target symp-toms," those specific symptoms (such as early morning waking, suicidal thoughts, and lack of interest in hobbies) that they and others will monitor to gauge the effectiveness of the medication. Monitoring target symptoms also helps those who question the necessity of the medication to understand that it addresses a specific illness and is not just a "feel better" pill. A fuller discussion of antidepressant medication may be found in Appendix B.

As mentioned above, addictions treatment is a complement to the ongoing treatment of a person with depression. However, the addictions counselor has unique insight into the thinking, emotions, and behaviors of the individual with an addiction. A supportive counseling approach that combines these insights with an understanding of depression can facilitate the cognitive and emotional changes necessary for the depressed addict to overcome depression.

The counselor should be thoroughly familiar with the symptoms of depression. The depressed patient is not merely an addict showing "stinking thinking" and self-pity. Clinical depression is usually more severe than the substance-induced depression many alcoholics and addicts experience. Depression is an illness, and, as with addiction, understanding the illness leads the therapist to a more empathic and helpful approach to the person who suffers from it.

The counselor should be alert to any suicide potential in a depressed client. The risk of suicide in depressed patients is about fifteen percent. The disinhibiting effects of alcohol and other sedative drugs significantly increase this risk in the depressed addict or alcoholic (Fawcett et al., 1987). In patients with a history of suicide attempts, poor impulse control, or expressed suicidal thoughts, the counselor should be alert to signs of suicidal intent. Some patients act on their suicidal thoughts without warning; however, most show signs of intent. The following should alert the counselor to the possibility of suicide: (1) vague references to killing oneself; (2) a new intense interest in death or dying; (3) overt suicidal threats; (4) self-destructive acts such as cutting or burning oneself; (5) any significant change in a patient's mood, especially from a depressed to an overtly calm or accepting mood; and (6) the saving or storing up of antidepressant or other psychoactive medications.

For depressed alcoholics, suicidal thoughts may occasionally arise during inpatient addiction treatment. A patient suspected of suicidal intent should be placed under observation. If the counselor anticipates suicidal behavior, he/she should approach the patient, share his/her concern, and implement a suicide precaution plan. All patients with any disorder involving significant depression should be monitored for suicidal risk. Most inpatient addictions-treatment agencies have a suicide precaution plan that can be set in motion as needed. The plan that appears in Table 3.1, and is suggested by Cull and Gill (1982), is highly recommended.

TABLE 3.1

LEVEL OF ASSESSED RISK	LEVEL AND TYPE OF INTERVENTION
Severe	Extreme suicide precautions. Immediate inpatient hospitalization and one-to-one monitoring at all times. Psychotropic medication is likely.
Moderate	Serious but not extreme suicide potential. General suicide precautions—either hospitalization for further observation or maintenance on an outpatient basis with increased availability of environmental supports. Psychotropic medication likely.
Mild	Some suicide potential, although may be generalized without specific suicide ideation. Use clinical interviews to determine appropriate level of intervention. Possible interventions include maintenance in outpatient therapy. Increase availability in working with significant others to help them identify clinical signs of increased suicide risk. Psychotropic medication is possible but not likely.
Subclinical	Normal or subclinical range of assessed suicidal risk. Routine monitoring and supportive interventions. Reassess if clinical indicators suggest that the patient was underreporting suicidal ideation or intent.

These guidelines are offered as a general plan. Every patient should be individually assessed for suicide potential and an individualized treatment plan should be implemented. Any patient presumed to be a serious suicide risk should be transferred to a psychiatric facility and monitored closely on a one-to-one basis.

Need for Structure

Depressed alcoholics and addicts require a strong, structured approach to treatment even more than their nondepressed counterparts do. The daily treatment regimen should include much physical activity, regular nutritious meals, and regular support and encouragement from therapists and significant others. It is important to "keep it simple" for depressed patients, and a regular, predictable, sequential program of recovery can impart a sense of simplicity and order.

Need for Organization

Depressed patients' lives are often in disarray, and due to their illness, they may approach treatment and other activities in a haphazard fashion. They need help in sorting out their internal emotional lives, interpersonal relationships, and day-to-day living, as well as their approach to recovery. The counselor should assist the patient in setting treatment priorities, dealing initially with symptoms, conditions, and behaviors that are life-threatening and progressing toward developing attitudes and skills that will support long-term recovery and emotional growth. Depressed addicts need assistance in integrating various treatment approaches, which could include psychotherapy, pharmacotherapy, addictions treatment, twelve-step groups, and diet and exercise routines. They need to see the reason for and predicted benefits of involvement in each of these approaches, and they need help in tracking their responses to treatment for both the addiction and the depression.

Need to Address Losses

Depressed addicts and alcoholics often become excessively invested in relationships, dreams of success, or past achievements.

A particular relationship or fantasized goal can become so dominant that if it is threatened or lost, the patient experiences a downward spiral. To get well, the patient needs to find new meaning in life, more realistic goals, and perhaps new relationships. In short, the patient needs a new beginning.

Therapists should work with patients to ensure that they do not become overreliant on any one person, situation, or goal. Interest in a variety of activities and objectives should be encouraged. Therapists should also help patients to become more accepting of themselves and to work through the grief and loss of, for example, a former level of status or a happier, more productive time in their lives. They need to set aside "used to bes, could have beens, and what ifs." All of this can be bewildering for patients, but they should realize that confusion precedes clarity and that the outcome can be a new perspective on their lives.

Addictions therapy can assist the depressed patient in renewing his/her life socially, emotionally, and spiritually. The following case provides an example.

Case C

A fifty-eight-year-old executive with major depression and alcoholism completed three weeks of inpatient treatment and six months of outpatient therapy. He was placed on antidepressants but showed only a partial response. He complained of feeling listless, unhappy, and confused about the direction of his life. He was preoccupied with the idea that he was "washed up" because he had not been promoted to vice president in his company, and he reported being jealous of younger executives who were passing him by. His wife had left him during his active alcoholism, and the thought of involvement with another woman was alien to him.

His counselor employed a cognitive and supportive therapeutic approach. An hour-by-hour daily schedule of activities was developed, which included regular exercise, daily reading of contemplative recovery literature, twelve-step group involvement four times a week, and intensive outpatient therapy. The patient was advised to establish a daily meditation program and did so. He was also encouraged to take the focus off himself through a charitable activity. He became actively involved in establishing a shelter for the homeless in his community. During the therapy hour, the counselor employed a cognitive approach to help him work through his fears and form a less catastrophic view of his life situation. This new perspective expanded, and he was able to embrace the benefits of middle age, such as the development of wisdom and a lifetime of rich experiences. He was assisted with mourning the losses of his youth and dreams that probably would not come true, and was able to see that the fulfillment of such dreams was not necessary to his happiness. In addition, his fears of taking the risks of romantic involvement were systematically processed and challenged. He joined a local dating service for professionals and met a woman for whom he developed deep feelings. He reported a greater sense of meaning and spirituality from his meditation program and found his charitable work immensely satisfying. For the first time in a decade, he felt hopeful about the future. He continued his antidepressant medication, and a number of his depressive symptoms remitted entirely.

In this case, the patient was able to make use of the addictions therapist's information and suggestions and develop an effective daily program to manage both his depression and his addiction. His therapist anticipated and focused on key issues often seen in a depressive illness and, in this case, the results were dramatic.

Through a combination of cognitive therapy and supportive interpersonal therapy, the depressed addict can be helped to make progress towards wellness in both of his/her disorders. After initial treatment, he/she needs regular psychotherapy and a highly structured aftercare program. Pharmacotherapy may also be indicated. The patient needs a good diet, regular physical activity, and rest.

The prognosis for the depressed patient is usually good. Depression, like addiction, is a very treatable illness.

BIPOLAR DISORDERS

Bipolar disorder is much less common than major (unipolar) depression. Bipolar disorder affects only about 1 percent of the population compared with the 10 to 20 percent affected by major depression. Because of this low incidence, combined with the successful pharmacological treatment of this disorder over the past few decades, an addictions counselor rarely sees an untreated manic patient.

Cyclothymic disorder is similar to bipolar illness in that both involve up-and-down mood swings, but they are less extreme in cyclothymic disorder. Bipolar disorder may also involve psychotic symptoms, such as hallucinations or delusions. The relationship of cyclothymic disorder to bipolar disorder is thus analogous to the relationship of dysthymic disorder to major depression. Cyclothymic disorder is responsive to the types of treatment approaches used in manic-depressive illness.

The mood swings of active alcoholism have led many alcoholics to be misdiagnosed as manic depressive (although manic-depressives are rarely misdiagnosed as alcoholics). Bipolar illness does occur in conjunction with chemical dependency but less often than major depression does. In a typical clinical scenario, the addictions counselor encounters a bipolar person with alcoholism whose symptoms are stabilized on lithium or another mood-stabilizing drug. When properly medicated, these patients are not difficult to treat. Their medication, however, needs to be closely monitored by a psychiatrist.

Bipolar patients with symptoms that are not well stabilized present a special challenge to the treatment team. The symptoms of mania or hypomania may become evident during the detoxification and stabilization phase of addictions treatment. The manic patient may show an elevated, euphoric, expansive, angry, or irritable mood. Rapid or pressured speech, along with racing thoughts, flight of ideas, and inflated self-esteem are common. Manic patients show an increase in energy level and a decreased need for sleep, often staying awake for days at a time. In interaction with others, they can become intrusive and inappropriate. A playful or festive mood may change abruptly to anger, irritation, and verbal abusiveness. Approximately half of patients with bipolar disorder experience delusions or hallucinations, usually of a religious or sexual nature. Untreated mania can result in severely disabling life difficulties. The patient may become involved in compulsive, risky business schemes and sexual adventures. Patients may, for example, abruptly leave their jobs and travel around the world or become involved in grandiose plans, for example, to eradicate poverty or cure AIDS.

Manic episodes may be mild, moderate, or severe and can occur with or without psychotic features. The clinical presentation and course of mania differ markedly from patient to patient. For example, some patients show a pattern of euphoric mood, grandiosity, hyposomnia, loquaciousness, and higher productivity in daily activities. Other patients show a predominately angry or irritable mood, a high level of distractibility and psychomotor restlessness, and excessive involvement in pleasurable but risky or painful activities. Mania can be caused by medical conditions or substance abuse and is equally common in men and women. Single episodes of this disorder are rare; it is generally considered an episodic, recurrent illness. Patients with this disorder show significant variation in their patterns of cycling among the manic, depressed, and euthymic phases of the illness. Some patients show a pattern of "rapid cycling," defined as four episodes of mood disturbance in a twelve-month period. There are also reports of ultra-rapid cycling and even ultra-ultra-rapid cycling.

Treatment Considerations

There is little clinical literature on the psychotherapeutic treatment of mania. However, it is generally agreed that counseling can be an important adjunctive treatment for all phases of this illness. The most important contribution that a counselor can make for a manic patient is to thoroughly treat the addiction. Persons with bipolar illness need help in learning to live with their mental illness and accepting responsibility for their treatment, including medication. There is often denial about the bipolar illness along with denial of the addiction, and the individual often needs first-step work to reach acceptance of the bipolar disorder as well as the addiction. Like addicts, these patients may only be able to see the positive aspects of their manic episodes and remain in denial about the negative consequences. The following case is an example of this type of double denial.

Case D

A thirty-two-year-old physician's assistant was referred for inpatient evaluation of both cocaine addiction and mood symptoms, including markedly pressured speech, delusions of grandiosity (for example, believing he had the authority to write prescriptions), and inability to sleep. He had been abstinent from cocaine for two weeks following his third arrest for driving under the influence. The outpatient department referred him for inpatient treatment when the evaluation team concluded that his mood symptoms were beyond any that cocaine dependence alone could explain.

A complete psychiatric evaluation supported this impression. The patient was diagnosed with bipolar disorder and a trial of mood stabilizers recommended. He resisted this diagnosis, although he acknowledged that a psychiatric evaluation a year before he began drug use had also resulted in a recommendation for mood-stabilizing medication.

When confronted with the unmanageability of his life due to the mood disorder, he would insist that he was "not crazy." When confronted with the unmanageability of his addiction, he would explain that his use of cocaine was "normal" for someone in his "socioeconomic strata." His denial about both illnesses was virtually delusional. Finally, through an intervention involving his family and his lawyer, he agreed that the only way out of his current legal difficulties was to comply with treatment, including mood stabilizers. Within two weeks after starting lithium, the patient was able to listen to the feedback of his peers about the seriousness of his addiction and the positive effects of the medication on his symptoms. By the time of discharge, he had fully accepted both his bipolar disorder and his cocaine dependence and was ready to comply with all outpatient recommendations.

In this case, the techniques (direct confrontation and feedback) usually effective in cracking denial were ineffective due to the patient's double denial of the mental disorder and the addiction. However, another technique of addictions treatment (intervention) was effective in gaining initial compliance with both the psychiatric and the addictions treatment.

Most bipolar patients are maintained on lithium or another mood stabilizer such as carbamazepine (Tegretol) or valproic acid (Depakote), and some may also require neuroleptic medication or antidepressants. These patients need to be encouraged to see their psychiatrist regularly for medication checks. Patients should learn to recognize the early signs of a manic or depressive episode (such as sleeplessness, rapid speech, and an increased urge to "pick up"), which they can take as warnings that medication may need to be adjusted. Because lithium has a number of physical side effects that can be very serious, these patients should receive regular medical checkups. The patient should realize the importance of staying sober. Relapse into alcohol or drug use often leads to relapse of manic-depressive illness. When this occurs, the patient is caught in an ongoing cycle of recurrent mania and active alcoholism. As with depressed patients, the counselor needs to maintain empathy, understanding, and support for the individual suffering from bipolar illness. Often low self-esteem, guilt, and fear are underlying dynamics for the symptoms of mania, including grandiosity. At best, the person with bipolar illness and an addiction is stuck with *two* illnesses that he/she must accept and learn to live with. It is no wonder that some patients report that they enjoy mania as an escape. Counseling must be supportive and empathic as well as directive and confrontive, to impress upon the bipolar patient the importance of compliance with both medication and a daily addictions recovery program.

CONCLUSION

Mood disorders and mood symptoms are common among individuals with chemical dependency and complicate the assessment and treatment process. The addictions counselor with a good understanding of these disorders and the techniques used in their treatment can guide the patient through a recovery program that will lead to long-term stabilization and growth.

Chapter 4

Anxiety Disorders

Anxiety disorders are characterized by anxiety and avoidant behavior. They affect about 15 percent of the general population, making them the most common psychiatric illness. Anxiety is probably the most painful emotional state a human being can experience. Individuals who suffer from anxiety disorders often report that they would prefer the most intense physical pain over the extreme anxiety to which they are prone. Everyone is familiar with the experience of anxiety, which is a symptom of nearly every psychiatric disturbance. In mild anxiety states the person may feel only moderate bodily tension, worrisome thoughts, or a feeling of vague apprehension. In extreme anxiety states the patient experiences unparalleled terror and a sense of doom and despair, as well as extreme physical discomfort.

Researchers and theorists have devoted considerable attention to understanding anxiety disorders. Psychodynamic theorists view anxiety as a sign that the ego is in danger from an aggressive or sexual impulse. Anxiety acts as a cue to the ego to mobilize defenses and contain the threat. Social learning theorists conceptualize anxiety as a conditioned response to a fearful situation. Cognitive therapists view anxiety as a misinterpretation of physiological sensations associated with the fight or flight response that accompanies normal fear. Attachment theorists hold that anxiety is biologically based, related to a disruption in maternal attachment, and signals fear of loss or separation in significant relationships.

Through recent research the physiology of anxiety disorders is becoming better understood (Charney, 1990). Specific areas of the brain—for example, the amygdala, hypothalamus, and locus ceruleous—are being implicated in the development of various anxiety disorders, along with neurochemical systems such as the norepi-nephrine system. Evidence also exists that early psychological stress and trauma can cause permanent structural changes in the brain that render the individual vulnerable to the development of an anxiety disorder.

Anxiety disorders tend to run in families. Furthermore, anxiety disorders and alcoholism appear to be linked, as first-degree rela-tives of individuals with anxiety disorders have been found to be at increased risk for alcohol abuse (Weissman, 1988). Epidemiolog-ical studies have also shown that individuals with alcohol or other drug dependence disorders are twice as likely to have anxiety disor-ders as the general population (Regier et al., 1990). Six of the anxiety disorders (generalized anxiety disorder, panic disorder, agoraphobia, obsessive compulsive disorder, social phobia, and posttraumatic stress disorder), found quite frequently among chemi-cally dependent individuals, will be discussed in this chapter.

GENERALIZED ANXIETY DISORDER (GAD)

Patients with generalized anxiety disorder show chronic diffuse or free-floating anxiety, along with continual worry, often about trivial matters. These patients experience profound muscular ten-sion and are unable to relax. They may experience headaches, insomnia, tremulousness, sweating palms, flushing of the face, fre-quent urges to urinate, and a host of other bodily complaints. Many patients have a rapid pulse rate, varying from 90 to as high as 150 beats per minute.

Patients with GAD show chronic apprehension. They appear to be constantly projecting into the future and continually worried that horrible things may befall them or their loved ones. These worries are associated with chronic autonomic arousal; the patient is constantly keyed up and tense. Since the patient fears and cannot control the future, he/she experiences a continual sense of threat and feels constantly on guard to ward off potential catastrophic events.

GAD patients complain of being easily distracted and having very poor concentration which make work and study very difficult. Patients often come across as self-conscious, nonassertive, and whining. Because of frequent and intense somatic complaints, these patients spend much time visiting physicians in search of relief from their distress.

Treatment Considerations

A good program for treating GAD could involve a combination of cognitive therapy, relaxation therapy, worry management, time management, and the development of problem-solving techniques (Brown, O'Leary, and Barlow, 1993). All these procedures can be carried out within the context of addictions therapy. Relaxation procedures such as Meichenbaum and Jarenko's (1983) Stress Inoculation Training and Transcendental Meditation (Bloomfield, 1975; Eppley, Abrams, and Shear, 1989) are especially effective at reducing anxiety symptoms.

Cognitive therapists have found that patients with GAD show two major types of cognitive distortions: *probability overestimation* and *catastrophic thinking*. In probability overestimation, the patient overestimates the likelihood of some negative event occurring. For example, one patient worried that her son would become involved in a horrible car accident every time he left the house with the family car. While this was certainly a possibility, the patient raised it to a probability and then constantly worried about it. With catastrophic thinking, the patient views an actual or potential negative event as disastrous and intolerable. For example, one patient viewed an upcoming possible layoff from his job as an indication that he would never work again in his life. He saw himself as totally without resources and unable to cope with life. Cognitive therapy techniques (such as those listed in Appendix A) can be employed to test the validity and reasonableness of the patient's irrational thinking and to supplant anxious cognitions with more reasonable ones.

Identifying and dealing with worries is another important part of the treatment of GAD (Rapee and Barlow, 1991). The therapist works with the patient to list the worries that commonly go through his/her mind and assists him/her in thinking them through within the safety of the therapy session. Then the therapist instructs the patient to think of the worst possible scenario for a particular worry and to focus on it continually for twenty to thirty minutes. Continually evoking the worry leads to a diminishment of the anxiety associated with it. This process is known as *habituation*.

Therapists can also assist the GAD patient to manage time more efficiently. Typically these patients are nonassertive, taking on more work than they can handle because they have difficulty saying no to others. Chronic worrying and anxiety can also lead to disorganized behavior and failure to plan the day efficiently. Having patients simply write down their daily agenda and prioritize activities and goals can be immensely helpful. Certainty and specificity usually reduce anxiety. Once patients know exactly what they are going to do and have a plan to achieve a goal, the diffuse anxiety associated with this disorder can drop to a manageable level.

Medications can relieve the most severe anxiety symptoms. As in panic disorder, benzodiazepines can be effective but should be avoided if possible. Buspirone, a new, presumably nonaddicting anxiolytic, can be very effective in controlling the symptoms of generalized anxiety. Unfortunately, persons who have previously been treated with benzodiazepines seem to benefit less from buspirone. Antidepressants can also be useful.

Patients with generalized anxiety disorder need constant reassurance that they are not "going crazy." Many of these patients are concerned that they have schizophrenia or another severe psychiatric illness. They struggle with the fear of loss of control. They may have deep conflicts over expression of hostility and aggression. Many have sexual conflicts. Because of their extreme neediness, these patients may require extra attention from addictions counselors in the form of supportive and directive counseling. GAD patients should receive liberal exposure to relaxation therapy. Regular exercise, good rest, and a proper diet low in caffeine are also in order.

Anxiety disordered patients should routinely be referred for psychotherapy in aftercare plans. Many patients respond well to insight-oriented therapy, cognitive therapy, and behavioral therapy. Aftercare plans should include training in an anxiety management program. Meditation techniques, particularly transcendental meditation, are especially useful with this disorder. Many patients show dramatic reductions in anxiety levels and a sharp decrease in the use of anxiolytic medication when they begin a program of meditation (Dillbeck, 1977).

PANIC DISORDER

Patients with panic disorder show sudden onset, discreet periods of extreme anxiety, and fear that may last from a few seconds to a few hours. These episodes are unexpected but in time may become associated with specific situations or triggers. During a panic attack the patient experiences often unbearable terror. He/she may have the following physical symptoms in varying degrees and combinations: chest pain, heart palpitations, choking sensations, tingling in hands or feet, sweating, flushed face, faintness, and trembling. Many of these symptoms are the same as those associated with alcohol or sedative withdrawal, and in some patients the onset of withdrawal symptoms can trigger a panic attack. In panic disorder, the patient usually harbors catastrophic thoughts and fears such as an extreme fear of dying, suffering a heart attack, or going crazy. Some patients are convinced that they are totally losing control over themselves and may injure themselves or others. Others are convinced that they will be publicly humiliated.

Panic attacks typically have their onset in the teens or early adulthood. Many patients suffering their first panic attack fear that they are suffering from a heart attack and admit themselves to an emergency room. Some patients are actually run through various medical tests for cardiac abnormalities. Despite the patient's fear, the cardiac symptoms experienced with panic attacks are not in any way related to the symptoms of an actual heart attack. A usually benign condition known as mitral valve prolapse (MVP) has been found to occur more frequently than normal with panic disordered patients. However, this condition is not currently considered to be a cause of panic disorder. Symptoms of MVP include palpitations, chest pain, fatigue, and lightheadedness. If MVP is detected, the patient should be reassured that panic symptoms will not cause heart problems.

Besides fearing heart problems, the panic victim may also be convinced that he/she is choking due to a feeling of profound tightness in the chest. Patients often feel that they are not getting enough air and may run outdoors or throw open a window and gasp vigorously. The patient usually experiences hyperventilation due to an increased rate of breathing in a panic episode. Hyperventilation leads the patient to feel lightheaded and very uncomfortable, often with a sensation of "pins and needles" throughout the extremities. Patients also feel confused and unable to concentrate, which further accelerates their anxiety. Some theorists view hyperventilation or faulty breathing as the central cause of panic symptoms (Ley, 1987).

Panic attacks vary in frequency and duration from patient to patient and may occur with or without agoraphobia (discussed in the next section). Some patients show panic symptoms all their lives. In other patients the attacks disappear as mysteriously as they appeared with no further episodes. In severe cases the patient cannot work and support him/herself. In milder cases the patient tolerates the attack and goes on living with relatively little inconvenience.

Treatment Considerations

Panic disorder occurs in about 2 percent of the general population and about 9 percent of alcoholics and addicts. Therefore the likelihood of encountering panic disordered patients in addictions treatment is relatively high. Many patients with panic disorder have not been evaluated or treated by a psychiatrist or psychologist before entering an addictions program. The patient may have been self-medicating the panic symptoms for months or even years. In such cases the patient often experiences a panic attack early in detoxification or in the first few days of inpatient treatment. Many patients are so frightened by the prospect of not having ready access to alcohol or other sedative drugs that they abruptly terminate treatment programs, often without explanation. They often do not know what is wrong with them, nor does the staff.

Because of the real possibility of an undiagnosed panic disorder, patients showing any of the above symptoms of panic should be promptly referred for psychiatric evaluation. If a patient experiences a panic attack during treatment, vital signs and other signs of withdrawal should be checked to ensure that the anxiety symptoms are not due to acute withdrawal requiring medical attention. The counselor should take a few minutes to see the patient for an individual session, preferably in the quiet of the counselor's office free from other distractions. The counselor should reassure the patient that symptoms of anxiety are common in early recovery, that his/her fears (going crazy, having a heart attack, dying) are unfounded, that the attack will pass, and that he/she will receive appropriate medical and psychological care. The counselor should stay with the patient until the attack subsides. If the facility has a relaxation program, the patient should be encouraged to try using this to reduce symptoms.

The prompt diagnosis and treatment of panic disorder can facilitate addictions treatment, as illustrated by the following case.

Case A

A twenty-year-old college student was admitted for chemical dependency treatment following a "bad LSD trip" characterized by panic symptoms and paranoid thoughts. He had used alcohol in an increasingly dysfunctional manner over the previous two years and had used "acid" three times in the six months since starting college.

The patient engaged actively in all aspects of addictions treatment and seemed comfortable with that diagnosis; however, episodes of panic symptoms persisted, apparently unrelated to withdrawal or flashbacks. He especially had difficulty with the twelve-step meetings he attended in the community, where he would become almost totally immobilized.

A careful evaluation by an anxiety specialist resulted in a diagnosis of panic disorder with agoraphobia. A concurrent program of behavioral treatment for the anxiety disorder was begun, including progressive relaxation and in vivo desensitization. The patient was encouraged to consider the twelve-step meetings his laboratory for applying newly learned techniques for managing anxiety. By the end of four weeks, he was ready to continue addictions treatment in an extended treatment program and had the skills and assurance to deal with panic and other anxiety symptoms as they occurred.

In this case, identification and treatment of a previously undiagnosed anxiety disorder not only enabled the patient to benefit from addictions treatment, it also provided him with additional tools for recovery.

Some patients may need antipanic medication to control the symptoms enough so that they can engage in and benefit from addictions treatment. The medication of choice for panic attacks is an antidepressant. These drugs are nonaddicting and, besides relieving depression, they have proven useful in blocking panic attacks. In most cases, benzodiazepines such as Valium, Ativan, or Xanax should be avoided in persons with addictions; however, these medications may be needed in occasional cases where panic symptoms are incapacitating and other treatments fail.

Many patients entering addictions facilities with a diagnosis of panic disorder are receiving an antipanic drug. Provided the panic disorder has been appropriately diagnosed and the patient is taking the medication responsibly, the addictions counselor's role is to help the patient understand that he/she can work a "good program" while taking medication. Without these drugs, many addicts with panic disorder will relapse to active addiction.

The panic-disordered patient can be treated in a relatively routine fashion in addictions treatment environments. Some may need additional one-to-one supportive counseling. Some panic-disordered patients are sensitive to crowds, and large addictions facilities may increase the frequency of their panic attacks. Requirements to speak before large groups can be limited in the treatment of patients who experience attacks during this activity.

Patients should be informed about the potentiating effects of caffeine. A strong cup of coffee may predispose a panic-disordered patient to an attack. Decaffeinated coffee or herbal teas should be substituted. Panic-disordered patients can benefit from engaging in relaxation therapy, and time should be allotted in their day so that they can do so comfortably. This may be progressive relaxation, autogenic training, imagery, meditation, regular repetitive exercise such as running, swimming, or some other activity. Aftercare is important for panic-disordered patients. They should be routinely referred to a mental health professional for treatment and ongoing monitoring of their disorder. For some panic-disordered patients, insight-oriented psychotherapy may be helpful in dealing with the psychological aspects of the disorder. Behavioral therapy, biofeedback-assisted relaxation, and hypnosis are among the many techniques psychologists employ to treat panic disorder, and some addicts with panic disorder can benefit from them.

Certainly an enlightened AA or NA group and a personal sponsor are important for these patients. Well-meaning but ill-informed twelve-step members can make panic-disordered patients feel guilty for taking psychotropic medication. Patients should be counseled to anticipate some animosity or puzzlement from fellow AA or NA members.

Current treatments for panic focus on this disorder as a learned reaction to bodily and mental experiences associated with the fight or flight response. Due to physiological and psychological vulnerabilities, certain individuals show a misfiring of the fear response during stressful life encounters. When this occurs, these patients then misinterpret their bodily experiences and, in the absence of an obvious stressor or threat, conclude that something is physiologically or mentally wrong with them. Cognitive-behavioral therapists focus on correcting the patient's faulty thinking and providing accurate information on the nature of the fight or flight response. This information can reorient the patient's attention so that anxiety does not spiral into full-blown panic.

There are many sources on the nature of panic (see, for example, Bourne, 1990; Craske and Barlow, 1993). In a supportive and matter-of-fact style, the addictions therapist can tell panic-disordered patients that they are experiencing a normal, not pathological, physiological process activated by an internal or external threat. The presence of anxiety is not a sign of sickness; it is an adaptive, health-promoting response to help the person escape danger. When the fear response is activated, adrenaline and noradrenaline are pumped throughout the body. These natural substances are responsible for many of the symptoms a panic-disordered patient experiences: a racing heart, sweating, blurred vision, a flushed feeling, and rapid breathing. Hyperventilation alone—a natural response that draws extra oxygen into the lungs—accounts for most of the sensations associated with panic, such as tingling, lightheadedness, and choking. Patients should be told that these sensations are benign and that symptoms of panic cannot lead to heart disease, psychosis, or death. A careful explanation of the physiological response associated with panic can tremendously reassure the patient, leading to appreciable symptom reduction and enabling the patient to make better use of primary addictions treatment.

AGORAPHOBIA

Agoraphobia is a serious chronic anxiety disorder that can occur with or without panic attacks. Agoraphobia is characterized by a marked fear of being alone or in public places where escape is difficult or help unavailable in the case of sudden incapacitation. Fears of helplessness or humiliation are common. Because of such fears, the patient's normal daily activities become increasingly constricted as avoidant behavior dominates his/her life. The central features of agoraphobia are severe phobic anxiety and phobic avoidance of a variety of situations. The most common situations agoraphobics avoid are crowded stores, tunnels, bridges, elevators, and public transportation.

As agoraphobia increases in severity, the patient avoids more situations, including seemingly benign ones such as walking around the neighborhood, eating in a restaurant, and going to a movie or sporting event. In the more severe cases, the patient becomes house-bound.

Most agoraphobics also suffer from panic attacks. Agoraphobia accounts for 50 percent of all anxiety-disordered patients seen in professional treatment settings. The age of onset is usually in the late twenties. The majority of agoraphobic patients are women (80 percent). By the time an agoraphobic patient seeks treatment, he/she has typically suffered with the disorder for many years. Patients with agoraphobia are usually reluctant to seek professional treatment due to embarrassment about the disorder and fear of being diagnosed as "crazy."

Many agoraphobics have a secondary disorder. Frequently this is depression, which often is a result of the severity and intractability of the agoraphobic symptoms. Alcoholism is also frequently found. Most agoraphobics report a history of stressful events that preceded the initial agoraphobic attack and a childhood history of loss and separation fears. The anxiety symptoms that agoraphobic patients experience are very similar to those of panic disordered patients. However, unlike patients with panic disorder, the agoraphobic develops a lifestyle of avoidance and constricted social interaction that severely limits his/her functioning.

Due to their phobic fears and the shame they feel about the disease, untreated agoraphobics present for addictions treatment somewhat less often than patients with other anxiety disorders do. The nature of the disorder precludes the ability to venture forth and seek treatment in a chemical dependency program. Like the panic-disordered patient, many agoraphobic addicts leave treatment against medical advice because they feel trapped.

Treatment Considerations

Agoraphobics are typically treated with behavioral therapy by psychologists who specialize in such treatment. Psychiatrists may prescribe antidepressant medication for the treatment of panic anxiety, but the agoraphobic symptoms may persist. One frequently used approach with agoraphobic patients involves *graduated exposure* to anxiety-eliciting situations. In this technique, the agoraphobic patient is exposed to those situations (for example, tunnels, airplanes, shopping malls) that provoke panic and other dysphoric feelings, beginning usually with the least threatening situation. As the number and length of exposure sessions increase, the patient slowly becomes habituated to the stimuli and begins to experience them without symptoms of panic. At the same time, the patient is educated about the nature of agoraphobia and the procedures of graduated exposure.

Goldstein and Stainbach (1987) have developed an effective program for treating panic disorder and agoraphobia. Agoraphobia is conceptualized as having its genesis in unresolved conflict from childhood and associated fears of abandonment, leading to unassertiveness and a sense of ineffectiveness. The patient deals with the resulting chronic anxiety and panic episodes mainly through an avoidant lifestyle. The patient learns to fear the onset of anxiety symptoms and becomes preoccupied with the bodily sensations involved in panic attacks. The fear eventually dominates the patient's lifestyle and leads to avoidance and irrational thinking. The patient becomes disturbed, isolated from others, and trapped in an escalating cycle of anxiety.

The program initially focuses on helping the patient develop deep abdominal, diaphragmatic breathing, the opposite of the shallow, rapid upper-chest breathing that agoraphobic patients often show. Next, the patient is taught to shift his/her focus from future-oriented catastrophic thinking to immediate physical sensation. For example, the patient is asked to turn his/her attention to the colors and textures in the immediate environment. This shift from anxious thoughts to physical sensations has a remarkable anxiety-lowering effect. Finally, the patient is asked to become alert to any anxiety-arousing catastrophic thoughts and to snap a rubber band worn around the wrist to remind him/herself to shift attention away from this thinking. These steps assist the patient to counter the panic symptoms of agoraphobia.

As the patient gains skill in clearing panic symptoms when they arise, the therapeutic focus widens to include expressing blocked emotions such as anger and guilt, developing assertiveness in social relationships, and challenging inhibitions. The preferred mode of treatment at this point is gestalt therapy, which focuses on enlarging the patient's awareness and acceptance of conflicts and fears. Family treatment and education are also considered essential. The families of agoraphobic patients can become quite disturbed and dysfunctional, much like the families of chemically dependent patients. Assisting family members in understanding the dynamics and manifestations of agoraphobia and its effects on family functioning has a profound healing effect for the patient and family, and helps ensure compliance with treatment guidelines.

Other strategies to combat agoraphobia include progressive muscle relaxation training and cognitive therapy. The success rate for the treatment of agoraphobia is approximately 50 to 60 percent. Treatment usually takes less than twelve months. The treatment of agoraphobia requires specific training and expertise. The goal of primary addictions treatment with the dual-diagnosis agoraphic should be to make the patient as comfortable as possible so that he/she can deal with the addiction.

The best way to put an agoraphobia patient at ease is to express understanding of his/her disorder. Agoraphobic patients are often wary that other patients will see their dysfunction as silly or, even worse, as a sign that they are going crazy. Frank discussion of the patient's dysfunction within the therapy group or treatment community is important. An agoraphobic patient will feel more comfortable if he/she feels supported and understood by fellow patients and staff.

In severe cases of agoraphobia, the patient may need an anti-anxiety drug to benefit from addictions treatment. In milder cases, all that is required is the clinical staff's patience, tolerance, and understanding. The patient may occasionally feel panic and have to leave a scheduled activity. If this occurs, someone should accompany the patient, offer reassurance, and encourage him/her to return once the panic has subsided. The patient should not be punished or ostracized for such behavior.

It is often helpful to house the agoraphobic patient in an area of the facility that is close to the dining area, nursing station, and therapy rooms. With a small radius of travel, many patients feel more secure and less intimidated by the inpatient environment.

Aftercare plans for the agoraphobic patient should routinely include psychiatric follow-up. There is a real possibility of relapse in agoraphobia symptoms, and relapse to active addiction may quickly follow. An agoraphobic patient in relapse may fear venturing out to attend AA groups or aftercare counseling sessions. To reduce this possibility, counselors should ensure that the patient is receiving appropriate treatment for agoraphobia from a competent professional.

OBSESSIVE-COMPULSIVE DISORDER (OCD)

This is a progressive and, if untreated, usually chronic anxiety disorder characterized chiefly by the presence of obsessions and compulsions. Some patients with this disorder appear to show only obsessions; however, most patients show both obsessions *and* compulsions.

According to DSM-IV (1994), obsessions are recurrent, persistent thoughts, impulses, or images that are usually experienced as intrusive and inappropriate and cause marked distress. Typically the person attempts to ignore, suppress, or neutralize the obsession with another thought or action. Often the obsessions have aggressive, religious, or sexual themes, although sometimes they seem completely nonsensical. Many patients have obsessions that they find repugnant and disgusting, such as thoughts of incest or murder. A chronic state of doubt and uncertainty usually accompanies obsessive thinking. For example, one patient was obsessed with the thought that he did not turn off the burners on the stove. Despite several checks that showed the burners were off, he was continually bothered by the thought, "Is the burner off?"

Compulsions are repetitive behaviors or mental acts aimed at reducing distress or preventing some dreaded event or situation. Compulsions are typically ritualistic, with compulsive washing and checking as the two most frequent. Patients with compulsions are often preoccupied with the idea that they have been contaminated by germs or soiled by bodily secretions. Compulsive washing is an attempt to combat this fear.

Patients usually recognize their obsessions or compulsions as excessive and unreasonable. The compulsions associated with this disorder can be clearly distinguished from the compulsive behavior seen in addictive substance use and from other compulsive behaviors often seen in addicts, such as compulsive eating, sex, or gambling. The latter behaviors are experienced as satisfying and pleasurable, although their repercussions are usually negative.

Obsessive-compulsive disorder usually has its onset in late adolescence or early adulthood. Typically, patients suffer for years before seeking treatment. It afflicts males and females about equally. It often occurs with other mental disorders such as depression, panic disorder, eating disorder, and phobias, as well as addiction (Eisen and Rasmussen, 1989). There are many theories on the causes of obsessive-compulsive disorder. Psychodynamic theorists view it primarily as a disorder in psychological development involving ego defenses such as isolation, undoing, reaction formation, and displacement to control unwanted instinctual urges. Evidence also exists for a neurological and biochemical basis for this disorder. Cognitive theorists have focused on the thinking patterns of patients with obsessive-compulsive disorder and have identified several dysfunctional cognitions manifested by these patients. They show unusually high expectations of negative consequences in their lives. They can harbor a belief that one should be entirely competent in all areas of one's life (McFall and Wallersheim, 1979). They develop the mistaken belief that they must live up to perfectionistic guidelines or they deserve punishment. They also develop the belief that certain behaviors and rituals can prevent problems. These patients believe they are responsible for conditions and variables that are beyond their control, and they tend to overpersonalize any problem situation. They exaggerate the presence of threat in any encounter and feel they have to be continually vigilant against potential harm.

Treatment Approaches

Treatment for OCD generally involves a combination of pharmacotherapy with serotonergic drugs (for example, clomipramine and fluoxetine) and specialized behavior therapy. The latter is a highly focused and specific approach to treating this disorder that requires special training. Typically, behavioral treatment for OCD involves two components, *exposure* and *response prevention*. With exposure therapy, the patient is asked to imagine or is presented with situations or objects that evoke obsessions or compulsions. For example, a patient seized with the obsession that touching a bathroom sink would contaminate him/her is encouraged to touch it repeatedly in the therapist's presence until the anxiety associated with this behavior subsides. In response prevention, patients are directed to face anxiety-provoking stimuli without engaging in ritualistic behavior. For example, a patient who ritualistically tapped the bedpost before going to sleep at night to ward off fears that something would happen to him/her or his/her family is asked to stop this behavior completely. Initially the patient may feel extremely anxious, but if refraining from the ritualistic behavior continues, the anxiety gradually subsides and the patient learns that the feared consequence does not become a reality.

Behavioral treatments for OCD are designed to disrupt the association between feelings of anxiety and those thoughts, situations, or objects that elicit the anxiety, as well as the association between ritualistic behavior and decreased anxiety. Patients are asked to face their fears vigorously without engaging in compulsions. This type of therapy is structured and rather labor and time-intensive. It involves extensive homework on the patient's part and often home visits by the therapist to aid in generalizing the effects of treatment to the patient's daily life. Often a family member or friend is used as a supervisor to monitor the patients progress. Behavioral therapy is effective, with over 75 percent of patients showing long-term improvement, and technicians, paraprofessionals, and counselors have all used it successfully. However, conducting behavioral therapy requires specific training. Addictions counselors can employ these techniques if properly trained, but for those who do not have specific training in treating OCD, it is best to refer the patient to an appropriately trained professional. If OCD is severe, it can prevent the patient's effective involvement in chemical-dependency treatment. Either pharmacological or behavioral treatment or both may be necessary before the OCD patient can take advantage of addictions therapy.

Addictions therapists should become familiar with the manifestation of OCD and should be alert to its presence in patients who have a family history of it or who show other symptoms of anxiety. Often, patients feel a great deal of shame and embarrassment about their symptoms and hide them from the therapist during the assessment process. Therapists can provide education, support, and guidance for patients with OCD. Counselors can offer information on the nature of obsessions and compulsions and the types of treatment available. Reassuring the patient that treatment is almost always effective can go a long way to bolster the patient's confidence and help resistive patients become amenable to involvement in appropriate therapies.

SOCIAL PHOBIA (SOCIAL ANXIETY DISORDER)

According to DSM-IV (APA, 1994), the essential feature of social phobia is a marked and persistent fear of social or performance situations in which embarrassment may occur. Exposure to such situations typically provokes an anxiety response which may take the form of a panic attack. If possible, the patient avoids the situation. Patients with this disorder are preoccupied with the fear of being humiliated or embarrassed in social situations. They experience symptoms typical of anxiety, especially sweating, blushing, and dry mouth. The social phobic's fears may be limited to a few specific social situations or are pervasive, leading to social isolation and incapacitation. Although almost any type of social situation can throw these patients into anxiety, the mostly commonly feared one is public speaking. Afflicted individuals often remain unmarried and may be grossly underemployed.

Nearly one out of five patients who present with an anxiety disorder are social phobics. There is a high comorbidity rate with this disorder, and social phobics may also suffer with generalized anxiety disorder and panic disorder. This disorder shows a relatively high prevalence in addicted populations; social phobics often misuse alcohol and other psychoactive substances in efforts to self-medicate anxiety (Chambless et al., 1987). In addition, social phobics often present with a concurrent Axis II diagnosis of avoidant personality disorder.

Treatment Considerations

Like patients with other anxiety disorders, patients with social phobia can benefit from a combination of cognitive therapy, exposure to feared situations, relaxation therapy, and medication.

Initially, it is important to offer the socially phobic patient liberal support and validation. Patients often terminate addictions therapy prematurely because of their high level of anxiety and because they feel misunderstood by and different from other patients. Many find the inpatient environment especially intolerable. In supportive therapy, the addictions therapist can process the patient's fears of social interaction. Often it is useful to make a list of the patient's worst fears and then probe for the thoughts that accompany these fears. Typically the socially phobic patient is in a constant state of doubt about his/her ability to make a positive impression on others. These patients lack confidence and a sense of competence in social situations and often have vivid memories of prior negative social encounters. They typically grossly overestimate the likelihood of being humiliated or rejected as well as the negativity of the behavior of others. For example, one patient was convinced that as soon as he opened his mouth in addictions group therapy, he would stutter and stammer and the other group members would laugh at him and ignore him. He was so convinced that he would make a fool of himself that he asked to be exempted from group therapy entirely.

A cognitive therapy approach can be immensely helpful with socially phobic patients. Patients can be taught the most common cognitive distortions (see Appendix A) and helped in seeing the irrationality of their fears and realistically assessing common social situations. Socially phobic patients tend to forget that others are not much different from them. It is important to remind the socially phobic patient that just as he/she is not out to hurt others, the same is true of other people with whom the patient interacts. Most people do not go around trying to humiliate others but, on the contrary, are considerate and usually want to help someone in distress. At the worst, they can be simply indifferent. The therapist can help the patient improve his/her reality testing and more realistically assess the danger inherent in any social situation. Role-playing in both individual and group therapy can augment informal discussions designed to increase the patient's empathy for and understanding of others. The group therapy environment particularly offers a rich opportunity for the socially phobic patient to confront his/her fears of humiliation. In the normal course of group interaction, with encouragement from the therapist and other group members, the patient can see that his/her fears are unfounded and that others are genuinely interested and supportive. In this way, addictions group therapy can be extremely powerful in offsetting the socially phobic patient's fears and reducing attendant anxiety.

Pharmacological treatment for social phobia may include a trial on an MAO inhibitor such as phenelzine (Nardil). Beta blockers such as atenolol (Tenormin) and propranolol (Inderal) have also been helpful for public speaking and performance anxiety.

POST-TRAUMATIC STRESS DISORDER (PTSD)

Post-traumatic stress disorder may result from any significant trauma. It may appear in victims of or witnesses to combat situations, natural disasters, and violent acts. Any situation in which the individual experiences outside circumstances overpowering his/her sense of control or well-being may lead to PTSD.

The reaction may be time-limited (acute) or delayed and/or protracted (chronic), lasting months or years beyond the traumatic event. The symptoms of post-traumatic stress disorder are as follows (APA, 1994):

1. A response of intense fear and helplessness to a traumatic event
2. A persistent reexperiencing of the trauma through recurrent and intrusive images, thoughts, and dreams, and acting or feeling as if the traumatic event were recurring

3. Persistent avoidance of stimuli associated with the trauma and numbing of general responsiveness
4. Persistent symptoms of increased arousal including sleep difficulty, irritability or angry outbursts, concentration problems, hypervigilance, and exaggerated startle response

Survivors of traumatic events regularly report symptoms such as extreme depression and dysphoria, sleep disturbances, an inability to concentrate, and feelings of guilt and shame for having survived the trauma while others perished or were seriously injured. However, not everyone who experiences a catastrophic stressor reports PTSD symptoms. For example, only 26 percent of Vietnam returnees reported appreciable psychiatric symptoms consistent with PTSD. About the same percentage of Prisoners of War (POW's) reported psychiatric disturbances. Over one-half of trauma victims do not develop PTSD.

Whether PTSD develops following a trauma depends on the individuals unique psychological and physical makeup. PTSD frequently occurs in the very young and the very old, possibly because in these age groups individuals are less adaptable and more vulnerable to stress. A person with a preexisting psychiatric disorder, such as an anxiety or mood disorder, is also at a greater risk to develop PTSD. The availability of strong social supports, the severity of the trauma, and any history of childhood trauma can also determine whether an individual shows PTSD following a trauma.

PTSD can be acute or chronic. In acute cases the symptoms develop rapidly, usually within six months following the trauma. With or without treatment, most cases of acute PTSD can be resolved and there are no lingering symptoms later in the patient's life. In chronic cases, PTSD symptoms can last six months or more and the onset of symptoms may be months or years after the trauma has occurred. In general, the longer the symptoms last, the more severe the disorder and the poorer the prognosis. Some cases of PTSD result in total disability.

Along with the most common complaints of recurring dreams and emotional numbing, patients with severe PTSD experience a variety of secondary problems. The patient's family suffers from the patient's distress or lack of interest and responsiveness. Likewise, the patient's education or job might suffer due to absenteeism, poor work performance, or interrupted school agendas. Many PTSD victims develop abusive drinking or drug use to deal with their symptoms. In PTSD victims who are also addicted, there is a marked acceleration in the drinking or drugging behavior and a sharp decline in psychological and physical functioning following the catastrophic stressor.

Treatment Considerations

Mild to moderate cases of PTSD can be dealt with without much difficulty in inpatient addictions treatment. Severe cases may require hospitalization and psychiatric treatment, which may include pharmacotherapy.

In the author's experience (mostly with Vietnam veterans, police officers, and sex offense victims), an additional adjunctive therapy group for PTSD victims has proven very effective in most cases. For Vietnam veterans especially, involvement in a group in which all members share similar traumatic experiences is effective in assisting these patients to work through the often repressed memories and feelings of the war.

The purpose of PTSD adjunctive therapy is to assist the patient in regaining self-confidence and self-esteem. Extensive discussion and ventilation of the thoughts and feelings associated with the original trauma can remove "blocks" or impediments to the patient's addictions therapy. In group or individual therapy, the traumatic events and feelings are recalled and worked through. Memories, including thoughts, sensations, perceptions, and emotions, are recalled and discussed. Care must be taken to have the therapy experience result in an *increased* sense of control over these internal experiences, as opposed to recreating the helplessness of the original trauma. A variety of feelings, including grief, helplessness, rage, and hopelessness, may be revived during therapy and need to be understood as memories with little connection to here-and-now reality. Support from peers and professionals can help the individual experience his/her ability to tolerate these feelings and develop a sense of mastery. Care must be taken not to "flood" the patient with too much painful material too rapidly or too soon. It is best to allow the patient to set the pace.

The principle behind the treatment of PTSD is to activate the feared traumatic memory while incorporating into it new information that is incompatible with the patient's fear structure, leading to the formation of new memories. The patient's reintegration of the traumatic memory is greatly facilitated by an accepting, safe, supportive therapy environment and by formal training in relaxation skills, such as stress inoculation, progressive muscle relaxation, or transcendental meditation.

As the patient is discussing traumatic material, initially he/she should be allowed simply to ventilate. Engaging the patient in *exposure* techniques—such as writing, role-playing, and deliberately calling to mind the original traumatic event—can facilitate discussion of the trauma memories. The therapist should direct attention to how the patient reacts to an interpretation of the traumatic event, which is usually what causes his/her problems. From a cognitive perspective, PTSD patients often engage in distorted thinking about their traumatic experiences. They may blame themselves, experience survivor's guilt, harbor the feeling that they have been unjustly punished, or conclude that they are inadequate because they cannot control the intrusion of painful memories. Patients can be told that distorted thinking keeps PTSD symptoms in place. Common cognitive distortions include: jumping to conclusions, exaggerating the meaning of the traumatic event, disregarding important facts surrounding the traumatic event, misattributing the causes of trauma, and overgeneralizing to conclude that the patient is doomed to suffer future trauma. The therapist can point out these distortions to the patient and challenge him/her with cognitive techniques such as decatastrophizing, reattribution, and guided association (see Appendix A), pushing the patient to provide evidence for his/her beliefs.

Reframing is also a very powerful intervention. For example, the patient's fear that something traumatic is bound to happen again can be reframed as a residual effect of the past trauma. Guilt and shame can be reframed as irrational cognitions based on rigid, faulty thinking. Rage and anger can be reframed as hurt and helplessness, especially for explosive patients. Finally, the trauma can be reframed as an experience that needs to be understood in the context of the patient's entire life. Although an important event, it need not totally absorb the patient's attention. Both cognitive interventions and reframing have the effect of distancing the patient from the traumatic event and cultivating an objective, rather than subjective, perspective on the trauma.

Except in extreme cases, pharmacotherapy is not regularly used in the treatment of PTSD. Some psychiatrists, however, have found benefits in the use of drugs such as propranolol and clonidine for the management of explosiveness, recurring nightmares, and intrusive thoughts. Selective serotonin reuptake inhibitors have also proven beneficial for these symptoms as well as irritability and depression. In cases of prolonged PTSD that is nonresponsive to psychological interventions, the counselor should have the patient evaluated by a psychiatrist to determine if pharmacotherapy would be useful.

The following case illustrates the effect that undiagnosed post-traumatic stress disorder can have on abstinence and recovery.

Case B

A forty-two-year-old computer programmer was admitted for detoxification from abuse of benzodiazepines, which were prescribed for the past six months by his doctor for sleep. Before this he had been sober for ten years, ever since his employer confronted him with his drinking at work. Over the years, he had attended AA meetings once a week and had no problem accepting that he was an alcoholic. He had always had difficulty with "nerves" and found it nearly impossible to speak at meetings, but he had come to enjoy the familiarity of the program and felt that he learned a lot just by listening. He knew that he was taking a risk when his doctor wanted to prescribe pills for his nightmares. He just could not see how he could live without relief from the terrifying dreams that would wake him up in the night and leave him shaking and in a cold sweat. He could never remember what they were about, but he was always left feeling as though he had done something wrong.

His withdrawal was difficult and he needed a great deal of support from his peers to make it through, but at least in the hospital the nightmares had stopped, until the Gulf War began. Even though he was in the hospital, there was no way to avoid hearing about the war. Not only did the nightmares return, but for the first time he began having flashbacks of combat in Vietnam. The reason for his nightmares and his lifetime of "nervousness" and avoidance of relationships suddenly became clear.

This man, like many others, had begun drinking to self-medicate his undiagnosed PTSD after returning from Vietnam. His alcoholism was identified and treated, but the PTSD continued in a chronic form with social and emotional withdrawal and generalized anxiety symptoms. The patient adapted to his symptoms and gained most of his life's satisfaction from his job until the papers, television, and people everywhere were focused on the troops being sent to the Middle East. Before this, without realizing it, he had successfully avoided situations that might trigger memories of his time in combat; now he was not able to do that and the nightmares began.

With the PTSD properly diagnosed, the patient was able to seek out other recovering Vietnam veterans, one of whom agreed to be his sponsor. He contacted the Veterans Administration and learned about a newly formed support group for vets with delayed reactions triggered by the new war. Although it was some time before the nightmares and flashbacks diminished, the patient gained relief in knowing that he was not "going crazy," and he became able to reach out for help for both the addiction and the PTSD.

Certainly not every case of post-traumatic stress disorder is so easy to diagnose and treat. Many patients resist the diagnosis. It is difficult for most individuals to reach out for help because acknowledging the need for help represents a degree of vulnerability, and any vulnerability can be terrifying to one who has been subject to the total vulnerability of a significant trauma. It is important for the treatment team to remain alert to signs of PTSD and to encourage the patient to keep an open mind as well.

CONCLUSION

The vast majority of patients presenting for addictions treatment with a coexisting anxiety disorder can be successfully treated. An understanding of the patient's disorder and its impact on the patient's functioning while in treatment is key to this success. The most controversial issue in the treatment of anxiety disorders in the addictions field is the use of psychotropic medications. Clinicians often term anxiolytic medicines "dry booze" and view these medications as posing serious threats to the patient's recovery. In many cases these criticisms are justified; antianxiety medications have been inappropriately prescribed by physicians and abused by patients. The author's position is that the use of anxiety-reducing medications should be reserved for only the most severe cases of anxiety disorder. Treatments such as biofeedback, relaxation therapy, meditation, and hypnosis should be thoroughly investigated before medication is considered. Addictions counselors can be helpful to the patient with an anxiety disorder by respecting his/her limitations and helping him/her find a way to work an effective recovery program.

Chapter 5

Schizophrenia

Schizophrenia is perhaps the most devastating of the mental disorders. Affecting about 1 percent of the general population, schizophrenia is a neurophysiologic illness characterized by fragmentation and breakdown in the continuity and interrelationships of thoughts, impulses, and behavior. The schizophrenic patient experiences profound internal and external chaos and loses touch with reality.

In its most virulent form, schizophrenia can render a person completely unable to function. However, the prognostic picture for the schizophrenic patient has brightened somewhat over the past four decades with the advent of antipsychotic medication. Recent long-term follow-up studies (McGlashan, 1988) show that schizophrenia is not necessarily the relentlessly progressive disease that earlier studies and clinical experience suggested. The deterioration seen in the early years of the disorder gives way to stabilization and slow, steady progress in the later stages. Advances in pharmacology have led to the development of neuroleptic medications with reduced side effects. The result has been greater patient compliance with medication regimens and less frequent relapse to active illness. The new medications also allow schizophrenic patients to appear more normal and therefore to live with more social ease (Siris, 1990).

Improvement in the psychiatric and medical treatment of schizophrenia has helped many patients lead more functional, productive lives. Many schizophrenic patients now live in communities in unsupervised or partially supervised arrangements. The movement toward deinstitutionalization in the late 1960s, which led to schizophrenic patients obtaining greater autonomy, has been a mixed blessing. Many patients, lacking the structure and stability of the psychiatric hospital, have lapsed into a marginal existence. Many live on the street, falling prey to crime and the elements. A significant number of nonhospitalized schizophrenics cease taking their medications, stop going to treatment, and relapse to the active phase of the illness.

The increased autonomy of schizophrenics has also led to a higher rate of drug and alcohol abuse among these patients. Chemical dependency severely complicates an already dysfunctional lifestyle. For schizophrenics who are in remission (the chief symptoms of the disease are absent and the patient is not overtly psychotic), alcohol and drug use increase their vulnerability and may lead to relapse to active schizophrenia.

For a variety of reasons, however, schizophrenics rarely seek chemical-dependency treatment. Often, these patients lives are so chaotic and they have such immense difficulty simply dealing with the problems of daily living that they may see addictions treatment as a luxury. Even patients with a better standard of living and a more supportive social and family network often cannot, for financial reasons, receive chemical-dependency treatment. Such patients' personal and family finances may be completely depleted due to frequent hospitalizations for treatment of schizophrenia.

Dual-disordered patients treated for schizophrenia in such settings as veterans hospitals, outpatient clinics, and mental health centers rarely receive chemical-dependency treatment. This situation is gradually changing as the mental health field realizes the widespread alcohol and drug abuse occurring in this population (Ridgely et al., 1987). Many day treatment centers and psychosocial rehabilitation programs have begun offering education and preliminary treatment for chemical dependency for schizophrenic patients (Radke, 1991). As further progress is made in understanding and treating this population, schizophrenic patients will be seen more frequently in chemical-dependency treatment programs.

Although many schizophrenic patients are so dysfunctional that they cannot benefit from chemical-dependency therapy, there are many who can. The level of functioning and the course of the illness vary considerably among schizophrenic patients (Pao, 1979). High-functioning schizophrenics hold regular jobs, marry, develop sustained friendships, and achieve financial stability. They are not overwhelmed by psychotic symptoms and do not have frequent relapses. They do not require extensive inpatient psychiatric hospitalization and can be managed on an outpatient basis. These patients enjoy a positive response to treatment and a good outcome.

This chapter focuses on managing chemically dependent schizophrenics who are functional and have developed at least a *social remission* of the illness. This means that these patients are capable of self-care and can live in unsupervised or partially supervised arrangements. The psychiatric symptoms are well managed by medication and the danger of suicide, homicide, or self-destructive behavior is extremely low. Such patients can be treated in a dual program or in a standard inpatient or outpatient chemical-dependency program.

SYMPTOMS

Schizophrenia is a psychotic disorder that is heterogeneous in its etiology, course, and manifestations in affected patients. Patient response to treatment also varies considerably. It is important to remember that schizophrenia is a chronic, relapsing illness. Even when symptoms are well controlled with medication, the patient and helping professionals need to be aware of symptoms that signal the need for psychiatric intervention. Schizophrenia involves disturbances in several areas of the patient's functioning—perceptual, social, neuropsychological, cognitive, and behavioral. The following are its chief clinical features.

Perceptual Disturbance

Hallucinations frequently are present in the acute or active phase of the illness. In schizophrenia, auditory hallucinations are the most common type. These may involve the voice of a supernatural being such as God, Christ, or Satan talking derisively about or to the patient. Sometimes the patient hears two or more people talking obscenely or threateningly about him/her. Visual hallucinations are less common. When they occur, patients typically experience them as vividly as normal people experience any visual perception. For many patients, hallucinations continue uninterrupted throughout their waking life and respite comes only during sleep. Visual and auditory hallucinations can occur together or separately. Olfactory, tactile, or gustatory hallucinations may also occur but are far less common than visual and auditory hallucinations. *Other perceptual disturbances* may also be present. These include: (1) continued or recurrent déjà vu feelings; (2) a sense of unfamiliarity with the environment; (3) hypersensitivity to light, sounds, or smells; (4) loss of appreciation of the passage of time; and (5) physical sensations such as burning on the skin or pressure in internal organs.

Delusions

Delusions are false ideas that are patently absurd and are not validated by others. Most delusional ideas involve themes of persecution, control, or destruction. The patient, for example, may have the persistent thought that satellites in outer space are controlling his/her thoughts and feelings. Patients may become convinced that the end of the world is imminent. Persecutory delusions are evident in the example of the patient who believes his/her relatives and friends are making fun of him/her and trying to ruin his/her reputation. *Ideas of reference* are a kind of delusion in which the individual finds personal meaning in the behavior of others or physical events that have no such meaning. For example, a delusional patient may believe a news broadcaster is speaking to him/her personally or that the broadcasters words or head movements have a special, secret meaning intended only for the patient.

Thought Disturbances

Schizophrenic patients tend to show a variety of types of disturbance in the thinking process. All show distorted, idiosyncratic logic that is impervious to the rational interventions of therapists and others. Most schizophrenics show a general impairment in the capacity for abstract thinking. For example, when asked to explain the proverb "Strike while the iron is hot," a schizophrenic patient might say that you should put your finger on a hot iron. Such an explanation is an example of the *concrete thinking* schizophrenic patients show. Similarly, the schizophrenic's language can be odd and even bizarre. *Tangentiality* is a disturbance in association evidenced by the patient's speech shifting from one topic to the next without getting to the point. One thought leads to an unrelated thought, and the patient lacks the capacity to control the flow of his/her thoughts and speech so that the conversation makes sense to a listener. Other thought disturbances include *thought interference* (or thought insertion), where the patient feels that some outside person or thing is placing thoughts into his/her mind. In *thought withdrawal*, the patient feels that some outside force is extracting or taking away thoughts from his/her mind. *Thought broadcasting* means that the patient believes his/her thoughts are being communicated to others without the patient verbalizing them. *Thought blocking* describes the patient's sensation that his/her thoughts are stopping abruptly.

Affective Disturbances

Typically schizophrenic patients show a *flattening* or *blunting of affect* (emotion); they may appear apathetic and uncaring. Some schizophrenics show *inappropriate* or *incongruous affect*, for example, laughing about an obviously sad or painful experience such as the death of a loved one. Some patients may experience extreme bliss at certain stages in the illness, and at other times overwhelming dread, apprehension, and doom.

Even patients whose symptoms are controlled by medications and whose illness is in remission may strike the counselor as odd. There may be something peculiar in the patient's affective expression and manner of relating to others. Antipsychotic medications appear to be more effective in controlling the thought and perceptual symptoms of schizophrenia than in treating the affective symptoms.

Behavioral Disturbances

Schizophrenic patients typically have little stamina or drive and show a low energy level. They are generally passive and show little initiative in dealing with life's demands. They tend to lead routine lives and are given to stereotypic language and behavior. For example, schizophrenic patients may follow a daily ritual, doing the same chores or activities day in and day out without variation. Their relationships with others are generally superficial and they typically have few friends. Many schizophrenics stay close with family members late into adulthood and restrict social contact to the immediate family. Severely disturbed schizophrenics may neglect personal hygiene and can be socially offensive. Schizophrenic patients can be very sensitive, particularly to rejecting or hostile behavior from others. The slightest sign of annoyance from another person can profoundly upset the schizophrenic patient and lead to withdrawal and avoidance of others.

These patients' behavior can be unpredictable and their mood and manner of relating can vary from one minute to the next. In interactions, the counselor may have the feeling that the patient is "not all there." Aloofness, awkwardness, and passivity all combine to make these individuals difficult to engage with socially.

Schizophrenia typically develops in stages. The first is the *prodromal* phase. Its onset is insidious and can occur over months or years. Symptoms include subtle behavioral changes such as social withdrawal, strange affect and thinking, reduced motivation, and diminished emotional responsiveness. Following this is the *active* phase, characterized by symptoms such as hallucinations and delusions. During this phase, the patient typically becomes dysfunctional and requires hospitalization and medication. A *residual* phase follows the active phase. Psychotic symptoms may continue but are usually less intense. Negative symptoms such as flat affect, poverty of speech, social inattentiveness, anergia, and anhedonia predominate at this time. Periods of exacerbation and return to the active phase may punctuate the residual phase.

Antipsychotic medication can dramatically reduce or eliminate many of the above symptoms. Counselors may never see these symptoms in successfully managed medicated patients; however, the medications tend to be more successful with hallucinations and thought disturbances and less effective with negative symptoms. The clinician needs to know, too, that schizophrenic patients rarely if ever show equal levels of disturbance in all the domains listed in this discussion. Over time the patient often accommodates to his/her psychotic symptoms and can function in daily living in spite of them.

TREATMENT CONSIDERATIONS

The overarching goal of chemical dependency treatment for schizophrenic patients is a stable life in which the symptoms of both schizophrenia and the addictive disease are under control. A relapse to active alcohol or chemical use can bring on a relapse to active schizophrenia and vice versa. Therefore, proper treatment is geared to controlling both disorders through carefully structured inpatient and continuing care. It is vital that chemical-dependency treatment interface with ongoing psychiatric management. This requires a high level of cooperation and collaboration between addictions counselors and mental health professionals, particularly psychiatrists.

The components of addictions treatment (forming a therapeutic alliance, learning the disease concept, accepting powerlessness and unmanageability, and developing recovery skills) are the same for individuals with schizophrenia as for those without. However, for each of these elements, the timing, methods, and course differ somewhat for the schizophrenic addict. The patient's difficulties with relationships, specifically ego-boundary confusion, impede the therapeutic alliance. Learning the disease concept can be useful in treating both the addiction and the schizophrenia. However, the techniques most often used to teach the disease concept involve abilities in abstract thinking, self-observation, and reality testing that many individuals with schizophrenia lack. Similarly, accepting unmanageability and powerlessness is difficult for someone who has always felt powerless and has never experienced his/her life as manageable. Finally, severely limited social and coping skills provide additional challenges for the patient with schizophrenia. Despite all of these factors, many patients with schizophrenia can benefit from chemical-dependency treatment provided that psychiatric consultation, psychosocial treatment, specialized education techniques, and sound aftercare treatment are incorporated. Discussion of each of these follows.

Psychiatric Management

For chemical-dependency treatment to be effective, the vast majority of schizophrenics need to be maintained on neuroleptic medication. The medication needs to be monitored by a psychiatrist

or at least a physician who is knowledgeable in the care of schizophrenic patients. The stress of therapy may require that medication
be increased for some patients. Since many neuroleptic medications
produce side effects, patients also need to be medically monitored.
The detoxification of patients with schizophrenia is complicated by
the interaction of neuroleptic medication with other psychoactive
drugs and, consequently, should take place in a hospital setting. Even
though most schizophrenics will have had a previous psychiatric or
psychological evaluation, an evaluation of the patient's functioning is
necessary at the initiation of chemical-dependency treatment. Regular contact with a psychiatrist throughout treatment is also highly
recommended. The patient and counselor should work closely with
the psychiatrist to identify *specific* target symptoms treated with
medication that would alert the patient and others for the need to
have medications adjusted. The patient is often the most knowledgeable about his/her symptoms and response to treatment, but may
need a good bit of guidance and encouragement to think about and
discuss what he/she is experiencing.

Psychosocial Treatment

A combination of individual, supportive counseling; group counseling; and formal or informal social-skills training is recommended
for schizophrenic patients. The general focus of counseling should
be on life management and problem-focused interventions. Chemical-dependency treatment provides an excellent opportunity to increase the patient's socialization skills, leading to better adjustment
and an improved quality of life after treatment. Specific attention
should be given to help the patient learn and practice the social
skills involved in twelve-step meeting attendance. Role plays in
which staff and peers model appropriate social behaviors can be
especially effective.

Highly confrontive treatment strategies are generally inappropriate for schizophrenic patients. They tend to lack the abstracting
ability needed to benefit from confrontation and can easily misinterpret the intent of these techniques. Supportive, directive approaches
are more effective. Similarly, highly emotionally stimulating techniques such as psychodrama and intense encounter groups are not
indicated. In therapy situations that are too emotionally charged,

schizophrenic patients can become overstimulated, leading to a worsening of symptoms.

Individual Counseling

Insight-oriented approaches are generally not useful and can lead to confusion for the schizophrenic patient. However, supportive counseling and guidance in dealing with life's problems and demands are appropriate treatment strategies and can prove very effective for increasing the patient's level of functioning (Karon and Vandenbos, 1981).

Individual counseling sessions should be kept very basic. A few easily defined goals should be selected and worked on. Appropriate goals include the patient's identifying and expressing negative and positive emotions, expressing personal needs, and verbalizing conflicts. The counselor can guide the patient through such problems of daily living as how to talk to the opposite sex, what is expected behavior at an AA meeting, how to handle conflicts with fellow patients, and how to get along satisfactorily in the inpatient treatment community. The counselor should keep in mind that schizophrenic patients have profound social problems and often have great difficulty with matters that the counselor may take for granted.

The most important feature of a successful counseling relationship for the schizophrenic patient is the development of trust. In the beginning stages of treatment the schizophrenic may seem excessively defensive and guarded, and it may take time and a great deal of supportive intervention for trust to develop. The counselor's being stable and predictable can help in the development of a therapeutic alliance. A regular meeting time and the inclusion of familiar routines during the session are useful.

These patients are extremely sensitive to other people and the physical environment. They are alert to signs of rejection and annoyance in the therapist. They may view the therapy with extreme anxiety or suspicion. They may see therapy as an intrusion in their lives. Initially, the counselor should spend considerable time discussing with the patient the goals of counseling, what is expected of the patient, and the importance of the patient's psychological comfort. The counselor should let the patient set the pace of therapy. Any gains in self-understanding, expression of interest in other people, or other signs of minimal progress should be liberally reinforced. The therapist should also respect the patient's need for physical and psychological distance in the counseling relationship and in the treatment community.

The counselor should not interpret the patient's fear of intimacy as a sign that counseling is not working or that the patient does not like the counselor. Psychologically, schizophrenic patients struggle with fear of loss of identity and separateness. The intimacy of the counseling relationship may make them feel extremely anxious. The counselor should realize this and allow patients some emotional distance. Chemical-dependency treatment environments tend to have emotionally charged climates that place great importance on intimacy and social bonding. These demands may create excessive anxiety for the schizophrenic patient, who needs his/her "own space" in the counseling relationship and in the treatment community.

Developing and stimulating the reality-testing function is an important component of counseling. The patient uses the counselor to understand reality and distinguish it from fantasy and leans heavily on the counselor to learn about him/herself. In a sense, the patient borrows from the counselor's personality to gain insight into his/her disease, learn what is socially acceptable, realize the impact of his/her behavior on others, and identify situations that heighten anxiety. The therapist becomes a partner with the patient to bring about self-understanding. It is important to remember that impaired-ego functions, including identity and boundary confusion, can complicate this partnership. As strange as it may seem, patients with schizophrenia may need frequent reminders and reassurances that they are separate individuals, apart from the counselor. Statements such as, "This is what *I* think; what do *you* think?" can support this process. The counseling relationship may resemble an adult-child relationship rather than the adult-to-adult relationship seen in more functional chemically dependent patients.

Many counselors feel uncomfortable with schizophrenic symptoms. When they occur, the counselor should not attempt to convince the patient of the irrationality of hallucinations or delusions. If possible, the counselor should ignore psychotic symptoms during the counseling session and keep the patient focused on the topic of discussion. If, however, the symptoms are disruptive to the counseling process, the counselor should try to help the patient arrive at a reality-based solution, such as discussing his/her medication with his/her doctor. For example, the counselor should acknowledge the patient's feelings if he/she states a belief that the nurses are poisoning the medication (the counselor might say, "That thought must seem scary") and encourage the patient to get more information that will help him/her understand this fear. Talking to the nurse, the doctor, or other patients who take medication, or learning more about the medication's side effects may help the patient form a broader reality base on which to interpret confusing thoughts and perceptions.

Group Therapy

Group treatment can provide an excellent opportunity to help patients learn what is appropriate and inappropriate in social interaction. This is important for schizophrenic patients if they are to derive benefit from AA attendance and aftercare group programs. The same general principles apply in group treatment as in individual counseling. In the group, the therapist may need to be more active and supportive with schizophrenics than with other patients. The group can also provide an excellent opportunity for the patient to deal with conflict and aggression. Many schizophrenic patients have deep problems with hostility and the expression of negative emotions, and learning how to verbalize anger and other negative emotions in a safe environment is particularly important for them. In the group, the therapist can help these patients work through disagreements and learn that confrontations and conflict will not harm them. However, the therapist should strictly avoid deliberately encouraging schizophrenic patients to ventilate anger or violent impulses. Techniques involving the use of bataka bats or punching bags to express anger may work with more highly functioning patients, but should not be used with schizophrenic patients.

The therapist should make every effort to build a high level of cohesion in the group, because schizophrenics' success in group therapy is associated with group cohesion. Every attempt should be make to reinforce any effort the patient makes at personal sharing with other group members. Sharing the experience of psychiatric symptoms with group members who genuinely want to understand can be quite effective in helping the schizophrenic patient to feel a part of the group.

Patient Education

Schizophrenic patients should receive a full regimen of addiction education. In addition, they should learn about the negative effects of neuroleptic and other psychoactive drug combinations. Relapse education should be a standard feature of treatment, with particular focus on the role of alcohol and drugs in precipitating a relapse to overt schizophrenia. A physician or nurse should be available to help the patient understand the need for regular medication and to explain the nature and course of side effects from antipsychotic medications.

The therapist should help the patient understand that a daily structure consisting of AA and counseling can reduce relapse to both addiction and schizophrenia (Minkoff, 1989). He/she should be cautioned to avoid high-stress situations such as overwork or intense emotional involvement. The therapist should also help the schizophrenic patient develop a plan in case of a breakdown in social support networks or such stressful situations as a geographical move or a death in the family. Any major change in the patient's life can precipitate problems, and patients should be helped to anticipate problems and make appropriate plans to address them. Evans and Sullivan (1990) describe a useful technique of "fail safe" cards. On one side of each card, the patient writes a situation that could lead to relapse, and on the other side, specific behavioral responses (for example, call sponsor, read Big Book of National Association of Alcoholics Anonymous, go to a meeting).

Ongoing Care

The goals of aftercare for the addict with schizophrenia are to continue the addictions-treatment process and to provide a social and treatment framework in which the patient can experience the inevitable relapses of both disorders without losing the continuity of the recovery process.

Probably the single most important factor in a successful aftercare plan is a supportive, sober living situation. Individuals with schizophrenia are easily influenced by environment and peers. Although few suitable halfway houses or group homes are available for dual-diagnosis schizophrenics, the effort to secure such a situation would be well spent.

Schizophrenic patients should be routinely referred to a psychiatrist who specializes in the treatment of their disorder. Ongoing daily treatment, often called day treatment, may be necessary for less functional schizophrenics. These programs are typically available at local community health centers. They usually include occupational and recreational therapy, both important to rehabilitation.

Patients should be made aware of AA meetings that are close to their homes and therefore easily incorporated into their daily routines. To minimize relapse, every effort should be made to help the patient organize a structured, simple lifestyle.

Studies have consistently shown that family counseling is important for the rehabilitation of schizophrenics. Family counseling to educate family members about addiction, reduce suppressed family conflict, and an increase in positive, open communication is essential to the success of an ongoing program for the schizophrenic addict. Codependency issues are complex for families of dually diagnosed individuals. The family may be accustomed to thinking of the patient as helpless or weak and may need a great deal of education and support to allow the addict to accept responsibility for his/her actions.

CONCLUSION

Individuals with schizophrenia and addiction live with two chronic, relapsing illnesses. Of all the dual diagnoses, they are probably the least well served by existing mental health and addictions services. With an effective addictions treatment program and a well-coordinated aftercare plan, the number and extent of relapses and hospitalizations can be reduced and the patients quality of life improved.

Chapter 6

Cognitive Disorders

Alterations in mental state can occur with any physical condition that leads to insult to the nervous system. These changes, formerly called *organic mental disorders*, are referred to now as *cognitive disorders*. Cognitive disorders are characterized by a clinically significant deficit in intellectual functioning or memory. The most commonly encountered cognitive disorders are delirium, dementia, and amnestic disorders, and these will be the focus of this chapter. Addictions counselors cannot provide direct treatment for cognitive disorders, but they can play a very important role in detecting these disorders and can make use of cognitive rehabilitation techniques to provide effective addictions treatment.

There are numerous medical causes of cognitive disorders. In addition, most of the major drugs of abuse (including alcohol, amphetamines, cannabis, cocaine, hallucinogens, inhalants, opiates, sedative hypnotics, and phencyclidine) can give rise to cognitive disorders during either intoxication or withdrawal. DSM-IV (APA, 1994) designates these disorders as substance-induced delirium, substance-induced persisting dementia, and substance-induced persisting amnestic disorders.

The addictions counselor is probably more familiar with cognitive disorders than most mental health professionals are. Delirium, a frequent complication of intoxication and withdrawal, and dementia are common among long-term alcoholics. These problems most often appear in detoxification settings, but it is important for counselors working in all phases of chemical dependency treatment to be able to recognize and understand the signs and symptoms of cognitive disorders. In most cases, early detection and action are vital for the patient's recovery. The counselor may be the first professional to detect cognitive dysfunction and can play an essential role in assisting the patient to receive prompt medical care. Referral to medical personnel can literally save the lives of some patients. For others, a prompt referral for evaluation and treatment may mean the difference between a return to full functioning and regression to irreversible brain damage.

DELIRIUM

Delirium is a rapidly developing disturbance in mental functioning, characterized by reduced ability to maintain or appropriately shift attention to external stimuli, together with disorganized thinking. Delirium is caused by insults to the central nervous system by metabolic, traumatic, or toxic agents. The course is typically fluctuating and may include reduced consciousness, perceptual disturbances, disturbance of sleep, change in activity, disorientation, and memory impairment.

DSM-IV (APA, 1994) describes delirium as:

1. Disturbance of consciousness (reduced clarity of awareness of the environment) with reduced ability to focus, sustain, or shift attention
2. Change in cognition (such as memory deficit, disorientation, language disturbance, and perceptual disturbance) that is not better accounted for by a preexisting established or evolving dementia
3. Development over a short period of time (usually hours to days) and a tendency to fluctuate during the course of the day
4. Evidence from the history and physical examination or laboratory findings of a general medical condition judged to be etiologically related to the disturbance

Addictions counselors are most likely to encounter delirium that is related to alcohol or other chemical intoxication or withdrawal. However, the possible causes of delirium are numerous and can only be fully assessed by a medical evaluation. Any delirium should be evaluated medically in an emergency setting, even if the cause is presumed to be known. As mentioned in Chapter 2, alcohol- or sedative-withdrawal delirium is potentially fatal and is considered a medical emergency. Head trauma, hypoglycemia, septicemia, and stroke all can appear in conjunction with intoxication and, left untreated, can lead to serious irreversible sequelae. Any condition that adversely affects the brain can cause delirium. Other causes are infections, epilepsy, head trauma, brain hemorrhages, poisons, endocrine disturbances, fever, heart disease, diseases of the liver or kidneys, and metabolic disturbances.

Delirium is a variable clinical entity. It is usually acute in its onset but may be slowly progressive. The symptoms of delirium may fluctuate greatly within each patient and may be quite different between any two patients. It can be very mild and hardly noticeable, moderate, or severely life-threatening, depending on its etiology. The delirious patient, especially in early stages, may present differently at various times of the day to different staff members. The counselor on an inpatient addictions unit may notice, for example, that progress notes for a twenty-four hour period reflect great variability in the patient's behavior and emotions. At staff meetings, various clinical personnel might describe very different impressions of the patient. Delirium should be suspected when there is a dramatic, abrupt change in the patient's level of awareness, thinking, or behavior, especially if the patient has no history of psychological disturbance. Very old or very young patients, chemically dependent patients, and patients being maintained on psychotropic drugs all carry a higher-than-normal risk of delirium.

The signs and symptoms of delirium are as follows:

1. *Memory.* Patients with delirium typically show a disturbance in recent memory or immediate recall. Less common is a disturbance in long-term memory.
2. *Perception.* Delirious patients generally show a disturbance in perception known as *disorientation.* Delirious patients are generally confused about time and place but oriented for person. They may experience illusions, misperceiving familiar objects (for example, mistaking a shadow for a person or a crack in a wall for a snake). Hallucinations (more often visual or tactile than auditory), crawling bugs, and little animals are also common.
3. *Thinking.* In delirium, patients may appear chronically distracted or aloof and uncaring about what is going on around them. Their thoughts and speech may be disjointed and disorganized. They may constantly repeat the same phrase or sentence (persevera-

tion). They show poor reasoning, judgment, and planning, as well as a lack of goal-directed behavior.

4. *Delusions.* Delirious patients may be paranoid and may have catastrophic thoughts such as a belief that the room is on fire. Often the delusions arise as the patient tries to make sense of visual hallucinations (secondary delusions). These patients (unlike patients with schizophrenia and other psychotic disorders) usually respond well to the reassurance that their delusions have no basis in reality.

5. *Affect.* Delirious patients may show blunted affect or affect that is dull, monotonic, depressed, or apathetic. Most often they show labile affect and an abrupt shift in the extent of emotional expression. Agitation or anxiety may be present; if so, the patient usually responds to calm reassurance.

6. *Behavior.* There is great variability in the behavior of delirious patients. Some behave very quietly and others show listless, restless behavior. Some become very agitated. Some patients show tremors and quick, jerky, irregular movements.

Treatment

The role of the addictions counselor is to identify delirium when it occurs and make a prompt referral to a medical-emergency center. The counselor may be able to provide the medical staff with information that is essential in evaluating the cause of the delirium. Certainly the amounts and times of latest drug use are important, but also important are details of recent activities, mental status, and physical condition. Names of relatives and friends who may be able to provide information about the patient's recent history are also helpful. Delirium is a medical emergency, and the counselor should keep in mind that issues of confidentiality are secondary to physical safety.

To determine the etiology of the disorder, physicians use a broad range of procedures, such as mental state examination, neurological examination, laboratory tests, electroencephalogram (EEG), and brain imaging studies. In treatment, the physician may use anti-anxiety or antipsychotic drugs to control the delirious patient's agitation or hallucinations. The patient may also need supportive medical care for complications of delirium such as fever, exhaustion, insomnia, and dehydration.

Following evaluation and treatment of the acute aspects of delirium, environmental factors need to be addressed. Keep the patient in a quiet, well-lighted, well-ventilated room. Playing music in the patient's room and providing calm reassurance is also helpful.

If the patient's symptoms frighten him/her, a brief explanation of delirium can help to reduce alarm. It is also helpful to keep a conversation going with the patient rather than let him/her fall asleep or slip into unconsciousness. Staff should repeatedly orient the patient by stating the patient's name, where the patient is, the time of the day, and what they are doing with the patient. A very agitated patient should have an attendant with him/her at all times. More aggressive patients may need physical restraint to avoid harming themselves or others.

Early treatment of delirium usually results in full recovery. Depending on the type of disorder, some patients sustain permanent brain damage, develop a psychotic condition, or die. Delirious alcoholic patients generally enjoy a return to full, premorbid functioning.

DEMENTIA

Dementia is a syndrome of acquired, persistent intellectual impairment with compromised function in multiple spheres of mental activity, such as memory, language, visuospatial skills, emotion, personality, and cognition (Cummings, Benson, and Lo Verme, 1980). It is the single most prevalent cognitive disorder and probably the one an addictions clinician most commonly encounters. For many patients it is irreversible, but with refinements in diagnosis and treatment, many dementias are now considered reversible.

Unlike delirium, dementia is characterized by a slow, insidious onset and a progressive loss of intellectual functioning. The prognosis for dementia is not as good as for delirium. Over the past decade, however, great strides have been made in the diagnosis and treatment of dementia, and many patients who would once have been doomed to progressive deterioration until death now have a brighter prognostic picture.

The DSM-IV (APA, 1994) criteria for dementia are:

1. The development of multiple cognitive deficits manifested by memory impairment (impaired ability to learn new information or to recall previously learned information), combined with:

2. One or more of the following cognitive disturbances:
   a. *aphasia* (language disturbance)
   b. *apraxia* (impaired ability to carry out motor activity despite intact motor function)
   c. ag*nosia* (failure to recognize or identify objects despite intact sensory function)
   d. *disturbance in executive functioning* (planning, organizing, sequencing, abstracting)

Dementia is characterized by central nervous system (brain) tissue damage that is usually detected in laboratory or neurodiagnostic procedures. It is a serious organic disorder that shows a lengthy course of progressive deterioration. Usually, death results from medical complications associated with the primary disease.

The most common cause of dementia is Alzheimer's disease. The etiology is not well understood, but Alzheimer's is clearly a disease process distinct from normal aging. Besides the direct toxic effects of alcoholism and those resulting from nutritional deficits, other common causes of dementia include vascular disease (strokes), medications, normal pressure hydrocephalus, cerebral mass lesions, infections, degenerative illnesses such as Huntington's chorea, and other metabolic abnormalities. The progression of dementia is dependent on the underlying causes, but can generally be described as having early, middle, and late stages.

Early Stage

In its earliest stage, dementia involves subtle, barely detectable cognitive and physical changes. It is almost never diagnosed at this stage but is often misdiagnosed as a functional depression. Patients suffering from incipient dementia may show any of the following symptoms: loss of energy, decreased ability to deal with stress, loss of enthusiasm for work or hobbies, lower sensitivity to other's feelings, inappropriate laughing, lack of appropriate response to severe losses (for example, death or divorce), disorganized behavior such as inattention to detail, deterioration in grooming habits, and early memory loss (which may be exhibited by increased reliance on lists or other concrete reminders). Other symptoms include increased difficulty in accomplishing physical and cognitive tasks, continual forgetting, and losing ones place in conversations. During a medical evaluation, patients may complain of numerous vague physical symptoms and a general feeling of malaise.

The normal forgetfulness that many older adults experience should not be confused with dementia. The former is not severe and does not result in serious life-functioning problems. Conversely, significant memory loss should not be written off as a normal sign of old age.

Middle Stage

As dementia progresses from the early to middle stage, cognitive losses previously only barely felt become unmistakable to both the patient and others. The patient knows something is definitely wrong with him/her. Impaired memory, especially short-term memory or immediate recall, is easily identified at this phase and is detectable through a mental status evaluation. When asked, for example, to remember a string of numbers forward and backward or a short list of words, the patient will show obvious difficulty. The patient will also show difficulty doing simple arithmetic calculations.

The patient's capacity to learn new information is reduced during the middle phase of this disease. Also, even though long-term memory may be grossly intact, the patient has difficulty constructing a logical sequence of memories. He/she may, for example, remember his/her birth date, date of marriage, and the circumstances surrounding such events, but may get the sequence wrong and state that he/she was married before being born.

On cognitive tests such as IQ tests and even in conversation, the patient shows a reduced capacity for abstract thinking, conceptualization, and other higher cognitive skills. When asked to describe how an apple and an orange are similar, for example, the patient may state that they are not alike. Other examples of concrete thinking may occur in proverb interpretation. When asked to interpret the proverb "Strike while the iron is hot," the patient may state that it is time to iron his/her clothes rather than articulating the meaning, "Act when opportunity presents itself."

The patient may become disoriented during the middle stage of dementia. Many patients suffer panic and anxiety when they forget where they are, even in familiar surroundings. For example, a patient may forget how to get home from the local grocery store and be found wandering helplessly through the streets.

Patients may present for treatment in chemical dependency facilities during the middle phase of dementia. Patients with alcohol-related dementia usually show a marked increase in functioning following detoxification and a few weeks of abstinence. The disorientation and cognitive dysfunction gradually clear, and studies have shown that the cognitive impairment due to chronic alcoholism gradually improves for several months following cessation of alcohol use. Dementia due to Wernicke-Korsakoff Syndrome, in contrast, may show little or no improvement or a gradual decline.

Late Stage

Patients with late-stage dementia are generally inappropriate for chemical-dependency treatment and require hospitalization or institutional care. They show gross memory loss, disorientation, poverty of speech, and loss of self-care abilities. Sometimes they have paranoid thinking and delusions.

In each phase of dementia, patients show great variation in the range and intensity of symptoms, emotional and behavioral changes, and the rate of progression of the illness. Because no two demented patients are alike, accurate diagnosis and *individualized* treatment planning and care are essential.

Treatment Considerations

Many, if not most, individuals entering chemical-dependency treatment experience some form of cognitive impairment for at least a few weeks due to toxicity and/or the effects of withdrawal on the brain (Meek, Clark, and Solana, 1989; Becker and Kaplan, 1986). Traditional chemical-dependency treatment is structured to facilitate the learning process in spite of deficits in attention, concentration, problem-solving, abstract thinking, concept shifting, and memory. Friedrich and Kus (1991) address some nursing interventions applied in these situations, including the use of repetition, encouraging the patient to ask questions for clarification, and offering patients notepads for recording thoughts, feelings, and questions. They emphasize the need for a physical environment with many visual reinforcers, such as posters and slogans. A predictable program structure, multi-modal teaching, and the use of concrete examples are also helpful. These approaches are based on the assumptions that the neurological deficits are temporary and that basic language and social skills remain essentially intact.

It is important for the addictions counselor to have the skills needed to determine when additional evaluation of cognitive functioning is indicated. All patients entering treatment can be assumed to have some degree of impairment. Such deficits are often related to depression (pseudodementia) or anxiety, rather than to actual dementia (Shelton and Parsons, 1987). However, the counselor should know that cognitive impairment is not easily detected from casual conversation. Patients' complaints of memory or other impairments should be taken seriously and evaluated by a professional. The addictions counselor should become familiar with administration of the Mini-Mental Status Exam and use it routinely to screen for cognitive deficits (Folstein, Folstein, and McHugh, 1975; reproduced in Kaufman, 1985; see also Chapter 2 in this book). Over time, in clinical practice, this tool can be used to estimate improvement with abstinence. Significant impairments found to persist past the first three to seven days of abstinence should be referred for neuropsychological testing to differentiate between irreversible conditions and those expected to improve with treatment or with time. Neuropsychological testing can also highlight cognitive and behavioral strengths and deficits as a basis for establishing individualized treatment plans and provide a baseline against which to measure future improvement or decline.

When the physician suspects dementia, the patient may receive a neurological examination, chest X ray, brain scan, urinalysis, and blood studies in addition to neuropsychological testing. Treatment goals for the medical treatment of dementia include addressing the underlying or associated medical conditions, restoring proper nutrition, and providing adequate exercise and physical activity. The physician may also treat any concurrent or related psychiatric problems. Some dementia patients have anxiety, depression, or psychotic disorders that require treatment with psychotropic medication and supportive therapy. Sleep problems may also require medication.

Standard chemical-dependency treatment needs to be supplemented for the patient with dementia, whether the disorder is permanent or slowly reversible, alcohol-induced, or of other origin. Tupper (1991) summarized treatment principles for cognitive rehabilitation that can be useful in modifying addictions treatment to meet the needs of the cognitively impaired. These principles are: (1) higher (or cortical) learning comes from repeated activity; with repetition, learning becomes organized into a functional system; (2) stimulations through multiple modalities and senses supplement each other in learning; and (3) consistent and systematic feedback is necessary. Following these principles, therapists should develop treatment plans and activities that are simple, concrete, and frequently repeated. The more sensory modalities employed (touch, sight, hearing) and the more diverse the learning approaches (lecture, role-play, reading, group discussion, writing), the more likely it is that treatment goals will be achieved and therapy will be effective with these patients.

Addictions counselors can help in treating the patient suffering from dementia by providing supportive treatment for agitation, anxiety, depression, and other negative emotional symptoms. Dementia patients need stability and reduced complexity in their lives; therefore, the treatment plan should be simple, focused, and realistic.

Patients suffering from dementia generally need to make emotional adjustments to accept and deal with their new limitations. Supportive psychotherapy can help the patient adjust to his/her illness. Many patients must take less intellectually or physically demanding employment, and the resulting perceived loss of status may lead to depression. Clinicians doing ongoing work with the demented patient should be alert for the symptoms of depression, a common complication of dementia, and refer the patient for a thorough psychiatric evaluation.

Individual counseling sessions should be frequent and brief. During these sessions the counselor should continually reorient the patient to the facility and the treatment program, as well as expectations, rules, and guidelines. A daily concrete structured program should be developed and written down for the patient. The goals and methods of the treatment plan should be worded simply and reinforced daily in individual sessions. Treatment plans should be limited, especially on concepts such as powerlessness, surrender, and defenses. Counselors should take time to explain abstract terms and give examples.

Patients with dementia should not be overloaded with reading assignments, lectures, physical activities, and meetings. Counselors should reduce the frequency and length of these patients' activities. Reading assignments should be brief. The patient should be encouraged to sit up front at lectures and other educational functions. Assigned seating further reduces confusion and provides stability and familiarity.

The individual with impaired memory needs to be taught to use memory support devices such as a notebook or cue cards. Visual-spatial abilities may also be impaired, and patients may need to be helped to structure their environment with visual cues that will help them get around safely and comfortably. On inpatient units, dementia patients should be housed close to areas such as the cafeteria and nursing station to reduce the complexity of their day-to-day functioning and minimize the chances of disorientation. To assist the demented patient with daily management, a peer "buddy" can be assigned to look after him/her.

In addictions treatment, first-step work needs to be modified for the demented patient. For the cognitively intact individual, the first step involves gaining awareness of the unmanageability of the addiction by recalling and sharing consequences of chemical use. When memory is impaired, focusing on the present and identifying current problems associated with substance use may be more effective. Another aspect of the first step, the concept of powerlessness, can be confusing for cognitively impaired individuals who lack the mental agility to grasp the subtle difference between powerlessness and helplessness. The concrete, straightforward approaches used with the thought-disordered patient can be of use here: "When you tried to stop using without outside help, you were unsuccessful; you need outside help for continued abstinence."

The fellowship of the twelve-step programs can be especially helpful for individuals whose cognitive deficits cause them to feel isolated; yet if they are confused and believe everyone else understands what is going on, bonding with the group can be difficult. Special work with slogans can facilitate these patients' group bonding. We have our patients work with a counselor to choose and write down three slogans that have special meaning for them. Hearing and using familiar slogans helps patients feel as if they are a part of the group. The routines and rituals of the twelve-step meetings, too, can provide comfort and a sense of belonging. It is important that the counselor take the time to talk with the patient about the experience of twelve-step meetings and to help him/her become comfortable about taking part. There are many meaningful ways to participate that do not involve sophisticated cognitive abilities. As the impaired individual becomes more skilled with participation in support groups, the rewards of attending increase.

Another approach that has proven helpful with demented patients is behavioral training (McEvoy and Patterson, 1986). Desired behaviors increase with prompting (including verbal instruction, modeling, and practice); positive reinforcement; and immediate feedback. Role-playing is an especially useful tool in teaching recovery behaviors. Situations can be relatively simple, such as meeting someone new at a meeting, and can increase in complexity, such as responding to an invitation to participate in a drinking activity. As with other approaches, practice and repetition are important for mastery.

Aftercare plans should assure that the patient is placed in a stable environment with adequate support and attention. Family members should be apprised of the patient's limitations and the patient's response to his/her condition, and be encouraged to have regular contact with the patient's physician. The family needs to remain aware of the patient's medical problems, daily life-management issues, and changes in the course of any concurrent psychiatric illness.

AMNESTIC DISORDERS

Amnestic disorders are characterized by the inability to learn new information despite normal attention, intact recall for remote information, and the presence of no other cognitive deficits (Benson, 1978). Common causes include Wernicke-Korsakoff Syndrome, strokes, hypoglycemia, and brain tumors.

According to DSM-IV (APA, 1994), the diagnostic criteria for amnestic disorder are:

1. The development of a memory impairment manifested by impairment in the ability to learn new information or the inability to recall previously learned information
2. Significant impairment in social or occupational functioning and a significant decline from previous level of functioning caused by memory disturbance
3. Memory disturbance occurring not exclusively during the course of a delirium or dementia
4. Evidence from the history and physical examination or laboratory findings that the disturbances are the direct physiological consequence of a general medical condition (including physical trauma)

Amnestic disorders can be transient or chronic. They are often preceded by clinical features such as confusion and disorientation, as well as confabulation. Patients usually lack insight into or awareness of their memory deficits. Some individuals may be aware that they have a memory problem but appear indifferent to it. Some individuals with amnestic disorder show psychological symptoms such as apathy, blunted affect, lack of motivation, and bewilderment. The onset of an amnestic disorder may be acute or gradual. Symptoms may be recurrent or persisting, depending on the etiology. The two most common substance-induced amnestic disorders arise from the prolonged abuse of alcohol and benzodiazepines.

Alcohol-Persisting Amnestic Disorder

This disorder, also known as Korsakoff Syndrome, is the chronic amnestic phase of the Wernicke-Korsakoff Syndrome. It is a condition of gross memory impairment and appears as a defective ability to consolidate, retrieve, and utilize newly learned information. This deficiency results in the patient's having reduced or no ability to use what is stored in recent memory, even though he/she can retain memories of immediate experiences (over a two- to three-minute period). Retrieval of remote memory is often poorly organized and integrated. On psychological tests, patients with this disorder show slowed perceptual processing, premature responding, and a diminished ability to learn from mistakes. Korsakoff patients usually do well on tests that tap overlearned information such as vocabulary and arithmetic, but do very poorly on tests that tap psychomotor speed and visual, perceptual, and spatial organization. Patients often show disorientation for time and place. Psychologically, they can appear apathetic, disinterested, and emotionally bland. Occasionally, transient periods of irritability and anger are seen. Improvement in this disorder tends to be steady but slow.

Treatment for this disorder involves administering high doses of thiamin. Many consider this disorder to be a dementia, and the treatment guidelines mentioned for managing the demented patient can apply equally to patients with this disorder.

Benzodiazepine Persisting Amnestic Disorder

Impaired memory can also result from prolonged benzodiazepine use (APA, 1990). This syndrome is similar to alcohol persisting amnestic disorder. The degree of impairment depends on the dose and route of administration of benzodiazepine use. Generally, higher doses and intravenous administration lead to greater impairment. Treatment guidelines for the management of dementia are also applicable to this disorder.

CONCLUSION

Chemical-dependency counselors can play a vital role in the diagnosis and treatment of patients with cognitive disorders. Armed with knowledge of the signs and symptoms of cognitive disorders, counselors can maximize the treatment response and significantly improve the quality of life of patients suffering with these serious conditions.

Chapter 7

Eating Disorders

Eating disorders have come into sharp focus during the past decade. Our society's obsession with thinness, media coverage of eating disorders, and the development of new self-help groups, have all contributed to increased attention to these disorders in both the professional and lay communities.

An appreciable number of patients with eating disorders also report drug or alcohol addiction. Some studies suggest the rate of addiction is 25 percent or higher, especially for bulimic patients (Mitchell et al., 1985). The cause of eating disorders, like that of addiction, is unknown. Psychological theories have emphasized a disturbance in the formation of the self and identity as basic to the pathogenesis of eating disorders. Biological theories have focused on the role of neurotransmitters in the brain and have likened eating disorders to a form of affective or mood disorder. Family theorists have focused on the central role of pathological family processes in the development of eating disorders. A variety of treatment approaches have emerged from these theoretical viewpoints. Regardless of theoretical orientation, state-of-the-art treatment for eating disorders involves a combination of medical treatment to stabilize the patient, behavioral treatment to help maintain optimal weight and normalize eating habits, and psychotherapy to alleviate underlying personality defects.

Addictions counselors regularly treat patients with eating disorders. The goals of treatment for these patients in chemical-dependency programs are (1) to continue and support effective primary treatment for the eating disorder, and (2) to teach the patient about the interrelationship between the eating disorder and the addiction as well as methods of coping with both.

Patients with serious medical problems associated with an eating disorder are not appropriate for chemical-dependency treatment.

Ideally, patients should have had some success in previous treatment for the eating disorder. However, there is evidence that specialized dual-diagnosis programs are effective in treating both disorders simultaneously (Yeary and Heck, 1989). The symptoms of an untreated eating disorder are so disruptive that they impede the patients ability benefit from addictions treatment. It is therefore important for the addictions counselor to be familiar enough with the signs and symptoms of eating disorders to be able to identify untreated cases and refer them for specialized evaluation and treatment. Of the two basic eating disorders discussed below, bulimia is far more prevalent than anorexia in chemically dependent patients.

ANOREXIA NERVOSA

Anorexia nervosa is a disorder involving a pathological preoccupation with gaining weight. Anorexia occurs in about 1 percent of the population, predominantly in women (therefore the female pronoun is used to refer to patients in this chapter). Only 4 to 6 percent of anorectic patients are male. Most patients develop the disorder between the ages of thirteen and twenty. Along with an intense fear of obesity, the patient experiences a psychological disturbance in body image. Anorectic patients see and feel themselves as fat even when they are grossly underweight. This misperception is so powerful that the anorexic adamantly refuses to allow herself to gain weight to normal or near-normal levels.

Anorectic patients' entire lives revolve around the task of decreasing body weight. These patients may engage in compulsive exercising, such as jogging, aerobics, and swimming to lose weight. They drastically reduce food intake and may refuse to eat in front of others. They may have peculiar eating habits. They may hide food, especially sweets, in secret places around their homes. When eating publicly, they may show ritualistic behavior. For example, they may cut up their food in extremely small portions or arrange the food in neat piles on the plate. The act of eating is surrounded with anxiety. Although the patient may show peculiar and childlike behavior accompanying food intake, typically when confronted about this, the patient denies it or does not see it as a problem.

Some patients' compulsive control over food intake is not entirely successful and they engage in secretive binge eating. (This occurs in 40 to 50 percent of anorexia nervosa cases.) Following such binges, the patient resumes a spartan regimen of exercise and severe dieting. Immediately after a binge, the patient may engage in self-induced vomiting or laxative or diuretic abuse. These practices pose serious medical risks. Continual vomiting can cause cardiac arrhythmia and even cardiac arrest, as well as damage to the upper gastrointestinal tract and erosion of dental enamel. Laxative and diuretic abuse can upset the body's delicate fluid and salt balance and cause permanent damage to the bowels and kidneys.

Almost all professionals who treat anorectic patients agree that these individuals show severe, long-standing personality dysfunction that predates the onset of the anorectic symptoms. On the surface, the anorectic patient may appear congenial, assertive, and pleasant. Unlike patients suffering from depression, anxiety, and other psychiatric disorders, they may appear in control of all areas of their lives apart from the compulsive attempts to reduce weight. Their amiability and social poise belie inner feelings of loss of control, inferiority, and extreme desperation. Far from being in control, these individuals feel like puppets dangled from the strings of life's demands. Psychologically, they feel incomplete, helpless, and ineffectual in conducting their daily affairs. They secretly feel phony in their relationships with themselves and others. They cannot identify and pursue the gratification of their needs, wants, and desires. They do not trust themselves, their perceptions, or their emotions. The anorectic patient harbors a deep fear of being a "nothing" and feels helpless to correct the situation. This helplessness gives rise to often severe panic, anxiety, and depression. To ward off these feelings, the anorexic finds the unique solution in control over the body. The anorexic acts and feels as if her body is separate from her self and hence is something that she can act upon. The environment and the self may seem uncontrollable, but the body can be controlled through strenuous efforts to reduce weight. Through these efforts, anorectic patients develop a feeling of power, autonomy, and even superiority. Their efforts at weight control become a concrete solution to an inner psychological problem.

Some theorists hold that the anorexic's rigid pursuit of thinness ensures her "little girl" status, and thus halts the normal separation-individuation process that occurs as people grow up, form their identities, and leave the family. The fact that anorexia often has its onset at the time of puberty reinforces this view. Through rigid control of weight, the anorexic attempts to remain a child by stunting physical and psychological growth, thus avoiding the complications and responsibilities of adulthood and the attendant chances of failure. Family therapists have noted that anorectic patients show excessive conformity and obedience, reinforced by the patient's family. Families of anorectic patients are typically described as very restrictive in the expression of feelings. Many anorectic patients complain that their families discounted or ignored their feelings as they grew up.

The anorexic is truly a deeply troubled individual. Along with the aforementioned symptoms, these patients typically are sexually maladjusted and may show little or no interest in sex. They can be extremely compulsive in all their activities: work, study, and daily living. Impulsive behavior, such as stealing, self-mutilation, and suicide attempts, may be present. Pervasive depressive symptoms may also be part of the clinical picture. A diagnosis of depression or personality disorder, such as borderline or histrionic, often is present with the anorectic patient. These patients are complex in the nature of their personality dysfunction and the frequency and diversity of symptoms.

Treatment Considerations

Effective treatment for anorexia nervosa involves medical management, individual psychotherapy, family counseling, nutritional education, and behavioral management. These patients are typically extremely resistant to treatment and, like alcoholics and addicts, often need much motivation and encouragement to enter treatment. Denial and other maladaptive defenses may be just as strong in cases of anorexia as they are in addictions.

Anorectic patients are considered appropriate for chemical dependency treatment when their nutritional state is normal, eating patterns are healthy, and weight is normal or near normal. All anorectic patients should have medical and psychiatric consent before entering the often stressful regimen of chemical-dependency treatment. Since psychotropic medications are generally seen as having limited value in the treatment of anorexia, the majority of these patients are not taking a psychiatric drug when admitted to addictions treatment. However, some are being maintained on an antidepressant, chlorpromazine, or amitriptyline, to assist in maintaining weight and to treat depressive symptoms, anxiety, or agitation.

Anorectic patients entering addictions therapy should be given much reassurance and supportive counseling. Admission to an inpatient unit may stir up traumatic memories of prior hospitalization for anorexia and the initial struggle to gain weight and deal with painful feelings. The inpatient addictions environment may also trigger fears of inadequacy or inferiority and competitive feelings. Counselors should do all they can to reduce the patient's anxiety and help her integrate into the treatment community.

Self-Acceptance

A major focus of treatment should be on helping the patient accept herself as she *is* and not as she *should* be. Anorectic patients feel they are somehow "not right." Therapists should acknowledge this belief and point out to the patient that all people have personality characteristics that they dislike. These patients often feel different from other patients and use this feeling to distance themselves from others and denigrate the treatment. The therapist should point out the anorectic patients' similarities with other group and community members. The common bond of addiction can overcome much of the psychological distance that anorectic patients feel.

In the push for self-acceptance, therapists should assist the anorectic patient to express *genuine* feelings, particularly hostile and angry feelings. These patients are very much out of touch with and fearful of angry feelings in themselves and others. They will go out of their way to avoid conflict and maintain a facade of pleasantness and control. This fear and avoidance should be acknowledged and gently worked through. Counselors should avoid strong confrontation with the anorectic patient. The patient is likely to view confrontation as harsh criticism and to be so sensitive to criticism that she may withdraw from the therapy process.

The first step in the twelve-step process of recovery poses another great problem for anorexics. With their compulsive need to control their bodies to offset feelings of helplessness, anorexics may have a particularly difficult time with powerlessness and surrender. Again, the counselor needs to be sympathetic to this difficulty and work intensely and closely with the patient in this treatment hurdle.

Address Beliefs

A common theme in initial addictions treatment is summed up in the phrase, "If your way was so successful, what are you doing here?" This idea graces the placards and posters of many chemical-dependency treatment programs. It points out the denial inherent in the addictions process and challenges the patient's attitudes and beliefs by emphasizing the results of these beliefs. In a similar way, the counselor can challenge the anorexic's view of her thinness by asking such questions as, "What has your extreme dieting behavior gotten you?"; "Is thinness really all it is made out to be?"; "Can one's self-worth be dependent on other factors besides body weight?"; or "Do you think you will really be happy when you obtain your desired weight?" Anorectic patients can be encouraged to check out their personal views about both food and drugs with other patients. The therapist should not disparage the patient's beliefs, but rather accept them and explore their utility with the patient and the group. The therapist can also point out that society is obsessed with thinness in the same way it is with alcohol. Group discussion about the importance of meeting one's own rather than society's needs can be helpful in clarifying and changing the patient's "people pleasing" behaviors and beliefs.

Inner Hurt

Anorectic patients have difficulty reviewing their emotional past and coming to grips with the intense emotional pain and loss they have experienced in their early lives. These patients have pervasive feelings of emptiness, isolation, and rage. Many have intensely ambivalent feelings toward parents whom they see as intrusive and controlling. Strong feelings of jealousy and rivalry with siblings are also often present. In group therapy, these early feelings of hurt inevitably surface both indirectly in the group process and directly through role-playing and family work. Acknowledging deep hurt associated with the family is much more difficult for anorectic patients than it is for other addicts. The therapist should work patiently and slowly with the patient to enable her to gradually acknowledge and express the pain of her early family experiences.

Group Therapy

In the therapy group, anorectic patients may appear less involved, more anxious, and more rigid than other patients. Open discussion of feelings is foreign to them and may make them intensely uncomfortable. It is important not to push these patients too far too fast in group therapy. The therapist should maintain strong support for and sensitivity to the patient's psychological needs.

It is also important for the therapist to inform the anorexic what will take place in group therapy before she enters the group. She should be assured that she will not be harmed in any way. The therapist should encourage the anorexic to be patient with herself because treatment gains are likely to come slowly. Anorexics feel very vulnerable in treatment groups. The group situation stirs up issues of competition, control, superiority, and other negative feelings that can overwhelm the anorexic. These patients should be cautioned that group therapy is not a quick fix and that they can expect to feel impatience, boredom, and anger toward the group or the therapist.

Individual Therapy

In one-to-one counseling, a cognitive approach has proven very effective in changing the anorectic patient's beliefs about thinness and body shape, alleviating her affective symptoms, and helping her return to normal or near-normal weight (Garner and Bemis, 1982).

Over the course of her life, the anorectic patient acquires and develops a system of beliefs, attitudes, and assumptions about what appearance, body shape, and weight are necessary and appropriate.

These beliefs support the anorexic's contention that she must always be both physically and emotionally in control and that she must strive for perfection. Two central beliefs emerge with anorectic patients: (1) weight loss will alleviate emotional and psychological difficulties, and (2) thinness is equivalent to being successful, competent, admired, and unique. In the patient's day-to-day functioning, her irrational, automatic thoughts support these core beliefs. Some examples are, "If I don't strictly control my weight, I will become fat and ugly"; "If only I lose a few more pounds, then I'll feel better and my life will be okay"; "If I stay thin, others will continue to envy me and like me"; or "If I let up, I'll fall apart." These automatic thoughts are held in place by a number of predictable cognitive distortions, including arbitrary inference, dichotomous thinking, personalizing, and selective abstraction (Bowers, Evans, and VanCleve, 1996).

Using a cognitive approach, the therapist works with the anorectic patient to help her become more aware of the underlying beliefs and attitudes that maintain her pursuit of thinness and fears of loss of control. As mentioned previously, these thoughts and beliefs can be gently but thoroughly and systematically explored, and their usefulness challenged. This process can raise the patient's awareness of how her thinking both maintains her dysphoric feelings and supports her frantic efforts to stay thin. Gradually more adaptable, flexible, rational thoughts and beliefs can supplant the maladaptive ones, thus severing the patient's association between her psychological concerns and the need to maintain a particular weight. Experience has shown that when an anorectic patient's dysfunctional beliefs are regularly and consistently explored and challenged, they gradually lose their sway over her feelings and behaviors.

Nutrition

Consideration of the medical and dietary management of the anorectic patient in addictions therapy is beyond the scope of this book; however, some general guidelines follow. Therapists should encourage patients to eat regular, balanced meals and include all food groups. Any peculiar ideas she has about nutrition can be discussed with a physician or nutritionist. Weekly weighing can provide the patient and staff with assurance that the desired weight is being maintained. Regular, sensible exercise should also be encouraged. It may help a patient at risk for purging to team up with a buddy or join others in an activity two to three hours after a meal.

Relapse

The therapist should point out to the anorectic patient that a return to either extreme weight reduction or alcohol or drug use can trigger either disease. High-risk situations for substance abuse or anorectic behavior should be identified and a relapse plan for both disorders instituted as a standard part of treatment.

BULIMIA

Bulimia is a chronic disorder characterized by episodic uncontrolled periods of rapid ingestion of food (usually sweets or junk food) typically followed by self-induced vomiting (purging) to prevent weight gain. Patients may also engage in prolonged fasting as well as laxative, diuretic, and cathartic abuse to control weight gain. Due to their abnormal eating habits, bulimic patients show frequent fluctuations in body weight. Bulimics are aware of the abnormality of their obsession with thinness and their eating habits, but feel totally unable to modify their feelings or behavior.

Bulimia occurs most frequently in females between the ages of twelve and forty. Bulimic behavior almost always occurs in the midst of efforts to reduce weight through severe dieting, which the patient begins because she is dissatisfied with her body shape. Bulimia may develop after a few weeks or a few years of dieting behavior.

The etiology of bulimia is unknown. Many experts believe that bulimia is a variant of an affective disorder. Most bulimics do show depressive symptoms; they may also show severe interpersonal problems, anxiety, compulsive and impulsive behavior, and personality disorders. A significant number of bulimics develop chemical dependency, most commonly with alcohol and amphetamines. Some studies show that substance abuse frequently occurs in the families of bulimics compared with the families of normal controls, suggesting the possibility of a genetic link (Bulik, 1987).

Bulimic patients show a wide range of levels of adjustment. Some bulimics show severe personality dysfunction, such as borderline personality disorder; others are very productive and well adjusted, apart from their eating behavior. Most bulimic patients function between these extremes.

Researchers and clinicians have noted a marked increase in the numbers of bulimic patients over the past fifteen years. Many theorists attribute this in part to our culture's devastating demands on women to be thin and equation of thinness with beauty, intelligence, and achievement. These demands have placed women under intense pressure to engage in any means to reduce weight. Coupled with this is the social prejudice against obesity. Society has become insensitive to and intolerant of the natural diversity in human body shape and weight. The notion that thin is beautiful has led to frantic efforts toward conformity among American women.

Although the exact cause of bulimia is unknown, there are a number of theories as to its origins. Cultural pressures, profound and enduring mother-daughter conflicts, poor interpersonal coping, and the physiological effects of semistarvation all appear to play a part in the pathogenesis and maintenance of this disorder.

According to the interpersonal stress model, bulimia is triggered by negative emotions, such as depression, anxiety, and anger, resulting from disturbances in social relationships. Some writers feel that the dysfunctional relationships many bulimics have are rooted in a conflict-ridden, mother-daughter relationship in which the mother projects her insecurities about herself and her body onto her daughter. The daughter pursues thinness out of feelings of anger and competition. The bulimic is trapped in a no-win predicament. If she does not become thin, she does not acquire the sense of power, autonomy, and achievement that she believes thinness provides; if she does achieve her goal, she wins out over her mother, inducing strong feelings of guilt. Conflicts over achievement, independence, and intimacy rooted in early family conflict can stay with the bulimic patient and color her interpersonal relationships throughout her life.

Bulimic patients may develop binge eating as a response to overwhelming negative affects that surface in interpersonal relationships. Purging behavior (vomiting after a meal), apart from the obvious goal of preventing weight gain, may serve as a self-punishment for overeating or other perceived wrongdoing.

Some writers (e.g., Wooley and Wooley, 1985) feel that semi-starvation resulting from intense dieting is a central cause of many of the bulimic's psychological and physical woes and may be the direct cause of binge eating. Initially, drastic weight loss from severe dieting produces feelings of well-being, happiness, and control. However, the body quickly develops a tolerance to a specific state of weight loss, and more weight-reducing behavior is needed to maintain the euphoric feelings. An escalating pattern of weight loss-euphoria-tolerance-more weight loss eventually becomes entrenched in the bulimic's behavior and leads to a loss of pleasure, depression, preoccupation with health, and extreme fatigue. The patient's efforts to normalize weight also typically produce profound feelings of dysphoria and fear of uncontrolled weight gain. The state of semi-starvation brought on by severe dieting makes the patient extremely vulnerable to cravings and urges to binge. This entire cycle is very similar to the addictive cycle for chemically dependent patients. If the starvation behavior continues for long periods of time, the bulimic experiences her world in an abnormal psychophysiological state. Much as the addict experiences his/her world abnormally in a drug-affected state, the bulimic's experiences or feelings generated in the state of semistarvation are similarly abnormal. If the bulimic cycle is maintained over a prolonged time, the bulimic patient comes to experience severe emotional and skill deficits that make recovery from the disorder very difficult.

Treatment Considerations

Bulimic patients presenting for chemical-dependency treatment should have psychiatric and medical clearance before treatment begins. Eating patterns should be normalized. Establishing normal eating habits usually takes patients about six months from the time of a successfully completed program to manage bulimia. Bulimic patients presenting with a coexisting psychiatric disorder, such as depression or borderline personality, should have had treatment for this condition before entering chemical-dependency treatment. Guidelines for the management of any coexisting disorder in addictions treatment can be found in other chapters of this book.

Addictions treatment, besides providing primary treatment for the addictive disease, can address the psychological conflicts and interpersonal problems that bulimics show long after modifying their eating behavior. Addictions treatment can buttress the efforts of the primary treatment and help offset relapse to bulimia. Patients can also learn about the interrelationship of the eating disorder and addiction and should learn ways to prevent relapse into either disease.

Initial Evaluation

In beginning treatment with the bulimic addict, the counselor should explore the patient's understanding of bulimia, dieting, and nutrition. Any peculiar ideas about eating behavior should be noted. The patient's feeling about her eating disorder should be explored, including what her symptoms mean to her personally in the context of her emotional development and personal struggle. This will help the counselor understand to what degree the patient has made efforts to learn about her disease and how aware she is of its seriousness.

The therapist should also probe to see if the patient can identify emotions, situations, or conflicts that led to bingeing or purging and to learn of any past attempts to avoid bulimic behavior. The nature and severity of urges to binge or purge should be noted. The therapist's overall interest should be how the patient is functioning in her day-to-day struggle with bulimia, how knowledgeable she is about her disease, and how much stress she is presently under. If the patient shows little or no knowledge of bulimia, severely lacks self-awareness, or is struggling hard with urges or cravings, then she should be referred to an eating-disorder specialist for evaluation and possible retreatment. The treatment for chemical dependency is most effective if the bulimic behavior is reasonably under control.

Nutrition

Bulimic patients should be encouraged to eat regular meals and include all food groups. Eighteen hundred to 2,400 calories a day is considered ideal intake to maintain normal body weight. Patients may have a tendency to delay eating and save their appetite for one large meal at the end of the day. This practice should be discouraged in favor of three to four spaced meals per day. To ensure that she is eating normally, the patient can be required to keep a daily log for the first week of treatment, including food and liquid consumed, feelings about eating, and any urges to binge or purge. Once normal eating patterns have been established, this practice can be discontinued. Bulimic patients should also be weighed regularly, preferably once a week. This will help identify any significant fluctuations in weight that could be related to a reemergence of bulimia.

Patients should routinely be referred to a nutritionist or physician to address any questions or concerns the patient or staff may have about eating behavior, weight control, and nutrition.

Medical Complications

The practices of self-induced vomiting, laxative, or diuretic abuse, and prolonged dieting can have serious medical consequences, including electrolyte abnormalities and other metabolic disturbances. Prolonged fasting can lead to dehydration, weakness, lethargy, and cardiac abnormalities. Purging can result in esophageal tearing and dental erosion. Because of these serious symptoms and conditions, bulimic patients should receive a thorough medical evaluation along with appropriate ongoing medical monitoring and follow-up.

Therapy Relationship

It is important for the bulimic patient to feel that the counselor understands her disease and her struggle. To promote trust and reassurance in the therapeutic relationship, the therapist should communicate to the patient his/her knowledge of the course and treatment of bulimia.

The general focus of treatment for bulimic addicts should be on developing self-acceptance. Bulimic patients feel that they have to be thin to be "okay." On every available occasion, therapists should explore other sources of self-esteem for the patient other than weight and body shape.

At a deep level, bulimic patients experience fears of independence and success that may stem from conflicting, competitive relationships with their mothers. Patients need assistance in overcoming their shame and guilt about success and learning that they deserve to be all they can be.

Many bulimic patients show intense conflict over the awareness and expression of hostile and aggressive feelings. Therapists should acknowledge this difficulty and gently work with the patient to assist her in expressing these feelings in group and individual sessions. Confrontive or provocative attempts to push the bulimic patient to express anger should be avoided.

Role-play, especially between mother and daughter or patient and spouse, may be helpful in promoting the affective expression of hostility. Group therapy may activate dormant conflicts about rivalry with the mother or other early conflicts. The therapist should anticipate these and be prepared to address them as they surface.

Like many addicts, bulimics may show deficits in social and coping skills due to abnormal ways of interacting with self and others throughout the active phase of the eating disorder. The bulimic addict has two strikes against her in these areas. The therapist may have to proceed slowly and patiently in helping the patient resocialize and develop the means to deal with internal and interpersonal conflicts.

Bulimic patients typically dislike their bodies. Therapists should encourage frank discussion of the patient's thoughts and feelings about her body. Actually modifying the patient's body image, however, is a difficult task that takes time and a very experienced therapist. It would be inappropriate for the addictions therapist to push strongly to change the patient's body perception. Instead, the therapist should explore the patient's belief and value system about her ideal body, her attitudes toward thinness, and what she imagines a thin body would do for her. Reassuring statements about the patient's physical appearance can have a beneficial, although limited, effect.

Cognitive Therapy

Cognitive and cognitive-behavioral therapy play a central role in the primary treatment of bulimia (Fairburn, 1985). Cognitive interventions can also be helpful to support therapy gains, control urges to binge and purge, and help the patient prevent relapse into active bulimia. The following sections offer considerations for cognitive interventions.

Record Keeping

The bulimic patient can be encouraged to keep a log of situations, feelings, and conflicts that lead to urges to binge or purge or to depression, anxiety, and other negative emotions that may render her vulnerable to relapse. This technique is a regular part of primary treatment for bulimia. Information from these eating logs can be used to identify problem areas to address in group and individual therapy and to plan for relapse.

Binge/Purge Urges

The stress of addictions treatment may activate previously inactive urges to binge or purge. If these cravings reemerge, patients can be directed to deal with them in the following ways:

1. *Distraction.* The patient should go for a walk, make a phone call, talk to another patient, schedule a brief counseling session, listen to music, watch television, or engage in another activity that distracts her from focusing on and giving into an urge to binge and purge.
2. *Delay.* The patient can say to herself that she will postpone the binging or purging behavior and substitute another activity in the meantime, such as going to a meeting, exercising, or reading from the Big Book. If the patient can delay the binge long enough, the urge to do it may subside.
3. *Coping Phrases.* Confronted with an overwhelming urge to binge or purge, the patient can use rational self-statements to help offset it. Some examples are: "The foods I am eating will not result in a large weight gain."; "It makes no difference how I feel now, I am okay and my weight is normal."; "Eating regular meals will not hurt me—it will make me better."; "If I vomit, I may not be able to stop it later."; or "Vomiting will only make me feel worse."

The patient should be encouraged to ride out the urge and view it as a temporary emotional and physical state that may be related to something going on in treatment. Rather than focus on the urge, the patient should be directed to look for its cause and explore associated feelings and conflicts in counseling sessions.

Distorted Thinking

Bulimics harbor deep, conflicted feelings over success, independence, control, and intimacy. They typically have difficulty in self-acceptance and have low levels of self-esteem. The following are examples of cognitive distortions bulimic patients may show and therapeutic interventions to help reduce them.

All or None Thinking. In this distortion, the patient evaluates behaviors or personal qualities in extreme categories. For example, a bulimic patient who has relapsed may judge herself to be a complete failure.

Therapists can challenge this irrational belief by exploring with the patient other positive qualities and past successes in dealing with cravings. It is also helpful to point out to the patient the progress she has achieved so far in treatment. The therapist can help the patient put the relapse into perspective against a background of hard-earned success in other areas of her life.

Catastrophizing. This refers to the patient's tendency to react hysterically to real or imagined setbacks and view them as evidence that the worst will happen. This is the "Chicken Little" approach to personal problems; if an acorn falls, it means that the sky is falling. For example, a bulimic patient with strong conflicts about the expression of hostility may become convinced that the entire group and treatment community will reject her when she challenges another group member. The therapist can counter this distorted, irrational thought by decatastrophizing. Ask the patient, for example, "So what if your group rejected you? Would it really be the end of the world? Would you survive? Does the possibility exist that you could eventually talk to the group and regain their trust and acceptance?" By constantly challenging and exploring the patient's catastrophic fears, the therapist can help the patient see that the feared situation may not be so catastrophic.

Magnification and Minimization. This refers to the patient's tendency to either downplay personal attributes or magnify personal problems, conflicts, and imperfections. For example, a bulimic patient may insist that her previous successes at avoiding bingeing or purging or maintaining normal weight are "really nothing," thereby severely minimizing her success. Another patient may view her social shyness and nonassertiveness as a severe crippling personality flaw that will prevent her from succeeding in life.

Therapists can address the distorted beliefs by questioning the evidence that led the patient to magnify or minimize a particular attribute. The therapist could, for example, ask the patient or group members to give reasons why the patient's ability to maintain normal weight is a substantial achievement. The therapist could also have the patient weigh the advantages and disadvantages of discounting her achievements. With the nonassertive patient, the therapist may ask her to engage in visual imagery, in order to see herself dealing with social situations very assertively. This "success imagery" can be very effective with shy or inhibited patients.

Should, Ought, and Must Statements. These refer to the patient's tendency to place restrictions on personal thoughts, emotions, and behaviors and to feel extremely guilty, anxious, or shameful if she does not live up to her own unrealistic expectations. For example, a bulimic patient with unresolved anger toward her mother might make the statement that she "should never feel angry or hostile toward her mother" and that she is a bad person for doing so. The therapist can challenge this "should" statement by questioning the practical value of it. ("Is it really possible for anyone to avoid conflict with her mother or father?") The therapist can also examine the advantages or disadvantages of a particular "should" statement by asking the patient to construct a list of the pros and cons of holding that belief. ("What will believing you shouldn't have anger get you?")

Cognitive therapy can be useful in treating the ongoing underlying emotional conflicts of bulimic patients (Garner and Garfinkel, 1985). Challenging, clarifying, and modifying the thinking processes of the bulimic patient can resolve the associated emotional pain.

Relapse

Occasionally a patient resumes bingeing or purging behavior in chemical dependency treatment. If this occurs, the therapist should reassure the patient that she has not "blown it" and point out that the episode was a temporary setback, a response to a difficult situation rather than a sign of personal failure or of an inevitable return to full-blown bulimia.

The following rational self-statements can be implemented following a relapse: (1) "This is just a temporary setback; I can get back on track today"; (2) "Abstinence from bingeing is just a moment away"; and (3) "Just because I made a mistake this once doesn't mean I have to return to my old eating patterns."

Relapses occurring in chemical treatment may be due to the stress of the therapy process. Relapses should be dealt with quickly and firmly. The therapist should meet with the patient, gently probe her emotional reaction to the relapse, and reassure her that all is not lost. The therapist should explore the antecedents to the relapse, including conflicts, emotions, and interpersonal stresses, and assist the patient with a plan of action to head off another relapse. This process is very similar to assisting a relapse-prone alcoholic or addict to develop a relapse plan in high-risk situations.

CONCLUSION

Eating disorders are relatively common among chemically dependent individuals. The addictions counselor needs to be familiar with the signs, symptoms, course, and treatment for eating disorders so that he/she can support the progress of diagnosed patients and identify undiagnosed patients who need to be referred for specialized treatment.

Chapter 8

Antisocial Personality Disorder (Psychopathy)

This and the two chapters that follow discuss personality disorders and their effects on addictions treatment and recovery. The addictions counselor is probably quite familiar with these disorders; the sixth of the twelve steps addresses "character defects" that are common in personality disorders. Not everyone with character defects has a personality disorder. Rather, when personality traits are grouped in a characteristic manner and lead to *functional impairment*, personality disorder is diagnosed.

Much has been written on the interaction between personality and addiction (O'Malley, Kosten, and Renner, 1990). Although there is no single "addictive personality," certain personality disorders (such as antisocial) seem to constitute risk factors for the development of addiction. In addition, personality disorders may influence the course of addictions, and dysfunctional character traits can develop *as a result* of addictions. Regardless of the sequence of events, addictions and personality disorders clearly occur concurrently in many individuals.

This chapter provides a framework within which to understand patients with antisocial personality disorder and guide them toward addictions recovery.

DESCRIPTION

Patients with antisocial personality disorder are often described as "con artists." Addictions counselors are familiar with the typical conning behavior of the addict or alcoholic and are usually quick to pick up on the same behavior in the antisocial patient or psychopath. However, conning behavior in the addict with antisocial personality disorder stems from pervasive, well-entrenched characterological problems that predate addiction. These patients can be extremely difficult to treat in chemical dependency programs or any other treatment setting.

According to Gray and Hutchinson (1964), the most significant characteristics of the psychopath are as follows:

1. They do not learn from past experience.
2. They lack a sense of responsibility.
3. They are unable to form meaningful emotional and social relationships.
4. They are impulsive.
5. They lack a sense of morality.
6. They are antisocial in their behavior.
7. Punishment does not alter their behavior.
8. They are emotionally immature.
9. They are unable to experience guilt.
10. They are self-centered.

According to DSM-IV (APA, 1994), antisocial personality disorder is not diagnosed until the patient is at least eighteen years of age. Some examples of behaviors in adolescence that may indicate psychopathy are truancy, delinquency, chronic school problems, persistent lying, chronic substance abuse, vandalism, theft, and cruelty to people or animals. Adult antisocial behaviors include chronic work problems such as the inability to keep a job, absenteeism, or impulsive decisions to terminate a job with no other prospects. In the home and community, psychopaths show an inability to function as responsible parents, neglect of children's medical and emotional needs, unlawfulness, promiscuity, a failure to meet financial obligations, and a massive disregard for the truth.

A diagnosis of antisocial personality disorder indicates that the above behaviors are continuous since the individual was fifteen years of age and are not secondary to some other type of mental disorder. Some researchers feel that the child who later develops antisocial personality disorder has an inability to experience inner stimulation (low cortical arousal) and a decreased ability to inhibit motor activity, much like the child diagnosed as hyperactive. This means that prepsychopathic children cannot rely on their own minds for inner stimulation and relief from boredom, nor do they have good self-control. To achieve some level of inner balance, they adapt to these deficits by constantly searching for stimulation.

Some authors consider "style of parenting" a contributing factor in the development of psychopathy. According to this theory, the prepsychopathic child receives inconsistent discipline from his/her parents. For example, a child fails to clean up his/her room and at various times is punished, not punished, or even told that this behavior is acceptable. The parents' mixed message confuses the child, who learns that the results of his/her behavior are unpredictable and that his/her actions have little or no effect on how others will treat him/her. The child also learns that by persisting in the behavior (for example, not cleaning up the room), he/she eventually gets the desired result (freedom from work). Following this line of thinking, the prepsychopathic child develops little concern for the future, sees little value in planning or goal setting, and learns that pursuit of immediate gratification is the only important thing.

This mode of operating creates obvious problems. Impulsive behavior can and usually does have dire consequences for the individual with antisocial personality disorder. The capacity to delay gratification is a hallmark of maturity in Western society. A person who does not develop this capacity will resort to a variety of devious methods to get his/her needs met.

Meloy (1988) comments on the role of hormonal, neurochemical, and genetic factors contributing to the etiology of psychopathy. Neurotransmitters involved in the regulation of aggression may play a particular, but as yet unknown, role in the development of antisocial personality disorder. This author has also traced the psychological development of psychopathy, conceptualizing it as resulting from maturation deficits due to impaired bonding between child and mother, with particular problems in attachment and identification. In later life the child experiences excessive aggression along with a limited capacity to bond psychologically with others.

The contributions of object-relations theorists have been helpful in understanding the origins of psychopathy, particularly severe homicidal psychopathy. A thorough grounding in object-relations

theory and self-psychology is necessary to appreciate these contributions to our understanding of the origins of antisocial personality disorder.

Minimal Negative Emotions

One characteristic of the individual with antisocial personality
disorder (psychopath) is a relative lack of negative affect such as
anxiety, depression, and guilt. Psychopaths rarely complain of any
extreme in emotion. Anger is probably the most evident negative
emotion but, unlike many addicted patients, the psychopath would
not describe the experience of anger as negative. In traditional
chemical-dependency treatment, a push for the expression of repressed emotions is one of the main functions of group and individual therapy. Similarly, the fourth and fifth steps of the Alcoholics
Anonymous program focus on an emotional housecleaning through
the sharing of negative behaviors associated with guilt, compunction, and remorse. In the sharing and caring climate of group therapy and AA meetings, the psychopath is a fish out of water. Most
clinicians and patients are incredulous when they discover how
emotionally shallow psychopathic patients are. They seem to go
through the most intensive therapy unscathed and can well with-
stand the anxiety-provoking confrontations that occur in addictions
treatment. They can discuss a life of crimes and infractions against
others without compunction. They show a severe deficit in the
ability to feel and, consequently, are unable to empathize with their
fellow human beings. This attribute alienates them from therapists
and other patients alike. Some psychopaths, however, particularly
those with high intelligence, sense the impact of their behavior on
patients and staff and actually *pretend* to feel concern for their
fellow patients in an effort to comply with treatment. The therapist
should be wary of any uncharacteristic breakthrough or sudden
expression of conscience in patients who carry a diagnosis of antisocial personality disorder.

Interpersonal Relationships

Perhaps due to their empathic deficit and inability to delay gratification, psychopaths view other people as a means to their ends,

rather than valuing them simply as humans with intrinsic worth. Psychopaths never develop the ability to love or form close emotional bonds with others. They live a life of emotional alienation and are seemingly immune to the problems of living this way. As a result of their emotional disengagement, they can manipulate others to their own gain in a manner that outrages most people. Their interpersonal relationships are therefore very disturbed. The psychopathic addict gets little sympathy from patients and staff and often has a disturbing effect on the treatment community. To the layperson, a psychopath may appear as a scoundrel or just plain no good. The professional counselor, however, should understand the psychopath to be a very sick individual. Uninformed clinicians can overlook this because of the nature of the disorder. The psychopath needs our empathy and understanding as does any suffering addict.

It will be clear from the next section that treatment of the psychopath demands some modifications in therapeutic approach.

TREATMENT CONSIDERATIONS

While it is possible for some addicts with antisocial personality disorder to achieve sobriety and some degree of recovery, the prognosis is quite poor. Counselors working with these patients need to have realistic and limited goals for treatment. They must always remember that one of the best motivators of change for these patients is to experience the *full* consequences of their behavior. With this personality disorder more than any other, as long as the addict can see some way to "get around," he/she will resist change. For this reason, the form of treatment considered most likely to effect change in these patients is intense, structured therapeutic community treatment lasting months or years (Reid et al., 1986).

In any setting, treatment of the psychopath is frustrating for both therapist and patient. Progress is slow and treatment is full of setbacks. Most psychopaths drop out of treatment. Those who persevere and attain some measure of internal or behavioral change typically show no gratitude to the therapist for his/her assistance. Throughout treatment the psychopath will con and manipulate the therapist. The therapist may, at various times, be amused by these patients, outraged by their lack of conscience, intrigued with the glamour of their high-risk lifestyle, or flattered by their praise of the therapist's skills and knowledge. In treating psychopaths, the addictions counselor should prepare him/herself for the possibility of becoming excessively fascinated by the course of therapy. Doren (1987) has provided a good outline of strategies for managing the psychopathic patient. The following sections draw heavily on his ideas as well as those of Barley (1986).

Misrepresentation of Facts

Typically one of the first issues encountered with the psychopath is the patient's misrepresentation, by omission or commission, of his past. With the psychopathic addict, the lying goes far beyond the denial or minimization seen in many patients early in addictions treatment; it is at times so fantastic as to strain the patient's credibility. I know of patients, for example, who have claimed to be involved with high-level political and professional people responsible for sensitive decisions involving billions of dollars. Psychopaths typically enjoy the effects their lying has on therapists. They are masters at "getting over" and think of it as a game. When their lies are discovered and they are confronted with their manipulation, they typically show no remorse or concern about their behavior.

Since it is difficult, if not impossible, to conduct treatment with inaccurate information, the first step in treating the psychopathic addict is to get reliable information on him/her from external sources such as family, spouse, employer, or the judicial system.

Avoid Intense Interest

Psychopaths, especially those who are affluent and intelligent, can be charming and even charismatic. They may lead interesting lives in the legitimate business world or the criminal underworld. Even those who are cognitively limited and spend considerable time incarcerated can fascinate the counselor with their stories of antisocial behavior. Some counselors find vicarious enjoyment in the psychopath's antisocial behavior and admire the patient for acting on impulses that most socialized individuals would avoid.

When a counselor becomes excessively enamored of the psychopathic patient, he/she loses objectivity and ultimately neutralizes his/her capacity to treat the patient. Any attempt to protect the patient from the consequences of his/her actions—such as defending his/her behavior at treatment team meetings or writing overly complimentary progress reports to parole officers, employers, and other third parties—can be seen as indications that the counselor has given in to manipulation. Addictions counselors should anticipate becoming fascinated with the psychopathic addict and make use of peer and other supervision to guard against this tendency.

Recurring Manipulation

Manipulation is a recurring theme in the therapy relationship with a psychopath, and the initial response to being duped by a patient is usually anger. However, as Doren (1987) points out, a psychopath's expending time and energy manipulating a counselor suggests that he/she has become involved with the counselor; a fragile and tenuous, but meaningful, social connection is formed. Counselors should expect manipulation, accept it, and use it. An example of using manipulation would be to point out to the patient that his/her behavior angers and frustrates the therapist and ultimately stops the patient from getting what he/she wants. The therapist can then suggest ways of asking for help that are more appropriate than manipulation.

Intimidation

Psychopathic patients can be psychologically and physically intimidating. The threats are usually subtle and take the form of insinuations. Counselors working in prison environments often hear veiled threats from their patients. Typically, patients comment on their power and influence and how they could make things "difficult" if the counselor does not meet their demands. Psychopathic patients may make all sorts of demands on the counselor, requesting, for example, that the counselor contact the patient's family, friends, or employers or provide assistance with legal matters. Threats are usually made when the counselor refuses these demands.

Studies show that physical violence toward the therapist is extremely rare. Psychological abuse from psychopaths, however, is quite common. A suggested intervention with an intimidating patient would be, for example, to say, "That kind of talk will not get you what you want from me. If I were you, I'd try another way to talk with me." Therapists should persist in this type of intervention and not give in to the patient's manipulation (Doren, 1987).

Criticism

Most therapists, especially inexperienced ones, want their patients to like them. Few patients openly criticize a therapist or confront counselors with their personal quirks. Psychopathic patients do this frequently. The psychopath may state, for example, that the counselor compares unfavorably with the patient's previous therapist. He/she may criticize the therapist's professional qualifications or clinical skills. For beginning therapists and those who are unsure of their abilities, this tactic can be very intimidating and demoralizing. Such critical behavior should be confronted. Most important, the therapist needs to anticipate this maneuver and place it in perspective as a sign of the patient's serious personality problems.

Flattery

Some psychopathic patients manipulate the counselor through flattery. The patient may tell the counselor that he/she is sharing privileged information because the counselor is the only person the patient can trust. He/she may state that the counselor is the only person in the world who really understands him/her. Therapists should be wary when psychopathic patients begin to say positive things about them. The patient is usually setting the counselor up for a con job. This is particularly true if the therapist's evaluation or impression of the patient is vital for legal or employment purposes.

Confronting Antisocial Behavior

Addictions counselors are accustomed to confronting addicts with their character flaws and con games. Indeed, much of traditional addictions treatment in group formats focuses on getting patients to honestly share their feelings about their behaviors during active addiction. Unlike most addicts, however, the psychopath does not see the error of his/her ways and has no particular feelings of remorse. This can be unbelievable to therapists and group members alike. The temptation for the therapist is to *make* the patient see the inherent wrong in his/her antisocial behavior. Much time may be spent trying to pin down the patient on past illegal and antisocial behaviors. Often the psychopath engages in offensive behavior (such as stealing and lying) in the treatment community, and the therapist may find him/herself in arguments with a patient who persists in lying about the offense. Specific offending behaviors should not be confronted in treatment, because it is usually impossible to prove, for example, that a patient stole something from another patient. Instead, it is useful to ask the patient if he/she *ever* engaged in a particular antisocial behavior. When the patient makes a general admission to a behavior, *this* fact should be the focus of the therapeutic interaction. The therapist should take a practical approach, exploring the consequences of the antisocial behavior to help the patient assess whether the act was worth the results. Confronting the psychopath with the image society has of him/her—a hapless, confused, disturbed person who steals and lies—creates cognitive dissonance in the patient, who views him/herself as "together" and competent. He/she then has to work to reconcile these opposing points of view on his personality. Nonphilosophical, nonemotional confrontations are generally the most useful therapeutic tactics with these patients.

Challenge and Control

Psychopaths show a constant need for external stimulation due to deficits in their ability to self-stimulate. Therapists can take advantage of this need by building challenges into the therapy process to pique their interest and keep them involved. Simply keeping a psychopathic addict in treatment and involved in the therapy process is a major achievement. The counselor can challenge the patient's capacity for abstaining from drugs by saying, "Staying sober requires skills that you simply cannot develop" or "Talking openly and honestly about your addiction seems to be beyond you." These examples illustrate ways the therapist can literally dare the psychopath to get something out of treatment. Psychopaths typically show a strong need to control therapist-patient interaction. They may dominate the conversation, shift the topic, practice one-upmanship, give the therapist the "silent treatment," and use a host of other maneuvers to stay in control. The psychopath is used to controlling social interactions and is very uncomfortable with the "one-down" position inherent in the therapy process. Paradoxical tactics such as those detailed by King, Novik, and Citrenbaum (1984) are often useful in harnessing the psychopath's attempt to control therapy through rebellious, oppositional, or passive-aggressive behavior. For example, asking the withholding, noncompliant patient to remain quiet and uninvolved in the therapy group may have the opposite effect of the patient speaking up and challenging the thera-pist's directives.

Social Skills Training

Psychopaths, particularly those frequently incarcerated, are accustomed to getting their needs met through intimidation and other aggressive maneuvers. Assertiveness and other social skills training can augment these patients' repertory of skills for getting their needs met. As in other aspects of treatment, with skills training the counselor appeals to the patient's "bottom line" mentality; acting more civilly with other people is a more efficient way of fulfilling needs. Through assertiveness training, the patient can learn to deal with other people in more prosocial ways, and this may have a positive impact on the patient's social interaction.

Role-playing is another social skills approach that can be useful with psychopathic patients. Research shows, for example, that when people role-play thoughts, feelings, and ideas that are opposite to their own, they are better able to understand another person's position and even internalize alternative ways to think, feel, and act. Having psy-chopathic patients practice feeling love and compassion, or imagine what feeling love and compassion might be like, may have the effect of making them more pleasant people with whom to interact. Psycho-paths are typically loners who do not form close emotional bonds with others. They see emotional involvement as intrusive and superfluous to their needs. Role-playing friendship, tender emotions, helping behav-iors, and other socialized ways of interacting may modify the psycho-path's behavior just enough to make his/her life and the lives of those around him/her more tolerable.

Finally and most important, *time* is on the side of the psychopathic patient. Studies show that these patients become more adjusted as they grow older, perhaps due to maturation or personality changes that ensue in middle age. If the patient can remain functional and sober long enough, he has a chance of living a better adjusted life in later adult years.

Meloy (1988) has commented on the extreme difficulty therapists, particularly novice therapists, have in treating severely psychopathic individuals, especially homicidal patients and those who present for treatment in forensic settings. Therapists often have difficulty empathizing with such patients and seeing them as genuine human beings. Therapists should be aware of the often severe blows to their own self-esteem that can take place in treating severely psychopathic patients. The psychopath can detect the therapist's internal conflicts, especially those surrounding hostility and aggression, and exploit them for his/her own reasons. Such patients can treat the therapy relationship as a struggle for domination and seek to triumph over the therapist.

Meloy also cautions therapists to be aware of a false identification that severely psychopathic patients can forge with the therapist. In such cases the patient appears to be developing a healthy identification with the therapist and appears to internalize the goals and objectives of the treatment. Such prosocial attitudes and behaviors, however, are superficial and short-lived. To spare themselves aggravation and misery and to maintain an objective view of these patients, therapists should be aware of the potential for apparent gains to prove illusory.

Cognitive Behavioral Approaches

Some authors have found that a cognitive therapy approach can be useful in the treatment of the psychopathic patient (Beck et al., 1990). With this framework, patients with antisocial personality disorder are seen as harboring a number of self-serving dysfunctional thoughts and beliefs. These include:

1. *Justification.* "Wanting something or wanting to avoid something justifies my actions."

2. *Thinking is believing.* "My thoughts and feelings are completely accurate simply because they occur to me."
3. *Personal infallibility.* "I always make good choices."
4. *Feelings are facts.* "I know I am right because I feel right about what I do."
5. *The impotence of others.* "The views of others are irrelevant to my decisions unless they directly control my immediate consequences."
6. *Low-impact consequences.* "Undesirable consequences will not occur or will not matter to me."

Through identification and exploration of these beliefs, the patient can gain a more realistic evaluation of the success or failure of his/her exploitive lifestyle. Experience has shown that psychopathic patients rarely appreciate the self-destructiveness of their manipulative lifestyle. Cognitive therapy approaches can help them broaden their thinking and see that they can benefit from learning a wider variety of ways to get their needs met. Through guided discovery (see Appendix A), for example, the psychopathic patient can assess the advantages and disadvantages of a dysfunctional assumption or behavior, laying the groundwork for him/her to adopt more prosocial ways of influencing others.

Medication

Medications are generally viewed as of limited effectiveness in the treatment of psychopathic patients. There is some evidence that depression encountered in these patients during treatment may be amenable to antidepressant therapy. However, it is important to note that the emergence of affect such as anxiety or depression in therapy is a sign of progress with the psychopathic patient. For extremes in impulsivity or aggressiveness, some patients can benefit from mood stabilizers such as Lithium or selective serotonin reuptake inhibitors such as fluoxetine (Prozac) or sertraline (Zoloft). As with other diagnoses, medication may be indicated for concurrent Axis I disorders.

CONCLUSION

Chemical dependency and antisocial personality disorder frequently occur in the same patient. Although change is possible in these patients, it is rare. The general goal of addictions treatment is to achieve at least an *appearance* of change so that the individual can live long enough to achieve actual change. Work with this patient population is fraught with difficulties but can be endured if the counselor keeps treatment goals realistic and remembers that the patient's best motivator is to experience consequences.

Chapter 9

Borderline Personality Disorder

A number of theorists have developed ideas on the causes and manifestations of borderline personality disorder (Druck, 1989). Although all differ in important ways, most depict the borderline patient as showing several common symptoms and conflicts stemming from psychological stress and trauma in early childhood.

According to DSM-IV (APA, 1994), borderline personality disorder is characterized by a pervasive pattern of instability in interpersonal relationships, self-image, and affect, as well as marked impulsivity indicated by five or more of the following:

1. Frantic efforts to avoid real or imagined abandonment
2. Intense and unstable interpersonal relationships alternating between extremes of idealization and devaluation
3. Identity disturbances with markedly and persistently unstable self-image or sense of self
4. Impulsivity in at least two areas that are potentially self-damaging (such as spending, sex, substance abuse, reckless driving, and binge eating)
5. Recurrent suicidal behavior, gestures, or threats, or self-mutilating behavior
6. Affective instability due to a marked reactivity of mood (such as intense episodic dysphoria, irritability, or anxiety, usually lasting a few hours and only rarely more than a few days)
7. Chronic feelings of emptiness
8. Inappropriate, intense anger or difficulty controlling anger (for example, frequent displays of temper, constant anger, and recurrent physical fights)
9. Transient, stress-related paranoid ideation or severe dissociative symptoms

Patients with borderline personality disorder suffer from profound arrest in their psychodevelopmental functioning that leaves them impaired in nearly all areas of their emotional and interpersonal functioning. They show impairments in the development of a stable cohesive identity, self-esteem, social functioning, the control of drives and impulses, and the capacity to regulate anxiety and modulate strong feelings. These deficits arise from early trauma, extreme frustration, and a conflicted and impaired relationship with the primary caregiver, in most cases the mother. Because these patients never developed a close, secure attachment to a caregiver, they have not developed a sense of inner security, stability, and completeness. Lacking the necessary emotional nurturing, in later years these patients experience a profound and fundamental sense of aloneness and emptiness. No person, thing, or ideal ever seems to fill them up, and they continue to feel separate, incomplete, and dependent. Their sense of self is fragile and highly vulnerable to any type of stressful situation. Of particular importance, especially for chemically dependent borderlines, is the patient's inability to "self-soothe," to attain an inner sense of quiet calm, safety, and stability. Without this capacity, the patient is in a continual state of anxiety and in later life turns to an external agent—for example, alcohol, drugs, or another person—to supply what the self cannot deliver. The patient is vulnerable to extreme separation anxiety when these external agents become unavailable.

The incompleteness, aloneness, and alienation that these patients feel give rise to an excess of hostility and aggression, affects that are already heightened due to the massive psychological trauma they have experienced in early life. The excess aggression renders these patients unstable in the face of the threats to their sense of self that they inevitably experience. The aggression can manifest in self-destructive behavior, such as sexual promiscuity, severe drug and alcohol abuse; self-mutilation behavior; or it can be directed at others as rage and violence. The borderline patient is enraged at him/herself for feeling disturbed and angry at others because they do not suffer as the patient does and will not set things right in his/her life.

BORDERLINE DEFENSES

The unique defensive constellation that borderline patients show falls under the rubric of splitting. Splitting is both a specific defense and a class of defenses, including *projective identification, primitive idealization,* and *devaluation.* These defenses develop as adaptations to the excess of aggression in the borderline patient's personality. They represent futile attempts to stabilize the patient's sense of self and preserve psychological order, and they account for much of the borderline patient's psychological pain and social alienation. The borderline patient suffers from a number of contradictory and mutually exclusive ideas, feelings, and impulses. Splitting defenses are processes that keep contradictory feelings and ideas isolated and separate. The price of these defenses is a lack of a sense of continuity in the self. The patient feels and acts differently under different conditions and responds to others in inconsistent ways.

Primitive idealization is the borderline patient's tendency to see others as totally perfect and good, thus protecting them from being corrupted by the patient's aggressive, sadistic feelings and ideas and enabling the relationship to endure.

Primitive devaluation is the psychological reverse of primitive idealization. The idealized person inevitably fails to live up to the patient's expectations. The patient becomes frustrated or disappointed in the relationship and gains a sense of power and triumph by dismissing and devaluing the person. This is a kind of psychological revenge that temporarily bolsters the patient's sense of self.

In *projective identification,* unacceptable and intolerable ideas, feelings, or impulses are projected outward onto others. Through this defense, the patient anticipates anger and rejection from others and thereby gains a rationalization for expressing his/her own anger, believing that this expression is self-protective. In treatment, the *therapist* may find him/herself feeling and acting in a manner consistent with the projected feelings.

All of these defenses serve to bolster a fragile sense of self and protect the patient from confronting the psychological realities of his/her life. These defenses reflect extremely immature, primitive, and rigid ways of interacting with others. The goal of psychotherapy with such patients is to relax these defenses and eventually supplant them with more mature ones that assist the patient in functioning more adaptively from day to day.

During times of extreme stress, some patients with borderline personality disorder may have psychotic episodes, become self-destructive, and require psychiatric hospitalization. More functional borderlines, in contrast, often strike the counselor as quite normal. They hold regular jobs, can sustain intimate relationships, and show little self-destructive behavior. It is only after an in-depth interview or a few therapy sessions that the counselor begins to see the fragile sense of self and chaotic internal emotional life. Severely disturbed borderlines generally do not seek addictions treatment. Those who do usually have had extensive psychiatric treatment and are appropriate for a dual facility if sufficiently stabilized. Mild to moderately impaired borderlines, more commonly seen in chemical-dependency treatment settings, are less likely than severe cases to pose serious self-destructive risks.

All borderline patients show a disturbance in identity. For example, when asked to respond to the question "Who are you?" these patients are characteristically at a loss for words, become agitated, and may frankly state that they do not know who they are. Indeed, much of the borderline's high-risk behavior is an attempt both to forge an identity and to cope with negative feelings associated with the lack of a cohesive sense of self. Because they do not know who they are, borderlines are often chameleon like in social interaction. They may mimic the qualities, speech, and behavior of those they idealize, including the therapist. They may appear to be entirely different people depending on the social situation in which they find themselves. Due to their desperation in the search for identity, many borderlines become involved in such groups as religious cults. Part of the appeal of these groups is that they supply a social niche, a set of beliefs and values, and other benefits that give the borderline a more solid sense of identity.

Borderline patients can show depression, anxiety, panic, psychotic features, paranoid episodes, and a host of other symptoms. The added stress of detoxification in addictions treatment settings can exacerbate the symptoms of this disorder. Thoughts of suicide and self-mutilation are common, but, in inpatient settings, actual suicide attempts and self-mutilation rarely occur.

A minority of borderline alcoholic patients may have a psychotic episode in treatment, with hallucinations, delusions, paranoia, and thought disturbances. These are typically transitory and usually respond to the administration of an antipsychotic drug. If these episodes occur repeatedly, the patient should be transferred to a dual or psychiatric facility. Sometimes patients experience brief paranoid episodes during therapy (Kernberg, 1975). These periods rarely require antipsychotic medication.

Regressive behavior is also frequently seen in these patients. Some patients present as fairly stable, but as therapy progresses and the frustrations and conflicts of treatment arise, they show symptoms such as anxiety, depression, and extreme anger. Adjunctive individual counseling sessions in times of crisis usually get the patient through these periods. As discharge draws near, many borderline patients have difficulty leaving treatment. They may become more demanding of the counselor's time and quarrel about aftercare arrangements. Short counseling sessions in a supportive therapy mode to discuss the patient's fears and concerns can help ensure a smooth transition to continuing care.

TREATMENT CONSIDERATIONS

Both individual and group therapy with the borderline patient can be difficult. Counselors managing these patients need to maintain close relationships with their supervisors. In addition, the services of a psychiatrist or psychologist are often required, especially for assessment of the patient and during times of acute crisis.

The following section contains both general and specific treatment guidelines for the management of the borderline addict in primary addictions-treatment settings. These guidelines are based on clinical experience and the literature on management of the borderline patient.

General Guidelines

1. The therapist should adopt a tolerant and empathic attitude with the borderline patient. The more the counselor under-

stands the patient's problems, the better the chances of success
in treatment.
2. The counselor should firmly set limits. Guidelines for expected behavior in both group and individual therapy, as well
as expectations of the patient in the treatment community,
should be clearly laid out and consistently enforced.
3. The main thrust of treatment should be on supporting the
patient while offering insight into the addiction.
4. The counselor should closely monitor the patient's mood and
behavior. Referral for psychiatric or psychological evaluation
is appropriate if the patient shows disorganized thinking, psychotic symptoms, or suicidal or other self-destructive gestures.
5. The patient should be routinely referred at discharge for ongoing psychotherapy with a psychotherapist knowledgeable in
the treatment of borderline and addictive disorders.

The overall tone of psychotherapy with the borderline addicted
patient should be highly empathic and aimed at assisting the patient
to gain insight into his/her addictive disease and associated psychological problems. The therapist should acknowledge the patient's
profound inner psychological difficulties and their influence on
his/her adherence to the primary treatment and involvement with
twelve-step groups. Borderline patients are typically envious of
other AA members who seem to develop sobriety sooner than they
do. Some borderline patients have difficulty trusting the wisdom of
AA and NA programs, while others idealize the program, expect
magical results, and inevitably become frustrated and disillusioned.
The therapist should be alert to these dangers and point them out to
the patient.

The therapist provides a kind of psychological model for the
patient and works at helping the patient identify with him/her.
Through interaction with the therapist, the patient learns to anticipate problems, rationally assess them, modulate extremes in emotions, and cope with life's necessities in a more rational and adaptive manner. Much of this can happen automatically as the
relationship between patient and therapist solidifies. The therapist
should acknowledge the patient's gains while at the same time
helping the patient see setbacks in a realistic light.

Borderline patients typically have pathological levels of hostility. Therapists should anticipate that eventually this hostility will be directed toward them. Patients are often envious of the therapist and are wary of being manipulated. The therapist should anticipate these responses, acknowledge them, and work through them with the patient.

A general focus of sessions can be on pointing out to the patient aspects of his/her functioning that he/she cannot or will not acknowledge. These can include contradictory thoughts, feelings, and behaviors; unrealistic expectations of self and others; and areas of functioning in which the patient is denying feelings or thoughts. Although these patients' individuality should be acknowledged their similarity to others in the group/program should also be reinforced to reduce alienation and promote identifying themselves as addicts in the twelve-step program.

The therapist should be alert to how the patient reacts to him/her, and specifically to the role in which the patient casts the therapist. Typically, the patient's mode of relating to the therapist mirrors the way the patient deals with other people in his/her life and reflects conflict-ridden and ambivalent early relationships. The therapist should focus on the "here and now," commenting on how the patient is recapitulating early pathological relationships. As the patient acknowledges these remarks, the therapist can take on a cognitive therapeutic approach to help the patient develop less distorted, more rational ways of relating to the therapist.

The patient should be continually reminded that he/she should discuss whatever is on his/her mind, regardless of how uncomfortable it is. Typically, borderline patients fear discussing feelings of hatred, envy, or hostility toward the therapist. They should be cautioned that withholding information in therapy or lying about aspects of their lives could disrupt their treatment and will hold them back in recovery.

Therapists treating a borderline addict should receive regular supervision from a clinician knowledgeable in the treatment of such patients. It is typical for a therapist to become bewildered, angry, and frustrated, and to experience a host of other negative emotions when dealing with a borderline patient. These patients are adept at drawing the therapist into their world and repeating the disappointment they have experienced at the hands of others in their lives. The therapist should be particularly alert to his/her wishes to rescue the patient. It is easy to fall into the trap of omnipotence with these patients. In such instances, the therapist sees him/herself as the main curative factor in the patient's life and the one who will finally set things right. The therapist should also be alert to strong feelings of anger or sadism toward the patient. The therapist's having strong emotional reactions toward these very troubled patients is the rule rather than the exception, and continued support and guidance from a good supervisor should be considered essential.

Individual Therapy

Perhaps the most common mode of psychotherapy with borderline patients is psychodynamic or expressive therapy, which has as its main focus the interpretation of problems and defenses. The goal of such therapy is a major change in the patient's personality. Alcoholism therapists who are not trained in intensive psychotherapy for borderline patients should avoid such attempts. However, even in treatment for addictions, the following guidelines are useful in the clinical management of the borderline patient.

It is necessary to establish a solid, clear treatment contract with the borderline patient. Borderline patients tend to present very predictable treatment management problems, and most of these can be adequately addressed through the establishment of a comprehensive treatment contract.

It is also important for the therapist to empathize with the patient's psychological plight, highlighting an understanding of the patient's deep problem with trust and his/her fear of engaging in therapy. The therapist should frequently discuss the patient's anxiety about pursuing a life without chemicals. Making specific plans for dealing with a relapse during treatment is extremely important; relapse is quite common with this population. The relapse plans outlined by Gorski and Miller (1979) can apply to the borderline patient. With borderlines, however, it is important for the therapist to determine whether a relapse is manipulative and, if so, to confront and explore the manipulation in therapy. The patient should be told that he/she is expected to maintain sobriety and that if the therapist determines the patient is not devoted to this goal, the treatment will have to be terminated and alternate arrangements made.

The therapist also needs to explain in the treatment contract what will be done if the patient acts out aggressively or self-destructively. The therapist should acknowledge that suicidal gestures or impulses may arise during treatment and tell the patient that when these occur, he/she should report immediately to the staff or, if an outpatient, to an emergency room. The therapist should remind the patient that suicide attempts are not effective ways of hurting the therapist or others in the patient's life.

In addition, the therapist should warn the patient that self-mutilation behavior will not be tolerated and may result in hospitalization. The patient should be told to voice any powerful feelings or thoughts related to self-mutilation instead of acting on them.

The therapist should emphasize that aggression toward anyone in the patient's life, including the therapist, is entirely unacceptable and that the therapist reserves the right to contact any person judged to be at risk of harm.

Finally, the patient should be told that he/she is expected to follow assiduously the guidelines of other health care professionals supervising medication or other modalities that are part of his/her addictions treatment. The patient should be warned against hoarding medications.

When the patient is apprised of all of the above and indicates he/she understands and agrees with these guidelines, the therapist can go on to implement the therapy.

Group Therapy

In group treatment, borderline patients are likely to stand out because of the behaviors characteristic of their disorder as well as their tendency to become upset by confrontation and negative feedback from other group members. It is of paramount importance for the therapist to avoid permitting the patient to be scapegoated for group conflicts and singled out and alienated from other members. The therapist needs to "be there" for these patients and support them during group confrontations. Whenever possible, the therapist should emphasize similarities between the borderline patient and other group members.

Of the curative factors inherent in group therapy (Yalom, 1975), borderlines respond most to *self-understanding, altruism,* and *instal-*

lation of hope. It is this writer's experience that the borderline patient responds well to learning about the dynamics of the addiction process and gaining insight into his/her personal behavior during active addiction. When working with a borderline patient in group, the therapist should emphasize interventions that raise the patient's level of understanding, especially about addictive behavior. The counselor should avoid, however, interpretive and insight-oriented remarks about the patient's borderline condition; this is best handled in psychotherapy.

Altruism involves, for example, the expression of care and concern by group members and personal sharing designed to help other group members. Borderline alcoholics respond well to help from the therapist and group members, and therapists should generate a high level of concern for this patient.

Installation of hope can be accomplished by sharing the success of other addicts in the program. The gaining of hope is very important for borderline alcoholics. Because they have suffered early psychic trauma, borderlines are filled with despair. The therapist should facilitate and support the group's attempts to cultivate hope in the borderline addict.

Borderlines are typically ambivalent about becoming part of the group. They desperately want to be accepted, but fear a loss of uniqueness and identity when they become "one of the group." The therapist should acknowledge this dilemma. Enlightened, empathic statements based on the therapist's knowledge of the borderline's conflicts in the group are powerful curative interventions that have proven effective with the borderline patient.

Cognitive Behavioral Approaches

Linehan (1993a, 1993b) offers immensely practical and effective guidelines for the treatment of borderline personality disorder, and the reader is referred to these works as essential reading. Her approach, termed *dialectical behavioral therapy* (DBT), includes a strong cognitive behavioral component. The following information and guidelines are based on her works.

The best way to understand the borderline patient is to see him/her as functioning from the core problem of *affective disregulation.* Borderline patients have diminished ability to stop themselves from engaging in inappropriate, often self-destructive behavior in response to feeling strong emotions. Likewise, they have diminished ability to respond to psychological challenges in a coordinated, organized, or goal-directed way. Finally, because they cannot "self-soothe," the physiological arousal brought on by strong emotions can be extremely uncomfortable and destabilizing. Borderline patients are extremely sensitive to emotional stimuli and take a prolonged amount of time to return to a stable emotional state after a stressor. Because of all of these, borderline patients do not trust themselves or their emotions, perceptions, and thoughts. Consequently, they seem to be in a continual state of distress and are often demanding and desperate in therapy.

During the beginning stages of therapy with a borderline patient, the therapist should: (1) work actively to decrease the patient's suicidal and self-destructive behaviors; (2) confront and work through behaviors that interfere with therapy; and (3) confront other destructive behaviors, such as high-risk sexual practices, out-of-control spending, and behaviors that undermine job performance. The heart of this approach is to increase behavioral skills that will help the patient attain inner quietude, manage conflict and stress in social situations, and achieve calmness and stability in the midst of strongly felt emotions.

It is important to help the borderline patient accept him/herself and whatever happens to be going on in his/her life and environment. This can be effectively approached through the development of *mindfulness*, an extremely valuable skill for the borderline patient. We suggest that the patient read *Wherever You Go, There You Are* (Kabat-Zinn, 1994) and *A Gradual Awakening* (Levine, 1979) to understand and internalize mindfulness skills. We have found that the practice of transcendental meditation (O'Connell and Alexander, 1994) is also extremely effective in reducing conflict, increasing emotional regulation, and decreasing a sense of distress, even with seriously psychiatrically disturbed patients. Teaching these or any other meditation practices requires that the therapist be familiar with the procedures involved. Also, the patient needs close supervision to minimize the unpleasant experiences that can accompany meditation practices.

Mindfulness involves allowing the mind to come naturally to its original stable state. The patient is told to do the following regularly, and especially in unpleasant situations:

1. *Observe.* Tell the patient to just "be" with the experience he/she is involved in without commenting on it, judging it, or trying to change it. Patients are told simply to witness the thoughts and emotions coming and going and to be innocently aware of sensations and perceptions. This sounds easy enough, but letting go and allowing evenly hovering attention to flow in stress situations requires much patience and practice.
2. *Describe.* When a feeling, thought, or perception arises, the patient is told to use words to describe the experience, such as: "Angry thoughts are flowing through my mind," "My heart is racing," or "A thought of hurting myself has just come into my mind." The patient is then asked to identify and label experiences.
3. *Participate.* The patient is encouraged to let go and enter whatever experience he/she is having. The patient is asked to not resist or refuse any particular experience and just to "be" with it. The patient is gently moved from judging and evaluating experiences to simply letting them happen without any sense of effort or urge to interfere with the process.

Implementing the above procedures can dramatically reduce emotional disregulation, especially if the patient practices regularly and in conjunction with daily meditation or another relaxation procedure. Through the regular practice of mindfulness and other meditations, patients learn to disembed their sense of self from thoughts, sensations, emotions, and perceptions. They can learn that they are *not* their feelings and thoughts and hence are not at the mercy of them. This realization can be very profound and can help promote a more anchored, stable sense of self.

Other Cognitive Behavioral Approaches

According to Beck et al. (1990), three basic assumptions exert a strong influence on the borderline patient's emotions, perceptions, and interpretations of events. These are: (1) the world is a hostile, dangerous, evil place; (2) I am incompetent and powerless to deal with it; and (3) I am basically unacceptable. These beliefs put the patient in a constant state of turmoil and crisis. Because of these basic beliefs, the patient needs to be constantly wary and to avoid or minimize risk-taking in daily living. At this level of thinking, these basic schemas can result in a wide variety of cognitive distortions, the most prevalent being *dichotomous thinking*. With this distortion, the borderline patient views him/herself and the world as discontinuous and discreet rather than continuous. For example, the patient may see him/herself as totally worthless and the therapist as omniscient, all-loving, and completely competent. A minor rejection in a relationship may lead the patient to conclude that rather than love him/her, the other person hates him/her. Through dichotomous thinking, patients can conclude that they will always fail in life, there is no point in living, and they will always be dysfunctional, so that the therapy process and their lives in general are a waste of time.

Alerting the patient to these distortions in thinking, pointing out their "all-or-none" quality, and helping him/her shift to a more realistic, continuous mode of thinking are important in treating the borderline. The therapist can ask the patient, for example, to rate his/her feelings on a scale of 1 to 10, or to rate negative events in terms of what percentage of the time they happen. The therapist should continually probe the patient's verbal report for examples of experiences or events that contradict his/her dichotomous thinking and point these out. The therapist should work gently but persistently at eroding the patient's distorted beliefs and gradually move him/her toward more rational, realistic, flexible styles of thinking and perceiving. At the same time, the therapist should acknowledge and validate the patient's fears of the therapy process and of change in general.

Medication

The use of medication in the treatment of borderline patients, especially with the chemically dependent borderline, is a complex topic. There is no drug of choice to treat borderline conditions, and many psychiatrists avoid the use of medication altogether. Addictions counselors should be aware, however, that antipsychotic and antidepressant medications do have their place in the treatment of the borderline patient. Antipsychotic medication is useful in the treatment of psychotic episodes, and antidepressant medication has been found useful in treating depressive symptomatology in borderlines. Selective serotonin reuptake inhibitors such as fluoxetine (Prozac) have emerged as potentially useful medications for the control of impulsivity in some borderline patients. Borderlines with affective instability or other problems in mood regulation have been found to benefit from the use of lithium carbonate, carbamazapime (Tegretol), and other medications to stabilize mood (Gardner and Cowdry, 1989). Alcoholism counselors should familiarize themselves with the nature of these medications, including their side effects (see Appendix B), in order to understand their medicated patients and recognize signs that they may need psychiatric reevaluation.

CONCLUSION

The prognosis for the borderline addict depends, as it does for any addict, on the patient's level of functioning, family functioning, support at work, and availability and use of aftercare outpatient counseling. Like psychopaths, borderlines tend to become more functional as they age. Research shows that borderline addicts do about as well as nonborderline addicts in abstinence and life functioning up to a year after treatment (Reeve, 1990).

Clinical experience with borderline addicts suggests that these patients can do well in traditional addiction-focused counseling (Reeve, 1990). Some reasons for this might be:

1. The developing identity of being an addict may increase self-cohesion and reduce anxiety and confusion associated with identity conflicts.
2. The concrete structured nature of many inpatient and outpatient alcoholism programs, as well as the clear, concrete guidelines of AA and NA, seems to provide much-needed guidance and practical advice on daily living. This may reduce inner chaos and provide limits for the borderline's behavior.
3. The availability of fellow addicts and sponsors in the formal and informal social structure of AA and NA provide for feelings of safety, acceptance, and support during the borderline patient's many crises.

Borderline patients should routinely be referred for outpatient psychotherapy with a knowledgeable psychotherapist along with standard aftercare addictions treatment.

Chapter 10

Other Personality Disorders

Personality disorders are common in chemically dependent populations, and the presence of a personality disorder usually complicates the course of addictions treatment. Further, many patients in addictions treatment show the traits of several different personality disorders. For these reasons, the present chapter provides information on the personality disorders not discussed in previous chapters, although addictions therapists see them less frequently than they see antisocial and borderline cases. With the information in this chapter, therapists can become acquainted with the wide variety of features common to all character disorders and can acquaint themselves with guidelines useful in the treatment of these conditions.

Personality disorders are characterized by inflexible, maladaptive responses to stressful situations. They are enduring patterns of perceiving, relating to, and thinking about the environment and the self which indicate a deep disturbance in the ability to work, love, and relate to others in meaningful, intimate ways. Patients with personality disorders often lack the ability to empathize with other human beings. They are deficient in the capacity for self-awareness and have an extremely difficult time viewing themselves as others see them.

Usually the psychopathology affects the people in the patient's life more than it does the patient. Personality-disordered patients tend to have strong defenses that spare them extremes in anxiety, depression, and other negative emotions. Patients with personality disorders more often than not come to treatment at the request of a family member, employer, the courts, or another external source. Interpersonal problems on the job, in the home, or in other environments, rather than internal problems, tend to be the presenting problems. However, personality-disordered individuals are not immune to anxiety, depression, and other negative emotions. When they present for treatment voluntarily, it is usually because their characteristically strong, nearly impervious defenses have begun to break down. In chemically dependent individuals with personality disorders, the addictive process can erode the effectiveness of these defenses, exacerbate internal negative feelings, and lower the quality of social relationships. These distresses can have the *positive* effect of increasing the patient's motivation to change, comply with treatment, and resolve interpersonal difficulties.

This chapter explores the remaining personality disorders listed in DSM-IV (APA, 1994). (See Chapter 8 for antisocial personality disorder and Chapter 9 for borderline personality disorder.)

PARANOID PERSONALITY DISORDER

According to DSM-IV, the patient with paranoid personality disorder shows a pervasive distrust and suspiciousness of others, as indicated by four or more of the following:

1. Unfounded suspicion that others are exploiting, harming, or deceiving him/her
2. Preoccupation with unjustified doubts about the loyalty or trustworthiness of friends or associates
3. Reluctance to confide in others because of an unwarranted fear that the information will be used maliciously against the patient
4. Reading hidden demeaning or threatening meanings into benign remarks or events
5. Persistence in bearing grudges; unforgiving of insults, injuries, or slights
6. Perception of attacks on the patient's character or reputation that are not apparent to others, and quickness to react angrily or counterattack
7. Recurrent, unjustified suspicions regarding the fidelity of a spouse or sexual partner

The central feature of this disorder is a long-standing, unjustified distrust and suspiciousness of other people. The paranoid personality-disordered patient takes no responsibility for his/her feelings. This disorder is believed to mask an underlying pervasive sense of inadequacy that the patient projects onto others to avoid personal humiliation. In daily functioning, these patients may show ideas of reference. They tend to overpersonalize events, believing, for example, that when things go awry someone is plotting against them or wants to cause their ruin. They are constantly on alert for any sign of attack or threat. When severely stressed, their thinking can become delusional.

Most people readily recognize the paranoid patient. He/she can be a distasteful person, usually with few friends. These patients can be litigious and excessively moralistic. They have vivid memories of all of the perceived injustices done to them, and these memories provide a rationale for feelings of being put upon by others. Paranoid patients impress others as being rigid, inflexible, and intolerant of differing views. They can appear as bigots. They tend to single out certain ethnic, racial, or socioeconomic groups and project blame for society's ills upon them. They also show a disdain for weak people.

Paranoid patients have unconscious, intense conflicts over dependency and intimacy, and a real fear of love and its effects on them. Typically, they lack intimacy. They have a deep belief that others are out to hurt them and are continually on the alert for confirmation of this belief. If a paranoid patient does become intimate with someone, he/she usually drives the other person away with constant accusations, suspiciousness, and jealousy. Others may find the paranoid individual detached, unemotional, and grim. These individuals are usually quite stubborn and cling tenaciously to their opinions and beliefs, which are often rigid and irrational. They see danger at every turn. They cannot stand to be criticized and are always poised for a counterattack. They view life as a continual struggle, and this engenders strong anger. Paranoids are convinced that their view of life is right and that others are wrong and devious in their motives and behaviors. They come across as lacking a sense of humor. They cannot be objective about themselves and cannot laugh at themselves. They tend to be excessively interested in power, social status, and position.

From a cognitive perspective, paranoids are guided by beliefs such as: "You cannot trust other people," "I must be constantly on guard against others' inevitable manipulation or abuse," and "Don't show your true feelings." From a psychodynamic perspective, these patients project their own internal conflicts and defects onto others, which reduces their anxiety and discomfort and offsets a deep sense of incompetence and inferiority. To others they seem to be continually fighting something and, indeed, most of their psychological energy is tied up in attack and defense. Paranoids approach any encounter in life, especially the therapeutic one, cautiously and suspiciously.

Treatment Considerations

Paranoid patients are difficult to treat. They are excessively concerned with confidentiality and may constantly question the therapist about their records. In group therapy, they may feel that the therapist is secretly trying to make them sicker. They can react to any imagined slight from the therapist with anger or jealousy.

It is important for the therapist to be honest, straightforward, and respectful with paranoid patients. Therapists should not challenge the patient's paranoid beliefs; instead, they should acknowledge these beliefs and empathize with the patient.

The general approach to treatment should be to gradually build a stable therapeutic alliance and gently explore the patient's interpersonal relationships, focusing on the development of trust and intimacy, however fragile this may be initially. The therapist should focus considerable initial efforts on developing rapport and a collaborative posture with the patient. The overall goal is to assist the patient in developing a more realistic, less rigid style of attribution and perception. Therapists should not push the paranoid individual along too quickly in treatment. The paranoid patient considers the therapist "guilty until proven innocent," and it takes him/her a considerable amount of time to trust the therapist. Patients should be allowed much input into setting the agenda during the therapy hour. The patient's initial fears and concerns should be respectfully acknowledged and gently addressed. From a cognitive behavioral perspective, increasing the patient's sense of competence in conflict situations and building skills to deal with interpersonal stressors are important considerations in treatment. Through role-playing and general discussion, the therapist is in a powerful position to help the paranoid individual better understand others and see them in a more realistic light.

Addressing cognitive distortions can also be quite helpful. Paranoid individuals often show *dichotomous thinking.* For example, they tend to see others as either totally trustworthy or completely untrustworthy. They need to see that there are gradations of trust. The therapist can help the paranoid individual learn to realistically determine who is clearly untrustworthy, who can be trusted to some degree, and who is generally worthy of trust (Beck et al., 1990).

Another cognitive distortion paranoids often employ is *emotional reasoning.* The paranoid individual concludes, for example, that if he/she feels anxiety, fear, or threat in a social encounter, the other person must be criticizing or attacking him/her. The patient needs to learn that his/her feelings are not necessarily facts and that they are determined partly by the patient's internal perceptions, beliefs, and thoughts, not just by the actions of others.

Medications such as pimozide (Orap) can be effective with paranoid personality-disordered patients who develop delusional disorders. Prozac (fluoxetine) and other selective serotonin reuptake inhibitors have shown effectiveness in reducing symptoms of severe suspiciousness and irritability.

SCHIZOID PERSONALITY DISORDER

According to DSM-IV (APA, 1994), individuals with this disorder show a pervasive pattern of detachment from social relationships and a restricted range of emotional expression in interpersonal settings, as indicated by four or more of the following:

1. Does not desire or enjoy close relationships, including being part of a family
2. Almost always chooses solitary activities
3. Has little, if any, interest in having sexual experiences with another person
4. Takes pleasure in few, if any, activities
5. Lacks close friends or confidants other than first-degree relatives
6. Appears indifferent to the praise or criticism of others
7. Shows emotional coldness, detachment, or flattened affect

Schizoid personality disorder is characterized by a lifelong pattern of social isolation. These patients show very little emotional expression. Their feelings are constricted and blunted. They show immense discomfort in human interaction and appear cold and eccentric to other people. Socially they are aloof and distant. When one talks to a schizoid patient, one gets the impression that the patient is preoccupied. Indeed the hallmark of this disorder is a well-developed inner fantasy life to which the patient turns for the gratification that he/she cannot acquire in human interaction.

Schizoid patients have few, if any, friends. They typically work solitary, low-stress jobs (for example, night janitor). They lack sexual maturity and rarely engage in dating or other forms of courtship. They have very few social skills, appear awkward and stiff in conversation, and show no trace of openness or spontaneity.

These patients see little or no need for human companionship and nurturance. They view themselves as self-sufficient loners. They do not understand the complexities of other people's feelings, thoughts, and behavior, and see no need to understand. They are in massive denial of their own emotional needs, feelings, conflicts, and concerns. Psychologically, they are simple and concrete. They prefer repetitive, predictable lifestyles that would strike others as boring. For schizoids, others are, at best, an inconvenience and, at worst, a source of considerable trouble and threat, so they keep their distance. They seem quite happy lost in their internal world, but they rarely are happy. Their life of isolation comes at a high price, as they are never able to fully develop as human beings or appreciate the subtleties of the human condition. Those who seek therapy usually do so because of some significant stressor in their lives, often because the necessity of interacting with others for more than just a brief time has caused anxiety. Schizoid patients generally make a poor impression on others, and others may not want to become involved with them. Their continual pattern of isolation leaves them at a distinct social disadvantage.

Treatment Considerations

Schizoids are difficult patients to engage in treatment since they place little value on human relationships; however, a considerate therapist can help them. The chief focus of treatment is on building trust and acceptance to allow the patient to open up. The eventual goal of treatment is to have the patient realize that he/she can get needs met through interaction with others. This is very difficult with schizoid patients because they show deep, very strong conflicts surrounding interpersonal dependency. A therapist may have to be content with far less than getting the patient to invest in a human relationship. The kinds of interventions used with schizophrenic patients may be helpful with schizoids as well, especially techniques that emphasize routine and predictability. In group therapy, other members see these patients as peculiar, and their lack of involvement can incite anger. The group therapist should help prevent the group from scapegoating the schizoid patient by supporting the patient and giving the group information about his/her conflicts.

The therapy relationship can provide a corrective emotional experience for the patient and serve as an effective platform for him/her to model and internalize new social skills and sensitivities. The general goal of treatment is to get the patient to become more socially active and develop extratherapeutic support systems. The therapist should remain active and involved, but proceed slowly and cautiously. Eventually, the patient's fears of the intimacy of the therapy process can be identified and addressed.

From a cognitive therapy perspective (Beck et al., 1990), the focus can be on addressing and modifying the dysfunctional thoughts that keep the schizoid patient isolated and unmotivated, so he/she may be able to pursue meaningful social relationships. Beck et al. identify such automatic thoughts as the following in schizoid patients: "It's better to do things by myself," "It's better to be alone," "I have no motivation," "Why bother?" "Who cares?" "I don't need anyone," or "People are trouble." These thoughts can be countered with more functional ones such as, "Why not bother?" "What do I have to lose?" "Is it imperative that I be alone *all* the time?" "What do I have to lose by including others in my life?" or "I don't need motivation to get things done—I can just do it." Besides countering dysfunctional, automatic thoughts, the therapist can liberally use role-playing to teach the patient what is acceptable and appropriate in informal social interaction and to address the patient's anxieties and concerns.

The therapist may find these patients boring, simplistic, and frustrating, just as other people do. Often, however, these patients do have something enticing about them, such as a special skill or avocation, and spending some therapy time exploring it can benefit both therapist and patient. In the inpatient addictions treatment environment particularly, these patients require much support. Moving from a solitary lifestyle to the buzzing, often dizzyingly intense social interaction in the inpatient environment can leave these patients reeling and they often need much assistance in handling this.

Medication is not often used in the routine treatment of the schizoid patient. Sometimes antidepressant medication can reduce social isolation and detachment, and some very dysfunctional schizoid patients can benefit from a low dose of antipsychotic medication.

SCHIZOTYPAL PERSONALITY DISORDER

Schizotypal personality disorder involves a disturbance in perceiving, thinking, and communicating with others. These patients are typically unaware of their own feelings, yet are quite sensitive to the feelings and intentions of others, especially anger and rejection. These patients are generally very superstitious and often imagine themselves to have psychic powers. Their speech can be quite odd, and therapists and other patients alike can have great difficulty understanding what schizotypal patients are saying.

Schizotypal personality disorder as described in DSM-IV (APA, 1994) involves (1) a pervasive pattern of social and interpersonal deficits marked by acute discomfort with and reduced capacity for close relationships, together with (2) cognitive or perceptual distortions and behavioral eccentricities as indicated by five or more of the following:

1. Ideas of reference (excluding delusions of reference)
2. Odd beliefs or magical thinking that influences behavior and is inconsistent with subcultural norms (for example, superstitiousness, belief in clairvoyance, telepathy, or "sixth sense"; in children and adolescents, bizarre fantasies or preoccupations)
3. Unusual perceptual experiences, including bodily illusions
4. Odd thinking and speech (vague, circumstantial, metaphorical, overelaborate, or stereotyped)
5. Suspiciousness or paranoid ideation

6. Inappropriate or constricted affect
7. Behavior or appearance that is odd, eccentric, or peculiar
8. Lack of close friends or confidants other than first-degree relatives
9. Excessive social anxiety that does not diminish with familiarity and tends to be associated with paranoid fears rather than negative judgments about self

Experience with schizotypal patients in inpatient treatment has shown that, despite their problems, they can be treated successfully and generally do not have extreme problems relating to the community or therapy group. Most show strange manners of speaking, and when questioned, most admit to bizarre perceptions, hallucinations, and paranormal experiences. Initially, many of these patients come across as guarded and, in verbal interaction, show a tendency toward intellectualization as a defense. However, they are usually amiable and compliant. In the emotionally charged climate of the inpatient chemical-dependency unit, these patients may feel very much out of sorts and have real difficulty relating to other patients and staff in a warm, emotional way.

Patients with this disorder are described as peculiar, odd, or even bizarre in their style of functioning. They tend to live on the fringes of the social environment. Schizotypals show a high level of social anxiety and appear continually anxious in most social situations, particularly informal ones. They can appear standoffish, even cold in their emotional style. Others quickly discover that there is something "strange" about schizotypal patients and often feel uncomfortable around them.

Treatment Considerations

It is important for clinicians to keep in mind that they should treat these patients with respect, tolerance, and understanding, and must not ridicule them for their behavior or perceptual experiences. Counselors should realize that these patients do not have control over their peculiar perceptions and manner of relating. They are not feigning crazy behavior. With encouragement, however, they can learn to act in ways that minimize their alienation from other patients. Handling the patient's odd perceptions requires tact on the therapist's part. The therapist should generally discourage schizotypals from openly sharing bizarre perceptual experiences with other patients, because this tends to alienate others in the treatment community. Learning to avoid the expression of bizarre perceptions will also help the patient act in a more socially appropriate way. The schizotypal patient is unlikely to voice appreciation for the counselors help, and the counselor should not anticipate an emotionally close relationship with this type of patient. During times of stress, these patients' symptoms may worsen. The therapist can refer the patient to a psychiatrist for possible neuroleptic medication at these times.

Schizotypal patients have an active fantasy life. They spend much time "lost in their heads" or in solitary pursuits. They have learned in their social development that they cannot get their needs met through relationships with people and rely instead on their own devices. Therapy should focus on helping these patients cultivate the hope that they can get acceptance, love, and other needs met through interaction with other people. The therapist should reinforce even very small gains made in the therapy process. Anxiety-arousing interventions should be kept to a minimum. The therapist should take care that the patient is not alienated or scapegoated in the group therapy process and should actively help the patient express feelings, conflicts, and anxieties. Since schizotypals prefer not to relate to others, the therapy environment can provide a rich opportunity for these patients to establish some level of intimacy and to deal with the anxieties, conflicts, and insecurities that can arise in any social relationship.

From a cognitive perspective (Beck et al., 1990), therapy can focus on identifying and uncovering automatic thoughts and dysfunctional beliefs that the patient harbors. Some examples of automatic thoughts include, "People are always watching me," "I know what others are thinking or feeling," "I can sense the evil in others," or "Something horrible is going to happen here." These thoughts often have little or no basis in reality, and this needs to be pointed out to the patient. Discussing such thoughts with the patient and exploring alternative ways of thinking about psychological events can improve reality-testing skills, which are deficient in schizotypal disorder. According to Beck et al., schizotypal patients suffer primarily from the cognitive distortions of *emotional reasoning* and *personalization.* With the former, the patient believes, "If I feel it, it must be true." This defect in logic can be pointed out to the patient. The patient needs to learn that just because he/she feels something does not necessarily mean that it is a reality beyond the feeling. With personalization, the patient sees him/herself as responsible for events beyond his/her control or influence. When this distortion is identified, the therapist can push the patient to come up with objective evidence for the belief. Once the patient's automatic thoughts, dysfunctional beliefs, and cognitive distortions are identified and explained, the patient can be taught to "catch him/herself" when they arise and can learn to attach less significance to them.

For patients with moderate-to-severe schizotypal symptoms and depression, low doses of antipsychotic medication can prove beneficial. Antidepressants such as amoxapine (Asendin) and fluoxetine (Prozac) have also proven helpful for some schizotypal patients.

HISTRIONIC PERSONALITY DISORDER

Although excessive emotionality and attention seeking occur in many individuals with addictions, they are the essential features of histrionic personality disorder as indicated by at least five of the following (APA, 1994):

1. Discomfort in situations in which the patient is not the center of attention
2. Interaction with others often characterized by inappropriate sexually seductive or provocative behavior
3. Rapidly shifting and shallow expression of emotions
4. Consistent use of physical appearance to draw attention to self
5. A style of speech that is excessively impressionistic and lacking in detail
6. Self-dramatization, theatricality, and exaggerated expression of emotion
7. Suggestibility, i.e., easily influenced by others or circumstances
8. Considers relationships to be more intimate than they actually are

These patients come across as colorful, excitable, and extraverted. Beneath their sensual exterior, they have enormous difficulty developing and maintaining intimate relationships. This disorder is more common in women than in men.

Histrionics are emotionally shallow and unstable and can show extremes in behavior from temper tantrums to tearful outbreaks. They seem to be continually trying to impress people with their looks and talents. These patients are charming, engaging, attention-seeking, and seductive, and they strike others as superficial and capricious in their style of relating and depth of feeling. They can be given to irrational emotional outbursts and displays of temper. They can be quite sensitive to and astute in understanding the problems of others, but are notably low in awareness of their own psychological difficulties. Histrionic patients can be quite dramatic in their mode of self-expression and day-to-day behavior. They are almost obsessed with their self-image and excessively dependent on others for validation and affirmation. In social situations, they tend to be the life of the party, but when such attention is withdrawn or turns negative, they can easily become fearful and depressed. From a cognitive perspective (Beck et al., 1990), these patients have core beliefs such as "I am basically unattractive," "My happiness depends on attention and admiration from others," "I am superior to others," and "Others should submit to my wishes." At a deeper level, histrionic patients harbor the unsettling belief that unless they are continually interesting and entertaining, others will abandon or reject them.

Two frequent cognitive distortions of histrionic patients are *catastrophizing* and *emotional reasoning*. Emotional reasoning, especially, leaves them in constant turmoil because they believe their emotions to be accurate reflections of reality when, more often than not, they are overblown displays of psychological vulnerability. If the histrionic patient feels severely threatened or overwhelmed, he/she can engage in abrupt, often dramatic self-destructive behavior followed by a quick compensation back to relatively stable emotional functioning. Usually, this behavior is designed to punish others who have not fulfilled the patient's needs or expectations. In the addictions inpatient environment, these patients tend to stand out from others and may foment problems in the patient community. In group therapy, less emotionally demonstrative patients often see histrionics as being full of psychological wisdom. Any type of treatment, including addictions treatment, is likely to be eventful for the histrionic patient.

Treatment Considerations

The single greatest challenge to the therapist is to control his/her reaction to the histrionic patient and see the outward behavior for what it is—a defensive cover for real problems of intimacy. The therapist must be able to muster empathy for these patients if he/she is going to treat them successfully. Histrionic patients are very much out of touch with their feelings, and therapists can help them identify and understand their true feelings. Attempts to modify their outward behaviors are usually futile. Confrontation regarding their emotional shallowness would be counterproductive and should be avoided.

In depth-oriented psychological approaches, the therapist would identify, explore, and initiate working through the causes of such dysfunctional behavioral patterns as seductiveness, angry outbursts, manipulation, attention seeking, and superficial emotional relating. These behavioral and emotional patterns often served the patient well as protections throughout childhood, but inappropriately continue into adolescence and adulthood. Assisting the patient to see this and extricate him/herself from these patterns is a lofty but ultimately necessary goal in long-term treatment.

From a cognitive perspective, the general goal is to replace the histrionic's fickle, emotionally dominated problem-solving style with a more rational, skilled approach. Because these patients have a flare for the dramatic, liberal use of role-playing to challenge the patient's dysfunctional beliefs and thoughts is often successful. To offset catastrophizing, it is important to help the patient slow down, think through a stressful situation, and call to mind similar stressful episodes that he/she handled successfully in the past. A patient is rarely incompetent in all areas of life. Simply pointing out the patient's successes in handling other conflicts and transferring those feelings, thoughts, and skills to the present situation can be quite helpful in improving the histrionic's capacity to adapt and change.

Some histrionic patients develop depressive disorders and a significant number also develop anxiety disorders. Their responses to appropriate antidepressant and antianxiety medication vary. The monoamine oxidase inhibitors appear to be the most effective medications for extremely rejection-sensitive histrionic patients.

NARCISSISTIC PERSONALITY DISORDER

Narcissistic patients show a very unstable sense of self-esteem. They need constant positive reinforcement from their environment to keep even a minimal level of self-worth and to ward off depression, which they experience in response to even minor insults to their self-image. As a defense against their fragile self-image, narcissistic patients show a variety of behaviors that suggest they believe they are superior to others. They come across as grandiose and self-pre-occupied.

This pervasive pattern of *grandiosity, lack of empathy,* and *need for admiration* may be diagnosed as narcissistic personality disorder when at least five of the following criteria are met (APA, 1994):

1. A grandiose sense of self-importance (e.g., exaggerates achievement and talents, expects to be recognized as superior without commensurate achievements)
2. Preoccupation with fantasies of unlimited success, power, brilliance, beauty, or ideal love
3. Belief that he/she is "special" and can only be understood by, or should only associate with, other special or high-status people (or institutions)
4. Excessive need for admiration
5. A sense of entitlement; unreasonable expectations of especially favorable treatment or automatic compliance with his/her expectations
6. Interpersonally exploitive; takes advantage of others to achieve his/her own ends
7. Lack of empathy; is unwilling to recognize or identify with the feelings and needs of others
8. Envy of others or belief that others are envious of him/her
9. Arrogant, haughty behaviors or attitudes

These patients carry a sense of entitlement and act as if they are "above it all" when it comes to human frailties. This outward behavior belies an inner sense of inferiority and worthlessness that occasionally erupts into the patient's conscious life. These patients can react with rage to the behavior of others that they construe to be critical or offending. They appear hypersensitive to criticism and interpret constructive criticism or advice as personal affronts.

In group therapy in chemical-dependency treatment environments, these patients can have a difficult time as they interpret confrontation of their defenses as an attack on their self-image. Similarly, powerlessness, humility, and other concepts derived from the twelve steps are foreign to them, and subscribing to them is inconsistent with their self-perception. Since they see themselves as unique, they often have difficulty becoming assimilated into the therapy or twelve-step group. Accepting the identity of addict or alcoholic is likely to be an extremely difficult task.

Narcissists consider themselves special people, unfettered by informal and often formal social conventions. They expect, and seek, admiration from others and can fly into a rage if they do not receive it. They can be obnoxious, competitive, and self-obsessed. They are continually concerned with their social status, power, and prestige. Often, they go into vocations that provide the potential for power, visibility, and adulation. Having any desirable attributes, such as good looks, intelligence, affluence, or special skills, can seduce narcissistic patients into becoming "a legend in their own mind" and keep them entrenched in character pathology.

Extremes of anger and depression are common with narcissistic patients. They can rarely attain a sense of equanimity since they continually have to protect their special status. Under auspicious conditions, others see them as talented, secure, socially poised, and confident, even charming and charismatic. When their needs are threatened, however, they can quickly become rageful and arrogant. They show a marked deficit in their capacity to understand, empathize, and sympathize with others. They expect servitude from others and tend to see others as a means to their own ends.

Treatment Considerations

In treatment, these patients need support during the injuries to their self-esteem that inevitably occur in the therapy process. The long-term goal of treatment is to help these patients develop a stronger, more stable, realistic sense of self, integrating the extremes of grandiosity and self-loathing that they experience. The starting point of therapy for most chemically dependent patients, admitting powerlessness over chemicals and accepting the disease, could be considered the *end* goal for the narcissistic patient. If the therapist can get these patients to admit their powerlessness, identify as addicts, and resign themselves to having a chronic disease that requires a lifelong commitment to recovery, this should be considered a major breakthrough.

Twelve-step approaches to addictions treatment, although difficult, are often effective for patients with narcissistic personality disorder because these approaches focus on identifying and addressing character defects. Many of the character defects often seen in alcoholic and addictive populations, such as grandiosity, impatience, and self-centeredness, are core traits of narcissistic personality disorder.

Treatment goals include increasing the patient's empathy for others, decreasing the frequency and intensity of rage reactions, and assisting the patient in dealing with the hurt and loss associated with the many narcissistic insults he/she has experienced (Sperry, 1995). The therapeutic relationship provides an optimal environment in which to address the patient's deficits in relating to others. The counselor can gently and tactfully point out character and skill deficits and offer ways to address them. Narcissistic patients can be taught to anticipate situations that provoke their anger or render them vulnerable to a severe drop in self-esteem and to take action to minimize the psychological damage in these situations. Therapy is often a rocky road for narcissists, and it is difficult for them to talk openly about their personal shortcomings. They are often massively defended against feelings of hurt, shame, humiliation, envy, and grief. It can take a great deal of chipping away at defenses by both the therapist and the therapy group to get through to narcissistic patients and help them achieve a more realistic self-perception.

Beck et al. (1990) offer excellent guidelines on understanding and treating the narcissistic patient from a cognitive therapy standpoint. The goals of treatment include: (1) altering the patient's grandiose view of him/herself, (2) helping the patient become less reactive to others' evaluation, (3) assisting with more adaptive management of emotional reactions to evaluation or criticism, (4) enhancing the patient's awareness of the feelings and needs of others, and (5) decreasing or eliminating exploitive behavior. Emphasis is placed on helping the patient learn to cooperate better with others and become more realistic in expectations of self and others.

The dysfunctional beliefs of the narcissistic patient, such as that he/she is exceptional and entitled, can be challenged and supplanted with less rigid, more rational beliefs. Alternative beliefs offered by Beck et al. include, "Be ordinary; ordinary things can be very pleasurable," "I can enjoy being like others rather than always having to be better," "I can go for long-term respect from others instead of short-term admiration," "No one owes me anything in life," "Everyone has flaws," or "I am responsible for my own moods and feelings." Assisting these patients to see the negative impact of their assumptions and moving them toward more realistic, adaptive beliefs can be a powerful way to effect basic changes in their character pathology.

Therapists can also help narcissistic patients by discussing their own emotional reactions to the patient, albeit in a tactful, gentle, nonconfrontive way. Providing patients with accurate feedback on their impact on others can be very useful in increasing their empathy and building a more realistic sense of self. It is often helpful to turn the tables on patients when they become demanding or intolerant and ask them, "How would you feel if you were treated this way?" This can also be accomplished through role-playing, where the therapist role-plays the patients behavior and how the patient reacts to it.

Overall, it is important to do everything one can to assist these patients with *acceptance,* not only of their addiction, but also of their own and others' personal shortcomings. Therapy can focus on shortcomings related to circumstances that usually hurt or anger the patient. The therapist can challenge the patient's grandiosity by emphasizing the price of his/her special status. What does the patient lose and what does he/she miss by clinging to a sense of superiority? Does the patient suffer from loneliness? What is it like to be constantly on guard, protecting self-esteem and position? Patients' tendencies toward manipulativeness and exploitiveness can be challenged by reminding them that they are losing out on the many rewards of selfless giving. They can then be informed that involvement in a twelve-step program is an excellent opportunity to give to others.

Some narcissistic patients develop a clinical depression such as dysthymic disorder, which can be treated with appropriate anti-depressant medication.

AVOIDANT PERSONALITY DISORDER

The individual with avoidant personality disorder shows a pervasive pattern of social inhibition, feelings of inadequacy, and hypersensitivity to negative evaluation, as indicated by four or more of the following (APA, 1994):

1. Avoidance of occupational activities that involve significant interpersonal contact because of fears of criticism, disapproval, or rejection
2. Unwillingness to get involved with people unless certain of being liked
3. Restraint within intimate relationships because of fear of being shamed or ridiculed
4. Preoccupation with being criticized or rejected in social situations
5. Inhibition in new interpersonal situations because of feelings of inadequacy
6. View of self as socially inept, personally unappealing, or inferior to others
7. Unusual reluctance to take personal risks or to engage in any new activities because they may prove embarrassing

Patients with avoidant personality disorder come across as excessively shy and reserved. In the clinical interview, they may be seen as very anxious, but deferential and eager to please the interviewer. They are extremely sensitive to rejection from others and require strong guarantees of uncritical acceptance in interpersonal relationships. In many ways they resemble the schizoid patient, but unlike schizoids, they have a basic interest in and desire for social interaction. However, they avoid people to preclude the pain of rejection.

Patients with this disorder see themselves as socially incompetent and inferior. They are constantly wary of others and alert to any signs of criticism or disinterest. They have a low tolerance for any type of unpleasant affect. From a cognitive perspective, the avoidant patient seems to function with the belief that if someone else really found out who he/she was, the other person would find the patient intolerable and reject him/her. Because of this, the patient almost entirely avoids intimate situations. These patients experience an ongoing sense of dysphoria that appears to be a mixture of anxiety and depression. They isolate from others, preferring withdrawal and avoidance to the potential devastation of actively and assertively confronting life's challenges.

Treatment Considerations

The formation of a therapeutic alliance is often very difficult with patients with avoidant personality disorder, and the counselor should proceed slowly and cautiously. These patients need a great deal of supportive therapy, and they need protection in group therapy. They can benefit from assertiveness and other social skills training. They need to learn that many of their reservations about social interaction are irrational. They need to develop a "tougher skin" and to learn that feedback from others is not tantamount to criticism and rejection.

For the avoidant patient, joining a twelve-step group requires a major adjustment to his/her lifestyle. As addicts, these patients can no longer afford to shun people, but their tenuous social skills make the transition difficult. These patients need an understanding sponsor in AA or NA and ongoing supportive counseling to assist them in understanding the demands of a daily recovery program.

The counseling arrangement can be immensely helpful in desensitizing these patients to the anxieties inherent in interpersonal contact. The therapist should do all he/she can to make the therapy experience successful and minimally threatening. These patients can impress therapists as very fragile and anxious, and therapists may feel that they have to tread very lightly in dealing with them.

From a cognitive perspective (Beck et al., 1990), it is important to focus on these patients' tendency to catastrophize any social encounter. The therapist should work steadily at challenging the patient's fears of disapproval and rejection (Sperry, 1995). These patients often discount positive input from others and are poor evaluators of others' emotional reactions to them. They can be adept at manufacturing excuses and rationalizations to back up their avoidant behavior. These dynamics should be pointed out to the patient and the irrational beliefs challenged and tested.

Extremes in social anxiety can be treated with the MAO inhibitors or fluoxetine (Prozac) (Deltito and Stamm, 1989). However, patients may be reluctant to take medications and often have fears about them. Providing accurate information on the medications, their actions, effects, and side effects is especially important for the avoidant patient.

DEPENDENT PERSONALITY DISORDER

This disorder is characterized by a pervasive and excessive need to be taken care of that leads to submissive, clinging behavior and fears of separation, as indicated by five or more of the following (APA, 1994):

1. Difficulty making everyday decisions without excessive advice and reassurance from others
2. Need for others to assume responsibility for most major areas of the patient's life
3. Difficulty expressing disagreement with others because of a fear of loss of support or approval (not including realistic fears of retribution)
4. Difficulty initiating projects or doing things on one's own because of a lack of confidence in one's judgment or abilities, rather than a lack of motivation or energy
5. Going to excessive lengths to obtain nurturance and support from others, to the point of volunteering to do things that are unpleasant
6. Feelings of discomfort or helplessness when alone because of exaggerated fears of being unable to care for oneself

Dependent personality disorder is characterized by the patient's subordinating his/her life to that of another stronger individual. Such patients get others to take over their lives for them. They believe they cannot exist apart from the people they depend upon, and show an intense dislike of being alone. Emotionally, they are pessimistic, filled with self-doubt, and, at a deeper level, show a fear of their own sexual and aggressive impulses. Dependent personality-disordered individuals are often involved in dysfunctional relationships such as marriage to an alcoholic or addict. They act out the part of the long-suffering victim and desperately cling to the relationship for fear of being alone and abandoned.

These patients see themselves as needy and inept, and are seen by others as docile and extremely nonassertive. They have a tendency to develop depression and anxiety. They desperately need another individual to rely upon to make their situation tolerable. They have pervasive fears of abandonment and isolation. This fear gets infused into interpersonal relationships, and the patient becomes excessively concerned with being left to fend for him/herself. As a result, the patient is constantly on guard for any sign of disapproval or disintegration within the relationship. The fragile security the patient acquires through overreliance on another comes at a high price, since the patient never grows up emotionally or takes responsibility for meeting his/her own needs (Sperry, 1995).

Treatment Considerations

In longer-term chemical-dependency treatment, the therapist should expect dependent patients to attempt to transfer their dependencies onto the therapist. Even in short-term inpatient care, these patients show the tendency to reenact their clinging behavior with the therapist. The general goal of treatment is to help the patient grow to a more independent level of functioning, stand on his/her own feet, and develop an individual identity.

The therapist can harness the patient's dependency and redirect it to dependency on twelve-step programs. This is a healthy dependency that may eventually lead to more independent functioning for the patient. As an interim step in this direction, the patient can learn to depend on *several* individuals in both group therapy and twelve-step programs. The therapist can facilitate this process by setting firm limits on his/her availability while at the same time ensuring and encouraging support from others. Therapy should also focus on the appropriate expression of anger and other negative emotions. This can be accomplished, especially in group therapy, as the patient encounters the conflict that inevitably arises in group interaction. In these situations, the patient can be encouraged to recognize, accept, and assertively deal with his/her own and others' anger.

The therapist should be alert to the danger of falling into the patient's dependent trap and recapitulating in the therapy relationship what the patient does with significant others in his/her life. The patient's assumptions about the necessity of relying on others, his/her sense of incompetence and perceived weakness, and other dysfunctional beliefs need to be identified and worked through. The overall goal is to move the patient toward *interdependence,* or the realization that one can attain a realistic level of autonomy with minimal emotional discomfort while acknowledging a healthy reliance on and need for others. Liberal reinforcement of even small treatment successes is very important with this type of patient. Often these patients develop a concurrent Axis I disorder such as an anxiety or depressive disorder. These usually can be effectively treated with appropriate antidepressant medication.

OBSESSIVE-COMPULSIVE PERSONALITY DISORDER

This disorder is a pervasive pattern of preoccupation with orderliness, perfectionism, and mental and interpersonal control at the expense of flexibility, openness, and efficiency as indicated by four or more of the following (APA, 1994):

1. Preoccupation with details, rules, lists, order, organization, or schedules to the extent that the point of the activity is lost
2. Perfectionism that interferes with task completion (for example, the patient is unable to complete a project because his/her own overly strict standards are not met)
3. Excessive devotion to work and productivity to the exclusion of leisure activities and friendships (not accounted for by obvious economic necessity)
4. Overconscientiousness, scrupulousness, and inflexibility about matters of morality, ethics, or values (not accounted for by cultural or religious identification)
5. Inability to discard worn-out or worthless objects even when they have no sentimental value
6. Reluctance to delegate tasks or work with others unless they submit to exactly the patient's way of doing things

7. A miserly spending style toward both self and others; money is viewed as something to be hoarded for future catastrophes
8. Rigidity and stubbornness

Patients with obsessive-compulsive personality disorder show a limited range of emotions and impress others as emotionally cold. The patient places a high value on orderliness, cleanliness, and efficiency. These patients can come across as stubborn and indecisive. They alienate others through their inability to show tender feelings, their formal behavior, exact speech, and critical nature. This disorder is more common in men than in women.

Obsessive-compulsive personality-disordered patients typically had very strict upbringings. Such patients are usually employed in vocations that require precision, orderliness, and exactness (for example, accountant, dentist, or engineer). These patients have difficulty experiencing pleasure and show a proneness to depression. They always seem to be in a serious mood and come across as humorless. Mentally, they show extreme indecision due to their strong fear of making a mistake. Any important decision may involve in-depth preparation, continual checking and rechecking of options, and overconcern with the exactness of information. Such behaviors can lead to difficulty in vocational and domestic decision making. The obsessive-compulsive personality-disordered patient usually has a stable job and family life, but few friends. Psychologically, he/she shows isolated affect and tends toward intellectualization as a defense.

Patients with obsessive-compulsive personality disorder can be described as extremely stubborn, strong-willed, and proud, and are often tireless in their work and avocations. They harbor a deep fear of experiencing and showing tender emotions and generally keep their feelings to themselves. However, during periods of stress, they can have angry outbursts and are given to criticizing and complaining. They place a strong premium on perfectionism and, above all, control. They are extremely hard on themselves, expect themselves to live up to unrealistically high standards, and often hold others to these same standards. A deep fear of making mistakes fuels a tendency toward procrastination and passive-aggression. Inwardly, these patients view themselves as incompetent or helpless, and their outward behav-

ior can be construed as a way to compensate for this fear. They need
order and predictability, and when they do not get them, they can
become disorganized and overwhelmed.

Obsessive-compulsive patients are notoriously uncomfortable in
social situations, particularly informal ones. They have a stilted,
controlled social style. Their humor is often dry and sarcastic. They
are not good at introspection, and to others they seem immensely out
of touch with their feelings. During periods of stress, they can
become extremely guilty, self-critical, anxious, depressed, and prone
to rumination about real or imagined problems and shortcomings.
Such symptoms can lead these patients to seek professional help.
Abuse of drugs or alcohol contrasts markedly to their otherwise
orderly, rigid lifestyles. Drug and alcohol use seems to provide a
"breaking out" that allows the patient to give in to forbidden feelings, act out unacceptable wishes and impulses, and experience
affective extremes. When the patient is again sober, he/she can ratio-
nalize what happened during periods of intoxication as ego-alien,
drug-induced experiences for which the patient is not responsible.

Treatment Considerations

Unlike sufferers from most of the other personality disorders,
these patients may come to treatment with a sense that something is
very wrong with their lives. They may complain that they are
unhappy or desire greater emotional and behavioral freedom. The
emotionally charged psychological climate of chemical-dependency treatment is a very good environment for these patients.
Therapy should focus on evoking feelings and encouraging their
expression as well as identifying and confronting defenses. In group
interaction, extreme controlling behavior or criticalness can be
pointed out and discussed. Depression, if it occurs, usually responds
to the supportive and behavioral approaches discussed in the chapter on affective disorders.

The goal of treatment with obsessive-compulsive personality disorder is to reduce the patient's inner fears to a manageable level.
These patients are afraid of making mistakes, of being imperfect, of
feeling, and of being exposed to themselves and others. The
defenses and behaviors in which they engage are all designed to
minimize fear, chiefly through acquiring as much control as they

can. Objectives for this type of patient are to help the patient gain emotional balance, a greater sense of joy in life, and a greater acceptance of self and others, especially of character defects and imperfections. As therapists, we want these patients to feel less emotionally guarded around others. We want them to learn that it is okay to feel and to make mistakes, and that neither of these is the end of the world. Ultimately, the patient has to learn that his/her prized goal, control, is an illusion after all. No one controls life. We can only *influence* conditions. There are simply too many variables to control, and some are inevitably left out. Moreover, who controls the controller? How does the patient know that his/her controlling behavior is under control? The answer to this question is not mere philosophical speculation. It exposes a basic fallacy in the patient's belief system.

In addictions treatment, the patient is usually told to "let go and let God," accept the disease of addiction and surrender to the treatment process. Obsessive-compulsive disordered patients need particular assistance with these tasks. Liberal use of relaxation, meditation, and inner-child work can facilitate the process of letting go. The patient needs to learn how to achieve the spontaneity, pleasure, and freedom that drug use artificially provided in ordinary, natural ways through genuine, intimate, here-and-now interactions with others and him/herself.

Beck et al. offer several excellent treatment guidelines from a cognitive perspective (1990). They emphasize the importance of uncovering and challenging the basic irrational assumptions and beliefs these patients hold. Some of these are: "I must avoid mistakes to be worthwhile," "To make a mistake is to have failed and failure is intolerable," "I must be perfectly in control of my environment as well as myself," "Loss of control is intolerable and dangerous," and "If the perfect course of action is not clear, it's better to do nothing." Besides uncovering and challenging these beliefs, the therapist can point out these patients' tendency to engage in dichotomous or all-or-none thinking. Some examples of this are seeing oneself as either perfect or imperfect, good or bad, in control or out of control, right or wrong, decisive or indecisive. In addition, the therapist can enumerate and catalogue the many "shoulds" these patients harbor and systematically challenge them by asking, "Who says?"; "Where is this written?"; or "How do you know for sure this is true?" The goal is to expose the rigid, absolute nature of these thoughts and help the patient see that they are entirely arbitrary proclamations that he/she has simply become accustomed to generating.

The inclusion of cognitively oriented therapy in the patient's addictions treatment often helps to counterbalance the more evocative, emotional focus of many addictions therapy approaches. Obsessive-compulsive personality-disordered patients often do poorly with strongly affective approaches and need some help in "warming up" to the therapy process. Cognitive therapy approaches can provide just such help.

There is no medication designed specifically to treat obsessive-compulsive personality disorder. However, since anxiety disorders and depressive disorders are fairly common with this group, appropriate antidepressant and anxiolytic medication may be indicated.

CONCLUSION

This chapter has provided a brief discussion of each of the personality disorders not covered in earlier chapters. Even in patients who may not meet the criteria for a personality disorder, character traits can provide treatment challenges for the addictions counselor. An understanding of each individual's unique characteristics can lead to a more effective individualized treatment plan.

Chapter 11

Sexual Abuse

The sequelae of childhood sexual abuse can significantly complicate the course of the treatment of addictions. Childhood sexual abuse can lead to a full psychiatric illness, such as post-traumatic stress disorder, personality disorder, or dissociative disorder. Even in the absence of a major illness, childhood sexual abuse results in impaired self-esteem, interpersonal skills, and coping skills. Although sexual abuse is not a designated DSM-IV psychiatric disorder, it is a condition that merits clinical attention. Because it is so common in the histories of alcoholics and addicts, a separate chapter has been devoted to it.

Childhood sexual abuse, specifically incest, occurs in about 20 percent of the adult female population (Russell, 1986). It is found at an even greater frequency among individuals with chemical dependency. Some writers estimate as many as 75 percent of patients in addictions treatment programs have a history of such abuse. This high comorbidity rate may be explained in a number of ways: (1) Both addictions and incest tend to occur in dysfunctional families; therefore the same factors, whether genetic or dynamic, can cause addiction and incest to affect the same individual; (2) individuals who have been sexually abused in childhood may turn to substances as a coping mechanism; and (3) substance use may lower inhibitions and increase the possibility that an individual would act on incestuous impulses.

Whatever the reasons, chemical-dependency counselors are faced with many victims *and* offenders in their work with addicted individuals. Counselors who have learned to be nonjudgmental about their addict clients are newly challenged to confront their own social and moral biases when treating the victims or perpetrators of incest. It is incumbent upon the addictions counselor to be able to identify the sequelae of sexual abuse, to understand the impact of these factors on treatment and recovery, and to provide a treatment framework in which recovery from both addictions and incest can take place.

First, this chapter provides a background on sexual abuse, specifically incest, in our society. Next, the effects of incest on victims and treatment considerations for the addict with a history of incest are discussed. Finally, attention is given to the addict sexual offender and the treatment challenges that arise. Because the victims of sexual abuse are often women and the perpetrators are almost always men, the female pronoun is used for patients suffering from the sequelae of sexual abuse and the male pronoun for sexual offenders.

BACKGROUND

Although there are many forms of sexual abuse and not all incestuous activities may be considered abusive, Courtois (1988) tells us that "incest between an adult and a related child or adolescent is now recognized as the most prevalent form of child sexual abuse and as one with great potential for damage to the child." For the purposes of this discussion, *incestuous abuse* (incest) is defined as any sexual behavior that leads to the exploitation of a child by an older person for his/her own satisfaction without regard for the child's development (Steele, 1986). Incest as a traumatic event— one that produces stressful memories—is discussed later in this chapter. Compared with sexual abuse by a stranger, incest has a greater potential for lasting emotional damage due to the dynamics of betrayal, secrecy, shame, and conflicting loyalties; this, too, is discussed more fully later.

In a community-based probability sample, Russell (1986) found that 19 percent of the 930 women interviewed reported incest experiences. She believes that the prevalence of child sexual abuse has increased due to a number of factors, including child pornography, sexualization of the child, the sexual revolution, backlash against gender equality, untreated child sexual abuse, and the increased number of stepfamilies. The prevalence rate for boys is conservatively estimated to be from 2 to 9 percent.

Various social factors (such as social class, mother's employment, race, and religion) have been assessed as to their association with incest (Finkelhor, 1984; Weinberg, 1976; Wyatt, 1985). Some studies find an increased risk of incest among families in rural areas, while others show an increased risk among *high-income* families. It is clear from these studies that incest can occur in *any* family, regardless of race, religion, location, or class.

Although the exact nature of the correlation is not known, numerous studies have documented an association between chemical dependency and child neglect and abuse, including incest. Evans and Schaefer (1987) reviewed studies of chemically dependent women, showing the prevalence of reported incest history ranges from 40 to 70 percent.

Physical violence is seldom a factor in incest; verbal threats are usually sufficient to gain the child's compliance. Most incest victims are between ten and thirteen at the first incest experience; however, a third of first incidents occur before the child is ten. Most incest occurs repeatedly over a period of years and ends through the victim's efforts (such as leaving home or threatening to tell). Very few cases of incest come to light at the time they occur. There are many reasons for this silence, including the child's fear, parents' and law officials' disbelief, and the child's need to maintain family integrity.

EFFECTS OF INCESTUOUS ABUSE

The dynamics of incestuous abuse are important for therapists to understand if they are to appreciate the lasting effects that they see in adult patients. The definition of incest previously given emphasizes a disparity in power that the more powerful individual exploits in the incestuous interaction. The child victim participates out of fear, respect, and confusion, and because she believes what the perpetrator tells her. For example, a ten-year-old's father may tell her that it is important for her to learn about sex from him, at the same time telling her that if she informs anyone something disastrous will happen. The child complies because she has been taught to believe that adults know best and because she is afraid of the consequences if she should reveal the secret. Strong mixed feelings accompany her experience of the incestuous activity.

The family dynamics are often characterized by dysfunction, specifically an immature and demanding father and a fearful and passive mother. In these families, the daughter is often "parentified" and takes on caretaking roles that the mother is unable to assume. This can extend to taking care of the father's sexual needs. Similar dynamics are at work in cases of sibling incest or incest involving other family members. The children's emotional needs are considered secondary to those of the adults. Often, when the child does work up enough courage to reveal the incest, the family system's need to maintain the status quo is so great that she is not believed and is sometimes blamed for the activity. Incest takes place in families characterized by enmeshment, blurring of generational lines, role reversal, unmet dependency needs, touch deprivation, shame, and disrespect for privacy (Evans and Schaefer, 1987). The effects of incest differ depending on the child's preexisting personality and relationships, the availability of support immediately after the abuse, and the child's age at the time of the abuse. Some effects, however, are common to many cases and associated with frequently encountered difficulties in addictions treatment.

The effects of incest on the child's psychological development are numerous. The child does not have an opportunity to experience a safe environment in which to grow emotionally and develop personally. The child experiences a betrayal of trust in what should be one of the safest relationships in her life. Also, whether or not the mother knows about the incestuous activity, the child's ability to trust is further impaired by her awareness that the mother has failed to protect her.

The "secret" takes on special significance in the psychological life of the child. She often comes to believe that she has a great deal of power as a result of her secret and fantasizes that she could destroy others through exposure. When the child feels powerless as a result of the abuse, she maintains a sense of control through her fantasies about what she could do with her secret. A sense of negative power comes from the knowledge that the secret could destroy the family. In actuality, a secondary trauma often occurs when the child or adolescent, in anger or revenge, reveals her powerful secret and is ignored or punished.

Many victims of incest are left with reactions to physical touch and sexual activity that can make satisfying adult relationships difficult to achieve. Many harbor ongoing concerns about sexual adequacy or fear of homosexual thoughts or impulses. Body image is also affected, and in some cases sexual abuse is linked to eating disorders.

In many, if not most, cases of incest, the basic building blocks of relationships are distorted, and subsequent relationships often reproduce the original distortions. Coleman (1987) talks about "intimacy dysfunction" that stems from boundary problems while growing up and is correlated to chemical dependency. The same factors affect victims of incest. Boundaries, learned through interactions with parents, define physical and emotional space. Through experiencing boundaries, the child develops her sense of a separate identity and of her relationship to others. Evans and Schaefer (1987) describe the effects of boundary violation:

> When boundaries are violated by emotional, physical, or sexual intrusions, it is as if someone rips open the victim, reaches in and "steals their soul." In later relationships, they often experience a terror of being "swallowed up" and losing their sense of self for they have learned that closeness/touch "takes away" rather than "gives" to them. This struggle to protect themselves from intimacy feels like a life/death struggle for survival. Requests are seen as demands by these persons, closeness is perceived as losing oneself, and affection puts one in touch with the "empty gaping hole" inside: the "hole" that carries all the unmet childhood needs; for many experienced as a hollow bottomless pit of neglect and despair. (p. 151)

Attention to boundaries is the key to successful work with incest victims. Addictions treatment is complicated by the need to help these patients establish the basic building blocks of relationships while they participate in the recovery community.

Low self-esteem is another byproduct of early abuse. The child does not have the opportunity to feel valued for herself and comes to think of herself as valuable only as an object. There is often a sense of guilt, and when the child learns these sexual behaviors are not acceptable, she may wonder what it is about her that makes her deserve such treatment. The feelings of guilt can be worse if she inadvertently experienced pleasure due to physiologic arousal during the incest activities. A more or less constant view of life as being hopeless and of herself as worthless can develop, making it difficult for the patient to feel the hope of recovery.

Childhood sexual abuse can lead to emotional trauma, defined as a "state of discomfort and stress resulting from memories of an extraordinary, catastrophic experience which shattered the survivor's sense of invulnerability to harm," resulting in post-traumatic stress disorder (PTSD) (Figley, 1985). The symptoms of PTSD, described in Chapter 4, include numbing of emotional response, hypersensitivity, and impaired relationships. These stress reactions are less likely to occur when the child is able to get support from caring others soon after the event. Flashbacks, nightmares, and other intrusive feelings are often tempered by the use of chemicals and can increase during abstinence and recovery. This factor has been implicated in relapse for many addicts with PTSD due to childhood sexual abuse (Root, 1989). The patient who knows of or suspects a history of incest should be educated about the possibility of such symptoms increasing during recovery and helped to develop alternative coping skills.

Dissociative symptoms can also result from childhood abuse. Usually, these first arise during the abusive activity as the child tries to gain psychological distance from the feelings. The individual subsequently applies dissociation to other situations of stress or strong emotion in an effort to retain a sense of control. Dissociative symptoms can range from occasional fugue states to multiple personality disorder. Some signs and symptoms that should alert the chemical-dependency counselor to the possibility of a dissociative disorder include:

1. Multiple previous psychiatric or psychological diagnoses
2. Periods of lost time or amnesia in the absence of alcohol or drugs
3. Behaviors the patient cannot explain

4. Multiple nicknames unrelated to personal attributes
5. Changes in handwriting
6. Sudden changes in facial expression and voice
7. Episodes of staring and blinking
8. Wearing markedly different styles of clothing from session to session

Patients showing these symptoms should be referred for a complete psychiatric evaluation, preferably by someone experienced with the full range of dissociative disorders. The rule of thumb is that if symptoms are so disruptive as to impede progress in addictions treatment, they deserve special attention. Many patients can function quite well while experiencing periodic dissociative episodes. When these are identified, the patient can be helped to see their adaptive function and learn alternative coping skills. In some cases of severe dissociative disorders, especially when accompanied by self-destructive behaviors, treatment in a specialized hospital program to achieve initial stability may be necessary before attempting chemical-dependency treatment.

If the therapist suspects dissociative symptoms or a dissociative disorder, the Dissociative Experience Scale (DES) can be administered to determine if referral to an appropriate specialist or treatment program is warranted (see Chapter 2).

Treatment Considerations

It is not unusual for an individual to reveal a history of incest for the first time in chemical-dependency treatment. For some, suppressed memories first come into awareness during early abstinence. For others, the imperative to "get honest" and the experience of a caring and safe group encourage them to reveal the long-kept secret. It is important for the counselor to be comfortable with revelations of incest so as to provide the patient with the necessary reassurance. It is also important to keep in mind that the patient may have a tendency to "spill it all" in an effort to get over the trauma. This effort can backfire when the patient's revelations are not met with the expected response, and she can experience rejection, powerlessness, and isolation similar to that of the original trauma. The counselor should be open to discussing this material, but should also make sure the patient knows it is okay to take things very slowly. The counselor may even suggest that memories and feelings be shared little by little. The counselor and group members should not probe for this material lest the intrusiveness of the original trauma be recreated in therapy. Treatment of patients with PTSD is facilitated by helping them to experience control during the therapy; therefore, as much as possible, specific treatment for incest issues should be conducted apart from addictions treatment.

Five principles formulated for intervention in post-traumatic stress disorder (Scurfield, 1985) that help to organize the treatment approach to chemically dependent incest victims are:

1. Establishment of a therapeutic trust relationship
2. Education regarding the stress recovery process
3. Stress management and reduction
4. Movement back to or a reexperiencing of the trauma in an adaptive context
5. Integration of the trauma experience

These principles represent a progression of treatment, and although some work may be done in several areas at one time, significant progress should be made in each one before going on to the next. Regression and integration of the trauma should be left to specially trained and experienced clinicians. However, achievement of the first three tasks is well within the range of addictions treatment and can be considered *central* to successful addictions treatment with chemically dependent incest victims.

Establishment of a Therapeutic Trust Relationship

In the slow process of establishing trust, the victim of incest moves from a need for total control (or the illusion of control) to a willingness to share control of the therapy. This is similar to the acceptance of addiction, but differs in that the incest victim must learn or at best relearn how to trust. The framework of addictions treatment with a goal of abstinence provides a point of reference for the overall treatment and can give the patient and therapist a common goal around which to build trust.

Whether an abuse history is known or suspected, the establishment of a therapeutic relationship is essential to the success of addictions treatment. It is important to keep in mind that the therapy provides an opportunity for the patient to experience helping, caring, and nurturing in a nonabusive relationship. The patient needs to *learn* how to trust and should be given information about the process as well as opportunities to practice.

Both male and female therapists can work effectively with victims of sexual abuse. In the early sessions, issues related to the therapist's gender should be explored with the patient and her preferences and concerns elicited. It should not be assumed, however, that honoring the patient's preference eliminates the need for the therapist to earn the patient's trust. Whether the perpetrator was male or female, the patient has experienced betrayal by both the adult who violated her and the parent who failed to protect her, so that there are usually issues of trust with both sexes. Further, the patient may be more aware of her feelings toward one gender and may need help exploring negative feelings toward the other. A hazard that female therapists encounter in working with female incest victims is the tendency to over-identify. The therapist should take much care to ensure that she is responding to the *patient's* material. If the therapist tries to impose her own responses onto the patient, this, too, can be experienced as an intrusion.

The victim of incest wants to be able to trust others but may think of trust as "all-or-none." She may be very guarded and controlling up to a point, and then, in a flash of hope, release an outpouring of self-disclosure. To avoid renewed feelings of hurt, disappointment, and shame, the patient may need help to "put on the brakes" and encouragement to take small steps toward disclosure, allowing time for trust and sensitivity to build. There is a difference between exploring childhood trauma and acknowledging it. If acknowledgment is given with openness, acceptance, and sensitivity, the patient can learn that the incest material no longer needs to be kept secret, but that she can and should choose when to disclose material depending on what is best for her overall recovery.

It is imperative that the counselor be alert to the factors in this therapeutic relationship that could represent a recreation of the original trauma. Premature exploration of detailed sexual material is such a factor, especially if the patient feels as though these thoughts, feelings, and memories are being "pulled out of her." Again, education about the trust-building process and assurance that the patient can decide when and with whom to share her experiences, are indicated. At the same time, the counselor should assure the patient that he/she or another appropriate therapist will be ready to hear these things when *she* is ready to talk about them. If possible, before significant disclosure, the patient should be helped to explore her fantasies about what may happen after she talks about these things. Expectation of a magical result (such as being "cured" of addiction or instant relief from pain) is common, and the patient may need to be introduced to the possibility of other outcomes.

Confrontation is essential in the treatment of addictions; again, timing and a measured approach are needed in treating the patient who has experienced sexual abuse. Confrontation should be direct and gentle and should support the patient's healthy aspects.

Case A

> Five months into recovery, a thirty-one-year-old alcoholic woman with a pattern of rescue fantasies leading her into physically abusive relationships reports that at a meeting, she has met a man with a few weeks of sobriety and she is thinking about asking him to move in to "share the rent." Confrontation is clearly indicated—but how? "So you want to throw away five months of recovery on the jerk?" is on target but may not get through. More likely to be effective is the following: "In the time we have worked together, you have worked very hard to learn to take care of yourself and to face the difficult challenges of recovery. It appears that your disease of addiction and your need to care for others are working together to convince you that this time it will be different. The work is hard, the progress is slow, but it is important to stick with the winners. Try reading page 261 of the Big Book, get feedback from your sponsor, and then decide if this is what is best for you *and* your recovery."

Creating and maintaining boundaries in the treatment of the recovering incest victim is one of the primary tasks of the therapist and provides the foundation for establishment of a trusting therapeutic relationship. In treatment, boundaries often have to do with issues of time, place, membership (as in group therapy), money, and role. The victim of sexual abuse is extremely sensitive to boundary issues and needs, to experience the therapist and other helping individuals as equally aware. In addition, based on their life experience, sexual abuse victims may doubt the therapist's ability to set limits and maintain appropriate boundaries. In the early part of treatment and at times of transition, the patient can be expected to test limits in direct and often creative ways.

Case B

> A thirty-eight-year-old stockbroker with vague memories of "some hanky-panky" as a child entered into individual therapy to support her very early sobriety and to work on her relationships. The first-priority goal of abstinence was agreed upon and weekly individual therapy sessions begun along with twelve-step and early recovery groups. She always wrote a check at the end of the session, as was agreed, until following a session in which she began to share shame and guilt about past behaviors, she began to "forget" her checkbook and have difficulty talking in the sessions. When this behavior was interpreted as a means of creating distance from the therapist whom she had begun to trust, the patient resumed the routine of prompt payment as well as productive use of the sessions.

In treatment, the incest victim will watch for any sign of the therapist's departing from strict appropriateness. She may try to persuade the therapist to move away from the role of professional helper by giving gifts or by other personal gestures. Again, this is the patient's attempt to assure herself that this relationship is "safe" and she will not be abused. The abuse of power in the therapeutic relationship has been written about elsewhere (Redlich, 1986) but deserves special mention in this context. Therapists working with sex abuse victims need to be comfortable in their role as helping professionals and able to maintain appropriate emotional distance. Regular high-quality supervision should be obtained until limit-setting becomes effortless. The therapist has probably achieved this degree of comfort when he/she can graciously refuse an inappropriate gift and gently persuade the patient to talk about her thoughts and feelings. It is largely through experiencing the therapist as trustworthy that the incest victim allows herself to enter into a therapeutic relationship.

The hugging and touching that take place routinely in twelve-step meetings represent a special boundary problem for the adult victim of childhood sexual abuse. These patients often feel confusion and fear about physical touch, and social touch may elicit extreme anxiety and panic. It may be difficult for the patient to think of touch in nonsexual terms. The therapist needs to actively support the patient in her adjustment to this ritual. The hugging that occurs in meetings can actually provide an opportunity for the individual to examine her irrational responses to touch and practice learning to touch in a caring, nonsexual way. The therapist should encourage the patient to talk about her reactions and to try to understand them. It may be helpful for the recovering victim to attend primarily women's meetings until she is more comfortable with social touch.

The concept of "powerlessness" presents a special challenge to the therapist working with the incest victim in addictions treatment. The learned helplessness that often accompanies childhood victimization is a cognitive structure that leads the individual to live in a perpetual state of victimization. Curiously, the victim maintains a fantasy of control; she believes she is either totally helpless or totally in control. Both extremes are defenses against the unconscious rage the patient holds toward those who violated her trust. The concept of powerlessness provides an opportunity for the recovering incest victim to restructure this dysfunctional way of thinking and to learn what can be controlled and what cannot. More than other addicts, the trauma survivor may try to skip the experience of powerlessness and move on to that of surrender. Therefore, much attention needs to be given to helping the patient understand that powerlessness does not mean helplessness. The patient may fear helplessness as a recreation of the original trauma and at the same time resist the increased personal effectiveness that comes from accepting powerlessness over things that cannot be controlled. The therapist can use this paradox to help the patient reach acceptance by pointing out to her that she is actually behaving *helplessly* by attempting to control things that cannot be controlled.

Case C

A thirty-year-old flight supervisor with several arrests for drunk driving could not understand why she had to admit that she was powerless over alcohol. She knew she could not drink, and she knew what she needed to do to keep from drinking. She declared that drinking on the job could not be a problem because she had never done so, and to do so would put her job and her chances for promotion in jeopardy. Therefore, all she had to do was stay away from bars, parties, and other social events where alcohol was served. She was helped to see that, even if her scheme could work, it would put her in a social straightjacket for the rest of her life and would limit her opportunities for promotion in a field where much business is conducted in social settings. She did not actually internalize the experience of powerlessness for some time after this. However, she was able to see the advisability of entering a program where she would acknowledge that the problem was within her and that she would need others' support to learn to live with it.

Education Regarding the Stress Recovery Process

A knowledge of the process and some understanding of what to expect in recovery form an important foundation for therapeutic work with these patients. For the sex abuse victim in recovery, there should be as few surprises as possible. The therapist should make it clear to the patient that she needs to learn how to trust and that she needs to learn and practice stress-reduction skills before exploring feelings or memories. It is also important that the patient understand that she can recover with treatment, but some symptoms will get worse before they get better, especially during early abstinence.

In addictions treatment with the recovering abuse victim, the conceptual foundation of stress recovery is expanded to include the addiction recovery process and to show how stress recovery and addiction recovery work together. Because many of the concepts of recovery are opposite to much of what the abuse victim has learned from life, her learning may be uneven at first. It will be necessary for the therapist to repeat this information often until the patient is able to internalize it. Key concepts of recovery from incest and addiction include:

1. Recovery from addictions and incest is possible and leads to a fuller, more effective life.
2. Recovery is a gradual, step-by-step process and may involve temporary setbacks.
3. Priorities for treatment will shift from time to time. Severe or life-threatening problems generally need to be addressed before the incest.
4. Learning to trust is an ongoing process, and beginning this process is the beginning of recovery.
5. Numbing and flooding of feelings will continue for a while as the patient learns and practices stress reduction and other coping skills.
6. The survivor skills learned in childhood that are helpful need to be identified and the skills that are not helpful need to be unlearned.
7. Early goals for treatment include abstinence, the establishment of a broad social support network, and the development of nonchemical coping skills.
8. Later goals for treatment include reconnecting with childhood experiences, grieving losses, and learning to live effectively.

The recovery processes for addictions and trauma are similar in many ways:

1. Both begin with acceptance.
2. Both are plagued with many forms of denial.
3. Both are lifelong processes, taken one day at a time.
4. Neither can be done alone; both involve other people.
5. Both may involve setbacks.
6. Both require the development of coping skills.
7. In both processes, recovery involves changing self-concept.
8. Both involve changing relationships.
9. Both involve grieving for losses.

Many patients enter recovery with no conscious knowledge of abuse, but the therapist suspects abuse based on the clinical presentation. Education about the recovery process should include preparation for the possibility that abstinence will bring increased symptoms and lost memories may be regained. Most patients are aware of living in a dysfunctional family even if they do not remember any sexual trauma. This awareness can provide a useful bridge to introduce the patient to the principles of stress recovery and the need to learn new skills.

Stress Management and Reduction

The therapist should help the patient understand and build on her existing coping skills. Ineffective or maladaptive techniques, such as social isolation, need to be replaced. The specific skills needed will depend on the symptoms that are present. Anxiety, depression, flashbacks, obsessive thoughts, poor concentration, derealization, and craving are some of the symptoms that may be encountered. The patient should be helped to identify existing symptoms and new ones that emerge in treatment. The techniques for stress reduction can be derived from the standard approaches used in treatment of anxiety and depression. These include relaxation, meditation, breathing exercises, structuring of time, exercise, problem solving, social networking, assertiveness training, cognitive restructuring, self-affirmations, thought stopping, and self-talk.

Trauma Processing: Integration of the Trauma Experience

The addictions counselor can prepare the patient for the work to follow by emphasizing the stepwise process of recovery and the expectation that progress is likely to be uneven. Early in recovery the trauma may be reexperienced through flashbacks or nightmares. The goal at that time is to strengthen defenses and coping skills to diminish these intrusions until substantial abstinence has been achieved, a strong support network has been established, and coping skills are well practiced. Later in treatment, within the context of a therapeutic relationship and with a therapist trained and experienced in working with abuse victims, the trauma can be reexperienced and integrated.

Processing trauma need not be an overwhelmingly painful experience. Indeed, it should not be. In the hands of a skilled therapist, the patient can deal with reemerging sensations, thoughts, and other experiences related to the abuse in a controlled, safe fashion through the use of appropriate procedures such as hypnotherapy. The recently developed technique of eye-movement desensitization and retraining (EMDR) (Shapiro, 1995), which is gaining acceptance in the professional community, appears particularly well-suited for desensitizing the patient to past abuse. Both hypnotherapy and EMDR are highly specialized procedures that require intensive training and supervision. The addictions therapist interested in the processing phase of trauma resolution should pursue appropriate training and supervision in these and other modalities before engaging in this phase of the treatment of sexual abuse.

Working the Steps

Some aspects of the twelve steps present special problems and opportunities for the sex-abuse victim in recovery. We have already discussed the difficulties with powerlessness and acceptance (or sharing the control). Some additional issues are discussed below.

The concept of a higher power and spirituality can be troublesome for recovering sex-abuse victims. The sense of betrayal that they have experienced can carry over to their understanding of God and religion. As with atheist or agnostic individuals, emphasis on the practical and social aspects of the program may be sufficient for the purposes of early recovery. It may be necessary to point out that the patient has a child's view of God as an omnipotent protector and that a more useful view of God may come in time.

The "moral inventory" of the fourth and fifth steps can provide a healing experience for the recovering sex-abuse victim. These steps can help the individual place in context any sexual acting-out that may have resulted from the original abuse and have been facilitated by alcohol or drugs. Because of the inordinate amount of shame and guilt that victims experience, these steps should be approached only after a firm recovery base and a good therapeutic relationship have been established.

Cognitive Approaches

Cognitive methods to address the repercussions of sexual abuse can be powerful ways of reducing symptoms of distress and modifying the patient's dysfunctional beliefs about herself (Resick and Schnicke, 1992). Whatever the nature and extent of the past sexual abuse, she interprets it in the present. The patient's perceptions of herself resulting from the abuse are directly connected to such feelings as depression, shame, guilt, and self-hate. Typically, these patients conclude that they are fundamentally defective. The pain associated with such a conclusion often outweighs the suffering incurred during the actual abuse incident.

Patients who experienced childhood sexual abuse often develop specific beliefs about the abuse and their role in it. Some examples are: "It is my fault that this occurred," "I provoked it," or "I deserved it." These patients may also harbor the belief that they did not take responsibility for stopping the abuse and feel guilty for not doing so. Any pleasure or enjoyment the patient experienced as a result of the attention given to her throughout the abuse can also lead to a belief that she is a horrible person.

Dysfunctional beliefs also develop over time, long after the sexual abuse occurred. Some examples are: "I'm defective," "I'll never enjoy or have sex again," "People can tell that I have been abused," "I'll never be normal," "I'm different from other people," or "I hate myself and I don't deserve happiness." The dysfunctional cognitions developed by abuse victims have several predictable characteristics. They are usually negative, rigidly held, and based on a priori thinking. They are self-evident to the patient and generally go unchallenged. They are arbitrary and based on little or no actual evidence.

The counselor should probe for dysfunctional beliefs, assumptions, and thoughts, point them out to the patient, and begin to challenge them. Can the patient prove her irrational beliefs? What evidence can she muster to back them up? Can she distinguish between facts and opinions about or reactions to these facts? The therapist can also challenge the advantages of holding such beliefs. What do they get for the patient? What do they ultimately lead to? Another effective technique is to turn the tables on the patient and role-play a situation in which a friend of the patient describes her own abuse and her reactions to it. What would the patient conclude about her friend? Can she point out the inconsistencies and illogic in her friend's beliefs about herself? Can she see them in her own thinking?

When regularly and consistently applied, cognitive intervention addresses and supplants dysfunctional cognitions, and restructures the patient's beliefs about and emotional reactions to her abuse in a more adaptive fashion, resulting in less emotional pain.

THE SEX OFFENDER IN ADDICTIONS TREATMENT

As noted previously, both victims and perpetrators of sexual abuse are found in addictions treatment. This section discusses some of the special issues of the patient with *pedophilia*. Pedophilia is the term for sexual attraction to and relationships with children. The two most common types are *regressed* and *fixed* pedophilia.

In regressed pedophilia, an adult who usually functions well sexually can at times of extreme stress revert to aberrant sexual behavior to offset threats to his sense of masculinity. The regressed pedophiliac may feel powerless, angry, and ineffective. Often the regressed pedophile is intoxicated at the time of the offense. Under this condition the addict's defenses are down, behavioral disinhibition occurs, and fantasies are acted out.

Fixed pedophiliacs are emotionally arrested at an early psychosexual developmental stage. These men show a habitual compulsion to molest children. In many ways, this compulsion is similar to compulsive drinking, gambling, and other compulsive behaviors. The fixed pedophile seeks a long-term emotional relationship with a child and will engage in a process of seduction to win a child's trust. Most fixed pedophiles are passive, socially aloof men. They are heavily defended through denial and rationalization and typically show little guilt, compunction, or remorse about their behavior.

Treatment Considerations

Treatment of the sexual offender does not radically differ from the general principles and strategies of traditional addictions treatment. Sexual offenders are typically highly defended, emotionally constricted, psychologically immature men. They require an actively empathic, directive, and at times confrontive therapist to assist them in admitting to their problems and agreeing that they require an ongoing (often lifelong) treatment program.

Initially, the therapist must vigorously deal with the sexual offender's firmly entrenched minimization, denial, and rationalization defenses. Experienced addictions counselors are quite familiar with these defenses, since they are present in almost all addictive illnesses. The goal is to get the patient to admit *responsibility* for the offending behavior. Of particular importance is exploring how the sexually offending behavior is tied into triggers of active chemical use. Often untreated sexual problems remain powerful relapse factors; this should be pointed out to the patient. With regressed child molesters, the role of alcohol and other drugs in promoting the offending behavior should be explored. The counselor should focus on specific episodes of the offending behavior to discuss just how the patient renders himself vulnerable to acting out sexually. The patient should be an active collaborator in this process.

In cases of continuing child molestation, it is the therapist's duty to report known or suspected physical abuse to child protective services or other appropriate organizations. The therapist should openly share this responsibility with the patient. Knowing about the therapist's responsibility to report suspected physical abuse can provide a powerful impetus for the offender to discontinue molestation.

A careful probing of the sexual offender's childhood is important to uncover any abuse the patient may have experienced. Typically, these patients have been abused themselves, and have repressed and defended against powerful feelings associated with the abuse. The therapist can usually be certain that the offender is troubled by anger and rage and has psychologically mishandled and misdirected these emotions. Often, the anger is intimately tied in with the offending behavior, although the patient may not acknowledge this connection. The therapist should point to the dehumanizing, manipulative aspect of the patient's sexually offending behavior as evidence of extreme anger. If the patient is stable enough, role-playing and psychodrama techniques can be used to draw out anger, humiliation, and other feelings. These techniques can also allow the offender to empathize with and understand the victim. A twelve-step program such as Sex and Love Addicts Anonymous should be explored with the patient. If it can be arranged, the patient should attend one or more of these meetings while in treatment and report on his experiences in group or individual therapy. It should be explained to the sexual offender that the problem is chronic and lifelong, and a commitment to an ongoing daily recovery program is absolutely essential for his recovery from both the sexual disorder and the addictive disease.

Specific treatments for sexual offenders include aversion therapy, antiandrogen drugs, and hypnosis provided by qualified professionals. Offenders should be routinely referred to such professionals during early recovery.

As treatment professionals, addictions counselors must be aware of their personal feelings toward the sexual abuser and strive to view this behavior as objectively as they view addiction. This is not easy. Many otherwise very professional mental health and addictions personnel have profound negative reactions to sexual offenders and are unable to treat them effectively. Counselors who do not feel they can adequately deal with such issues in chemical-dependency treatment should refer the patient to a colleague.

In summary, the treatment of the sexual offender should: (1) identify the behavior, (2) assist the offender in taking responsibility for the behavior, (3) get the offender to commit to stopping the abuse, and (4) get the offender to agree to specialized treatment for his problem.

CONCLUSION

Both sexual victimization and sexual offense frequently occur amongst patients in chemical-dependency treatment. The skilled addictions counselor will know how to identify these problems and will help the patient enter into recovery for both the addiction and the sexual abuse or offense.

Appendix A

Cognitive Therapy Approaches

Cognitive therapy has emerged as an effective treatment for a wide range of psychiatric disorders (Beck, 1976). It is easily implemented in primary addictions treatment and has been found to be an effective approach for all types of addictions. Much has been written on cognitive therapy. This appendix is not a comprehensive summary of cognitive theory and techniques; rather, it includes approaches discussed in the existing literature that have proven particularly useful in the treatment of the depressed addict or alcoholic. The techniques offered here are applicable to a number of other psychiatric conditions as well, including anxiety disorders, eating disorders, and personality disorders.

A major assumption underlying cognitive therapy is that the depressed patient systematically and negatively distorts his/her view of the self, the environment, and the future. Depression is viewed as a disturbance in mood or affect that can be the result of distorted thinking and misperception. Depression arises when the person feels that he/she lacks some essential ingredient in the self that is necessary for happiness and well-being. The role of the thinking process in the etiology and maintenance of depression is the central focus of cognitive therapy.

The first order of business in a cognitive-therapy approach with a depressed patient is to slow the patient down and focus on the content of his/her thinking (Freeman, 1987). Depressed patients typically show characteristicly irrational thoughts that aggravate the depressive symptoms. Working collaboratively with the patient, the therapist should begin to point out distortions in the patient's *automatic thoughts*—those thoughts that arise spontaneously and regularly, preceding and exacerbating depressive symptoms. It is very helpful to go through a list of common cognitive distortions with the patient, exploring each one and checking to see if the patient shows evidence of it. (See the list later in this appendix; such a list also appears in Burns, 1980, pp. 40-41.)

The therapist can then point out to the patient that his/her thinking shows several general characteristics. First, thoughts tend to arise automatically and the patient accepts them as "fact"; the patient believes them and acts as if there is no other way to think. The therapist can reframe these distorted thoughts as hypotheses rather than facts and tell the patient that therapy will focus, in part, on testing the validity of these hypotheses. The therapist then notes how the distorted thoughts lend predictability to negative-feeling states. Here the relationship between cognition and feelings can be clarified; that is, negative, distorted thinking results in depressive feelings. The introduction of this idea helps the patient gain distance from his/her thinking. The patient takes a step backward to "think about thinking" and how it leads to emotional misery. The therapist can also note how the distortions are *reliable* and *predictable*, that is, the patient experiences the cognitive distortions in a *systematic* fashion. Every time an upsetting event or feeling occurs, the distorted thoughts can be reliably found in the patient's consciousness.

As the distortions are identified and explained, the therapist should select one or two central problem areas for focus. In cognitive therapy, it is important to prioritize the depressed patient's many problems, keep the focus narrow, and stick to a definite agenda in counseling sessions.

SILENT ASSUMPTIONS

After the patient learns how he/she employs distorted cognitions to create depressive symptoms, the therapist can move to an exploration of the roots of these distortions. These have been termed *silent assumptions* (Burns, 1980). Silent assumptions are dysfunctional rules for living that patients are typically unaware of, learned primarily in early childhood often in response to the inevitable stresses, disappointments, and losses of the childhood and adolescent years. These assumptions form a belief system that is represented by the type and nature of the patient's distorted thoughts. The therapist can begin to identify these assumptions by exploring the themes in the patient's distorted thinking. The therapist can use an inventory such as the dysfunctional-attitude survey to assist in identifying and exploring these assumptions (Burns, 1980, pp. 242-246). Ellis' (1962) lists of dysfunctional rules are another source for the therapist to use in identifying the patient's assumptions.

Whatever method the therapist chooses, the goal is to uncover the patient's belief system and expose and scrutinize it in the same way that automatic thoughts and cognitive distortions are explored. For example, a silent assumption of "don't talk, don't trust, don't feel" is familiar to the addictions therapist as a dysfunctional rule of living often seen in families with an alcoholic member. Although this assumption may have saved the patient much pain and helped ensure emotional survival in a disturbed family system, the persistence of this belief can lead to a great deal of unhappiness later in life. Typically, depressed patients have a number of such dysfunctional attitudes and beliefs in major areas of their lives. These are often connected with approval needs, love needs, achievement needs, and beliefs about dependency. Dysfunctional assumptions can lead to problems such as love and sex addiction, workaholism, perfectionism, extreme dependency, procrastination, and severe deficits in self-esteem. Uncovering and modifying dysfunctional beliefs are therapeutic efforts that get at the cause of the patient's depression. As the patient's beliefs, assumptions, and values become more rational and realistic, the foundation is laid for pervasive behavioral and emotional change.

Beck et al. (1990) have termed these silent assumptions *schemas*. Schemas are defined as cognitive structures for "screening, coding and evaluating the stimuli that impinge on the organism. . . ." Schemas are used to categorize and interpret experience in a meaningful way. Maladaptive schemas develop out of the awareness of the young child and result from negative learning from early stressful experiences. According to Young (1990), these schemas have several characteristics: (1) they are held to be self-evident, (2) they are self-perpetuating and extremely resistant to change, (3) they are irrational and dysfunctional, and (4) they can lie dormant for years until a negative-environmental event triggers them. When activated, they are associated with high levels of emotionality. Some examples of maladaptive schemas are: "I am unlovable," "Others will always leave me," "I will always fail," "Others will hurt me," "I cannot function on my own," "I will never be happy," or "I cannot let anyone really know who I am."

According to Young (1990), the maladaptive schemas or silent assumptions common in depressed patients are predictable and fall into six domains:

1. *Instability and disconnection*—the belief that one's needs for safety, stability, and nurturance will not be met
2. *Impaired autonomy*—the belief that one cannot function independently or protect oneself
3. *Undesirability*—the assumption that one is basically inferior, deficient, or defective, and therefore unattractive to others
4. *Restricted self-expression*—the belief that one should ignore one's own preferences or opinions and should not express them to others
5. *Restricted gratification*—the belief that one should not experience too much pleasure or gratification and that life is basically work and sacrifice
6. *Impaired limits*—the assumption that one should get what one wants and that others should give in to one's demands

In treating depressed patients with cognitive therapy, experience has shown that maladaptive schemas become more obvious to both patient and therapist as they identify and challenge the patient's cognitive distortions. For example, recurring automatic thoughts, when examined, often fall into a pattern, and the therapist can explore these with the patient to grasp what the automatic thoughts really mean or say about the patient. The beliefs or schemas these distorted thoughts reveal can then become the focus of cognitive interventions designed to challenge them and supplant them with more adaptive beliefs.

COGNITIVE DISTORTIONS

As stated previously, a major assumption of cognitive therapy is that the patient's thinking, rather than external or internal events and experiences, is the source of problems for the patient. Depressed patients have been found to show definite patterns of thinking errors. Such types of thinking are viewed as dysfunctional and maladaptive and are directly tied to the physical and emotional symptoms the depressed patient shows.

The following are descriptions of the major types of cognitive distortions seen in the depressed alcoholic or addict.

Catastrophizing

This has been termed the "Chicken Little" approach to life. It is a form of exaggeration in which the patient continually focuses on the possibility of danger and disaster. An alcoholic who thinks, "I'll die if I don't get a drink" or "What is the use in getting sober, I'll relapse anyhow" is showing catastrophic thinking. Catastrophic thinkers are convinced that the worst will *always* happen.

All-or-None Thinking

In this distortion, the patient views life in an extreme black-and-white fashion. For example, an alcoholic with two years of sobriety began to experience craving and urges to use. He concluded that he was a bad person and a failure. To him, any setbacks in his sobriety were evidence that he was not working with his program and was unworthy of sobriety.

Overgeneralization

The patient concludes that if an unfortunate or negative event happened to him/her once, it will happen again. A patient who is rejected in a relationship and concludes that this always happens and always will happen to him/her, is showing overgeneralized thinking. He/she has taken a single episode of rejection and arbitrarily concluded that he/she is doomed to rejection in all relationships in the future.

Selective Abstraction

The patient focuses only on the negative details of a particular situation, to the exclusion of any other information. The patient sees only errors, mistakes, and weaknesses, and cannot see his/her accomplishments. An addict who relapses and concludes that he/she has "wasted" three years of sobriety is showing selective abstraction. He/she does not consider either the positive learning that can come about through a relapse or the gains made in recovery.

Magnification and Minimization

The patient magnifies or exaggerates, for example, the qualities and accomplishments of others while minimizing and shrinking the significance of his/her own achievements or qualities. The patient continually compares him/herself to others and always comes up short.

Shoulds

The patient imposes unrealistic expectations that are difficult or impossible to live up to. Some examples are: "I should be a tolerant person," "I should be a perfect spouse," or "I should be able to control my anger at all times." This type of thinking can lead to significant guilt, frustration, and resentment. Alcoholics and addicts struggling to overcome character defects in the early stages of recovery often fall prey to this distortion.

Emotional Reasoning

The patient experiences a feeling state and uses it as a basis for erroneous conclusions. The patient who experiences a sense of guilt and then concludes that he/she is a bad person is showing emotional reasoning, as is the patient who feels overwhelmed and arbitrarily concludes that his/her problems are unsolvable.

Personalization

The patient assumes responsibility for a negative situation without any proof that he/she is responsible. An alcoholic who assumes that the happiness of his wife or children is dependent upon him is showing the personalization distortion. For example, a patient concluded that he was not an adequate father when he discovered that his son was having academic and behavioral problems at school. This thinking indicates a misplaced and exaggerated sense of responsibility that can leave the patient feeling a disabling level of guilt.

Armed with knowledge of the cognitive distortions, the therapist can be alert to their presence in patients. Likewise, patients can begin to identify and understand cognitive distortions and their role in creating depressive symptoms.

COGNITIVE INTERVENTIONS

Once the patient's cognitive distortions are identified, explored, and understood, the therapist can employ some specific strategies designed to assist patients in testing the reality of their thinking. The following interventions are designed to expose and uncover the faulty logic in the depressed patient's thinking and to assist the patient with more adaptive ways of perceiving and processing his/her world.

Questioning the Evidence

Depressed patients often draw negative conclusions based on little or no evidence. An alcoholic patient stated, for example, "I am embarrassed to be an alcoholic, people at work think it is pathetic." When asked what evidence he had to verify his thoughts, the patient could not readily identify any. He simply assumed others saw him as pathetic because he was a recovering alcoholic. Depressed patients do this all the time. The counselor can direct the patient to substantiate his/her conclusions. In many cases the patient may be projecting his/her ideas onto others or "reading into" comments that have no relevance to the patient.

Decatastrophize

When patients jump to negative conclusions, the counselor can counter these by exploring with the patient the impact of the fantasied catastrophe. For example, a depressed addict refused to speak up in treatment because she felt that the other patients would see her as an "idiot" with nothing to contribute to the group. The counselor challenged this fantasy by asking, "So what if you are an idiot? Is it the end of the world? Would the group refuse to speak with you? Would you never get sober? Would you commit suicide?" Such questions induce patients to follow their thoughts to natural conclusions. By thinking through the fear, patients often realize that they can deal with the fantasied catastrophe, and often the assumed catastrophe may be merely an inconvenience.

Replacement Imagery

Depressed patients often visualize events in a negative way. They "see" the worst happening. The counselor can take advantage of this tendency and have the patient visualize successful, positive outcomes to problem situations. The patient who is too self-conscious and unassertive to ask her boss for a raise can be directed to visualize herself as an assertive, competent person who is successful at this task. Regular positive imagery can be "contagious," and the more it is practiced, the easier it is for a patient to choose a more positive frame of mind. The patient can also use therapy sessions, especially group sessions, to rehearse positive imagery in role-play situations.

Reattribution

This is the preferred technique to offset personalization. When a patient complains that he/she is the sole cause of a family or relationship problem, for example, the therapist carefully and calmly points out to the patient that it is highly doubtful that a single person would be totally responsible for any given problem. Indeed, all problems can be seen as having multiple causes. By calling the patient's attention to the illogical conclusion that he/she is the originator of all his/her problems, the therapist redistributes responsibility for problems to others in the patient's life and the patient is then less burdened with guilt, anxiety, depression, and other troubling affects.

Scaling

Depressed patients with all-or-nothing thinking show a rigid, absolute style when coping with their problems. In this intervention, the therapist points out the patient's either/or approach to problems. The therapist then introduces the concept of a continuum or scale with which to gauge thinking and emotional reactions. For example, the patient can measure his/her depressive feelings on a scale of one to one hundred. This sensitizes the patient to subtle changes in mood as therapy progresses. The same technique is useful in helping the patient perceive his/her world in a more modulated fashion. For example, the patient who continually sees him/herself as a failure in competitive situations can be helped to see that failures and successes can be measured in degrees rather than in absolutes.

Guided Association

Depressed patients are often apprehensive about the future and anxious about specific interactions or challenges they are anticipating. On their own, patients rarely think through these imagined fears or rationally confront the fantasized consequences. In guided association, also called the "then what?" technique, the therapist helps the patient carry his/her fears to their logical ends by accepting the patient's conclusions about their fears and anxieties and taking them a step farther, asking, "What would happen next?" For example, a patient who is paralyzed with fear about asking his/her boss for a raise may be helped by thinking things through with the guided association technique. It may proceed like this:

Patient:	If I asked for a raise he would laugh in my face.
Therapist:	And then what would happen?
Patient:	He would throw me out of the office.
Therapist:	And then what?
Patient:	I would be so embarrassed, everyone in the office would laugh at me.
Therapist:	Okay, and then what would happen?
Patient:	Well . . . I don't know, that is about all I thought of . . . I guess I'd go back to work.
Therapist:	And then what?
Patient:	(Laughs) Well, I guess I would call my spouse.

With this technique, the patient's tendency to catastrophize and assume that disaster will happen is simply, but systematically, explored to test its validity. The patient is taught to think through his/her fears and not just react in a hysterical fashion to unsubstantiated claims.

OTHER TECHNIQUES

There are a number of other techniques that the therapist can employ to combat the dysfunctional thinking of the depressed patient. In *labeling of distortions,* the therapist stops the patient when he/she shows an example of irrational or distorted thinking and labels it as, for example, personalization or overgeneralization. The aim is to help the patient see that it is the process of thinking, rather than the situation, that is causing the distress. In *examining the advantages and disadvantages,* the therapist selects a particular assumption, emotional reaction, or behavior and focuses on the likely results of such a belief. The patient is asked to verbalize or write down and weigh the advantages and disadvantages of the belief or behavior. This helps the patient becomes more objective about his/her cognitions and perceptions and highlights the patient's need to modify beliefs, thoughts, and behaviors that are not useful. In *fantasizing consequences,* the patient uses mental imagery to depict a problem situation and describes his/her concerns and fears. The therapist can then use the guided-association technique to systematically go through the fantasy, assess the likelihood of the patient's imagined problems occurring, and explore more adaptive alternatives.

All the above interventions are designed to assist patients in testing the validity of their thinking errors. As patients do this, they begin to develop more flexibility and adaptability in thinking and become more creative problem solvers. As more rational and useful styles of thinking develop, depressive symptoms eventually lift, and much to the patient's delight, the mood begins to stabilize. As this occurs, the patient's belief in the cognitive approach to treatment increases, leading to even greater therapeutic success.

OTHER CONSIDERATIONS

In cognitive therapy, it is considered important to build small successes early on in the patient's treatment to bolster self-confidence and offset the sense of futility that depressed patients often harbor. Daily assignments to keep the patient active and involved in rehabilitation efforts are also quite important. The therapeutic activities listed in *The Feeling Good Handbook* (Burns, 1989) and *Mind Over Mood* (Greenberger and Padesky, 1995), are particularly useful for depressed patients. For severely depressed patients, cognitive therapy can be conducted concurrently with antidepressant therapy.

Medication Used to Treat
Dual Disorders

Addictions therapists regularly treat patients who are being maintained on a psychotropic medication and refer patients to a psychiatrist for consideration for such medications. Therefore, it is important for addictions counselors to be familiar with the major psychiatric medications.

Recent developments in biological psychiatry have led to important advances in the development of potent and effective medications to treat major psychiatric syndromes. Most of these medications have dramatically less-severe side effects than the psychotropic drugs that were standard before their introduction, leading to more effective treatments and greater patient compliance with medication regimens. The relatively high level of comorbidity of psychiatric disorders with chemical dependency, together with new research showing the effectiveness of combined psychotherapeutic and pharmacotherapeutic treatment, mean that the use of psychiatric medications to treat dual-diagnosis patients is becoming more prevalent. Perhaps too, because managed care generally means stays are shorter in both inpatient and outpatient treatment, there may now be a greater tendency to prescribe psychotropic medications to speed patients' response to available therapies.

PROCEDURES INVOLVED IN PHARMACOTHERAPY

When a patient is referred to a psychiatrist or other physician for consideration for medication, a predictable sequence of procedures

---

This appendix was developed in collaboration with Barbara Reeve, MD.

usually follows. First, the psychiatrist determines whether the patient has a condition that is appropriate to treat with psychotropic agents. Once a patient has been determined to be an appropriate candidate for a trial on a psychotropic drug, and following an accurate diagnosis of his/her condition, the physician chooses a medication targeted to the symptoms to be ameliorated. The choice of a particular drug is based on a number of factors, including: (1) the patient's response to medications in the past, (2) the response of the patient's close relatives to medications, (3) any medical conditions present, and (4) the patient's capacity to tolerate various types of side effects.

In the next phase, the physician educates the patient about the medication that has been selected. Proper patient education is critical for patient compliance with medication. Ideally, the patient should learn about: (1) how the drug works; (2) the time necessary for a therapeutic response; (3) the anticipated time period the patient will be on the medication; (4) the predicted response to the drug, including side effects; and (5) any related considerations, such as necessary changes in diet or behavior. Once the patient has learned about these aspects of the medication, drug therapy is initiated and the patient's response to the drug is monitored and evaluated. The patient then remains on the medication for a set time (*adequate trial*) and the effects of the drug on the patient's symptoms are evaluated. Maintenance on a psychotropic drug may lead to a full or partial remission of symptoms or no therapeutic response. Depending on the patient's response to the drug, the dosage may be elevated or decreased, the patient may be switched to another medication, or combined treatment (*augmentation*) may be initiated, which involves adding another drug to increase the effectiveness of the original medication. In some cases, all medications are withdrawn entirely and the psychiatrist may determine that the patient is not an appropriate candidate for pharmacotherapy.

PATIENT RESPONSE TO MEDICATIONS

Patients differ widely in both their psychological and physiological responses to a psychiatric drug. Some patients are desperate and have unrealistically high expectations of medications. They may become angry or despondent if they do not achieve the symptom relief that they expect. Some patients are hypersensitive to side effects and may find them intolerable and simply cease taking the drug.

Many patients are ambivalent about taking a psychiatric drug at all. They may view medication as a crutch or a sign of character weakness and a concrete reminder that they are "sick." Such patients may experience a plummet in self-esteem. Often significant others in the patient's life wittingly or unwittingly undermine the patient's pharmacotherapy by letting the patient know they do not approve of his/her being on medication.

A small, but significant, percentage of patients shift their focus to medication issues as a way of resisting or avoiding the therapy process. Such patients may begin dominating therapy time with discussions about the effects of their medications, problems with side effects, and interest in psychopharmacological issues. The therapist needs to address this shift. Many such patients abruptly drop out of therapy once psychiatric drugs relieve their symptoms.

THE ROLE OF THE ADDICTIONS COUNSELOR IN MEDICATION MANAGEMENT

Addictions therapists can help the prescribing physician better manage their patient cases in two ways:

1. They can provide the psychiatrist or physician with accurate information on the patient's addictive use of substances, a complete and accurate drug and alcohol history, and their clinical impressions of the patient. Patients often misrepresent themselves to physicians and may leave out vital information that would help the doctor in pharmacological management of the patient.
2. As the primary therapist, the addictions counselor is able to monitor patient response to medication as well as patient compliance. The counselor can be instrumental in initiating a reevaluation for patients who might not do so themselves. According to Preston, O'Neal, and Talaga (1994), patients should be referred back to the prescribing physician under the following circumstances: (1) inadequate or no response to medications, (2) partial response

to medications, (3) medical or psychiatric problems other than those for which the patient is receiving primary care, (4) relapse in psychiatric symptoms, (5) side effect problems, and (6) discontinuation of medications.

Once on a medication, patients show varying responses. There are often problems with the management of side effects. The patient may develop another psychiatric disorder or the medication may unmask previously unnoticed psychiatric symptoms. All these conditions warrant referral back to the prescribing physician for a reevaluation, and the addictions therapist can be instrumental in getting this done. Finally, after an adequate trial, it may be time for the patient to discontinue the drug. This issue can be addressed in treatment and with the prescribing physician.

Addictions therapists can be very helpful in ensuring patient compliance with the medication regimen. Therapists can provide education on the effects of psychiatric drugs and can support and reassure the patient while pharmacotherapy has time to take effect. Therapists can also be helpful in the management of any relapse to active addiction that a patient may experience. Drug or alcohol relapse usually interrupts the patient's regular medication intake. Alcohol and other psychoactive substances can also have the effect of lowering the efficacy of psychiatric medication, and some drugs interact with medications with severe, potentially lethal, results. Active use of alcohol and drugs concurrent with the taking of psychiatric medications usually exacerbates the psychiatric symptoms for which the medication was prescribed (Vogel, 1986). Addictions therapists can keep their patients informed of the risks of relapse and can help ensure that the patient returns to a recovery program and discusses the relapse with his/her prescribing physician.

ANTIDEPRESSANTS AND OTHER MOOD STABILIZERS

There are many medications that can be used to treat depression and bipolar disorder. Although many of the antidepressants appear to be chemically similar, the mechanisms of action are sufficiently different that a complete trial may involve several different antidepressants in sequence. Medications used in the treatment of affective disorders include the following.

Tricyclic Antidepressants

These are a large group of medications with somewhat differing mechanisms of action, but equal efficacy. Until the recent introduction of selective serotonin reuptake inhibitors (SSRIs), tricyclics such as imipramine and amitriptyline were considered the drug of choice in the treatment of depression. The tricyclics share similar, but varying, side effects. They all have some anticholinergic effects (dry mouth, blurry vision, constipation), sedation, and orthostatic hypotension (resulting in dizziness on standing). Weight gain and sexual dysfunction are also commonly reported. Appleton (1991) provides an excellent comparison of the effects and side effects of the tricyclics as well as the other antidepressants.

Other Heterocyclic Antidepressants

This group of medications was developed subsequent to the tricyclics. They include bupropion (Wellbutrin), fluoxetine (Prozac), maprotiline (Ludiomil), and trazodone (Desyrel and others). The introduction of fluoxetine (Prozac) and other SSRIs such as paroxetine (Paxil), sertraline (Zoloft), and venlafaxine (Effexor) has radically altered prescribing practices in this country. Their effectiveness is similar to that of the tricyclics and the side effects are much less troublesome, with little anticholinergic effect, orthostatic hypotension, or drowsiness. They are reported to cause weight loss and can cause insomnia, restlessness, and gastrointestinal upset, especially in the beginning. Although the full clinical benefit of SSRIs can take several weeks to establish, the patient often begins to feel some improvement within the first week. This is a clinical advantage over the tricyclics, which may show no positive effect for up to three weeks.

Monamine Oxidase (MAO) Inhibitors

Monamine Oxidase Inhibitors such as phenelzine (Nardil) or tranylcypromine (Parnate) have an antidepressant effect based on blocking the enzymes that metabolize epinephrine, norepinephrine, serotonin, and dopamine, leading to an increase in these substances. As a result, hypertensive crises, which can lead to stroke or death, can result if tyramine-rich foods (aged cheese, wine) are ingested. Similarly, combination with alcohol, over-the-counter cold preparations, or other antidepressants can present danger. These enzyme-blocking effects can last for over a week after the MAO inhibitor is discontinued.

Lithium

Lithium is the first-line treatment for bipolar disorder. Unfortunately, the response can take up to ten days, so in the early treatment of severe mania, a neuroleptic is often added. Lithium is very safe if the individual is free of heart or kidney disease. Some mild side effects can occur in early treatment or if the blood level of the drug is too high. These include nausea, diarrhea, stomach pain, mental fatigue, and tremor. Weight gain is often observed. Hypothyroidism is an occasional adverse effect of lithium therapy, as is kidney disease; these are easily monitored with blood testing in routine office visits.

Anticonvulsants

Anticonvulsants, including carbamazepine (Tegretol and others) and valproic acid (Depakene and others), have been found effective in the treatment of lithium-resistant bipolar disorder. They have a few more side effects than lithium, including drowsiness, dizziness, nausea, vomiting, and blurred vision. In addition, a rare, potentially fatal condition of aplastic anemia can result. Careful monitoring of blood levels and blood counts is essential for the proper use of these medications. A third anticonvulsant, clonazepam (Klonopin), has been introduced for mood stabilization in severe mania. This is a benzodiazepine and should be used with extreme caution in patients with known alcohol or sedative dependence.

ANTIANXIETY AGENTS

Most of the medications used to treat anxiety are benzodiazepines or other sedatives. With dual-disorder patients, these should be considered medications of last resort and used only in the most severe and refractory anxiety disorders, as they carry a significant risk of reactivating addiction. Tricyclic antidepressants have been found to have antianxiety effects and are a good first-line choice for the treatment of anxiety disorders in chemically dependent individuals. Buspirone (BuSpar) is a reportedly nonaddicting, antianxiety agent that can be quite effective for the treatment of generalized anxiety disorder. However, compliance and acceptance are limited in patients previously treated with benzodiazepines. Another suitable treatment for many patients with anxiety disorders is the noradrenergic agents. These medications, including propranolol (Inderal and others) and clonidine (Catapres), are effective in treating the somatic symptoms of anxiety and therefore breaking the "fear-of-fear" cycle. Hypotension (low blood pressure), slow heart rate, depression, and sedation are possible side effects; however, these medications are not considered addicting.

MEDICATIONS USED TO TREAT PSYCHOSIS AND THOUGHT DISORDERS

Neuroleptics

Neuroleptics are used to treat the symptoms of schizophrenia and related disorders, including hallucinations, delusions, and impaired-reality testing. They belong to a number of chemical groupings but have similar effects and side effects. Chlorpromazine (Thorazine and others) was the first of this group to be developed and serves as a reference standard for dosing. Others include thioridazine (Mellaril and others), trifluoperazine (Stelazine), thiothixene (Navane), and haloperidol (Haldol). Although sedation is a frequent side effect of many of these drugs, they are not considered addicting in that the doses needed to sustain an altered mood result in very unpleasant side effects. Nevertheless, practicing addicts sometimes do abuse these medications in conjunction with other drugs to create a "buzz." The potential for abuse needs to be actively addressed with the dual-diagnosis patient who needs these medications, but is not in itself a contraindication for prescribing them.

The side effects of the neuroleptics can be grouped in the following categories:

1. *Central nervous system effects*—sedation, depression, and a very rare but potentially fatal reaction called neuroleptic malignant syndrome
2. *Anticholinergic*—dry mouth, blurry vision, constipation, urinary hesitance, can precipitate glaucoma
3. *Extrapyramidal reactions*
   a. Pseudoparkinsonism marked by akinesia (slowed motor movements), rigidity, and tremors
   b. Akathisia, a motor restlessness characterized by pacing
   c. Dystonic reactions, which usually affect young males when first beginning treatment and are characterized by painful spasms of the eye, face, neck, and back
   d. Tardive dyskinesia, an involuntary-movement disorder usually involving the mouth (lip smacking, tongue darting) but also affecting neck, trunk, and limbs; appears in a small proportion of individuals treated with these medications and only after several months to years of treatment; often reversible; although it may get worse when the drug is first discontinued
4. *Cardiovascular*—tachycardia, orthostatic hypotension.
5. *Metabolic and endocrine*—weight gain, breast enlargement, impotence, amenorrhea, and hyperglycemia

Antiparkinsonian drugs

Antiparkinsonian drugs are used for the treatment of extrapyramidal side effects; benztropine (Cogentin and others) is the most commonly prescribed. Although these medications are very useful in reducing the extrapyramidal side effects of the neuroleptics, they have anticholinergic effects that *add* to the side effects of the neuroleptics. Amantadine (Symmetrel) has somewhat fewer side effects but a longer half-life, giving it a slow onset and making determination of the correct dosage somewhat more difficult.

USING MEDICATION IN THE TREATMENT
OF PERSONALITY DISORDERS

There is no specific medication treatment for personality disorders (Ellison and Adler, 1990). However, experience shows that some symptoms associated with personality disorders can be relieved with medication. First, a period of abstinence needs to be achieved. Many of the symptoms listed below resolve with abstinence. If symptoms persist, an accurate diagnosis needs to be established by a psychiatrist experienced in dual disorders. Often a mood disorder or anxiety disorder is present along with the Axis II diagnosis. If so, these illnesses should be treated appropriately. If a full Axis I diagnosis cannot be made, a careful assessment of symptomatology resulting from the personality disorder needs to be conducted. Six symptoms that often occur in personality disorders and can be helped with medications are transient psychosis, schizotypy, impulsivity, mood instability, dysphoria, and anxiety.

Transient psychosis may be characterized by brief hallucinations, delusions, ideas or reference, and depersonalization. Patients with borderline or paranoid personality disorder who experience these symptoms may benefit from treatment with neuroleptics.

Schizotypy is characterized by a mild, persistent cognitive dysfunction leading to poor reality testing, suspiciousness, anhedonia, and ambivalence. Patients with schizotypal, paranoid, or borderline personality disorder may show this symptom and benefit from neuroleptic medication.

Impulsivity is prominent in several personality disorders, including borderline, narcissistic, and antisocial. Lithium and the anticonvulsants have been shown to be of some help with this symptom.

Mood instability is a common symptom in many of the personality disorders, including histrionic, narcissistic, borderline, and avoidant. The antidepressants and the other mood stabilizers have been used to treat this symptom.

Dysphoria is defined as a state of low energy, fatigue, and depressive mood. When this appears, antidepressant medication may be indicated.

Anxiety is a troublesome symptom in that it is very common in early recovery, often associated with a protracted withdrawal syndrome. If extreme anxiety interferes with an individual's ability to participate in recovery and other treatment activities, treatment with tricyclic antidepressants or beta-blockers may be useful. As in the treatment of anxiety disorders, benzodiazepines should be the treatment of last resort.

SUMMARY

The addition of any kind of medication to the treatment plan of an individual with a dual diagnosis is a serious matter. Medication is not to be feared, neither is it to be taken lightly. A psychiatrist trained and experienced in working with the dually diagnosed should be consulted. The patient needs a great deal of education about the expected benefits and side effects of the medication, and needs help in understanding the role of medication in his/her overall recovery. The addictions counselor can be instrumental in helping the patient formulate questions to ask his/her physician. The counselor can also help the patient explore his/her attitudes about taking medication and help to formulate realistic expectations.

Appendix C

Selected Sample Treatment Plan Activities

ANXIETY DISORDERS

- Patient will practice abdominal breathing and progressive muscle-relaxation exercise two times daily. Keep a written log of experiences in relaxation and discuss in an individual therapy session.
- Patient will construct a list of common worries, rank them for the level of anxiety they provoke, and develop a written action plan to deal with each worry.
- Patient will develop three rational coping statements and practice them in anxiety-provoking situations. Discuss in treatment group.
- Patient will read handout on the physiology and psychology of panic and prepare a short summary of it to present in treatment group.
- Patient will identify a time when he/she was confronted with an anxiety-provoking situation and did not panic. Patient will discuss how he/she handled this situation and how these skills can be applied to a panic situation.
- Patient will list the advantages and disadvantages of having the following belief: "I must be in control of my feelings and actions at all times." Discuss in treatment group.
- Patient will develop a list of at least ten irrational thoughts associated with anxiety and will develop at least ten rational counter-thoughts and practice them. Discuss in individual therapy session.

MOOD DISORDERS

- Patient will develop a daily plan of activities, including exercise, work schedule, leisure activities, and meal planning, and

follow this while in inpatient treatment. Discuss in treatment group.
- Patient will identify and list at least five depressive thoughts and develop at least five rational counters. Patient will practice rational counters and discuss experiences in individual therapy session.
- Patient will review history of depressive episodes, listing those feelings, thoughts, situations, and stressors that accompanied these episodes, and will develop an action plan to deal with a potential recurrent depressive episode.
- Patient will review a list of cognitive distortions, identifying the ones he/she uses and situations in which they arise.

EATING DISORDERS

- Patient will list personal beliefs about thinness and discuss them in treatment group.
- Patient will list at least five feelings that precede a binge/purge and five feelings that follow a binge/purge. Patient will discuss feelings in treatment group.
- Patient will develop five cognitive coping statements to assist in preventing a binge/purge behavior.
- Patient will develop comprehensive action plans, including developing coping statements, delaying and distracting activities, and substitute activities to prevent relapse to active bingeing/purging.
- Patient will practice conflict and anger-management strategies in role-play with other group members and therapists.

PERSONALITY DISORDERS

- Patient will interview ten other patients in the treatment community and ask them to give one statement about patient's personality, strengths, and weaknesses. Patient will write them down and discuss results in treatment group.
- Patient will discuss advantages and disadvantages of attempts to get along with others.

- Patient will discuss common irrational thoughts and self-talk patient engages in throughout informal social situations, identifying fears and concerns, and discuss in treatment group.
- Patient will agree or disagree with this statement: "If someone disagrees with me, it means they don't like me." Patient will discuss reasons for his or her choice in treatment group.
- Patient will write down his or her reaction to the statement, "The world is screwed up and people are out to get you." Patient will list any personal evidence to back up this belief and will discuss in therapy group.
- Patient will brainstorm all the events, situations, and factors in childhood he or she can think of that had an impact on his or her personality development. Patient will then list what traits or behaviors he or she can change and will ask group members for input and advice on how to change.

ANTISOCIAL PERSONALITY DISORDER

- Patient will list the advantages and disadvantages of believing this statement: "It's my way or the highway." Discuss in treatment group.
- Patient will list the major benefits and liabilities of the following behaviors: (1) intimidating others, (2) impulsive behavior, and (3) irresponsibility.
- Patient will list five different alternatives to manipulation for getting needs met.
- Patient will list five problems he might encounter if he harbors this feeling: "I want what I want when I want it."

BORDERLINE PERSONALITY DISORDER

- Patient will practice mindfulness meditation three times daily, write down experiences, and discuss with therapist in individual session.
- Patient will develop emergency action plan to prevent self-mutilation and self-destructive behavior. Discuss in individual therapy session.

- Patient will interview ten group or community members and list three different ways the patient is similar to other patients.
- Patient will develop emotion-management plan, listing several activities (i.e., relaxation, meditation, brisk walk) to cope with extremes in feelings.

SCHIZOPHRENIC DISORDERS

- Patient will list five fears and concerns involved in being intimate or trusting others. Discuss in individual therapy session.
- Patient will review history of relapses to the active phase of schizophrenia and addiction, list those triggers associated with relapse, and collaborate with therapist to develop an action plan to prevent future relapses.
- Patient will discuss his/her beliefs, attitudes, and concerns about antipsychotic medication. Discuss in individual therapy session.
- Patient will interview three treatment group members and solicit advice for handling conflict in family and social situations.
- Patient will discuss the impact of taking alcohol and street drugs while on medication and list five disadvantages of this practice.

References

Chapter 1

American Psychiatric Association. (1994). *Diagnostic and statistical manual of mental disorders,* 4th ed. Washington, DC: American Psychiatric Association.

Caragonne, P. and Emery, B. (1987). *Mental illness and substance abuse: The dually diagnosed client.* Rockville, MD: National Council of Community Mental Health Centers.

Gottheil, E. L., McLellan, A. T., and Druley, K. A. (1978). *Substance abuse and psychiatric illness: Proceedings of the Second Annual Coatsville-Jefferson Conference on addiction.* New York: Pergamon Press.

Harrison, P. A., Martin, J. A., Tuason, V. B., and Hoffmann, N. G. (1985). Conjoint treatment of dual disorders. In A. I. Alterman (Ed.), *Substance abuse and psychopathology.* New York: Plenum Press; 367-390.

Kalb, M. and Propper, M. S. (1976). The future of alcohology: Craft or science? *American Journal of Psychiatry, 133,* 641-645.

O'Connell, D. F. (Ed.) (1990). *Managing the dually diagnosed patient: Current issues and clinical approaches.* Binghamton, New York: The Haworth Press.

O'Connell, D. F. and Patterson, H. (1996). Recovery maintenance and relapse prevention with chemically dependent adolescents. In M. A. Reineke, F. M. Dattilio, and A. Freeman (Eds.), *Cognitive therapy with children and adolescents: A casebook for clinical practice.* New York: Guilford Press; 79-102.

Penick, E. C., Nickel, E. J., Cantrell, P. G., Powell, B. J., Read, M. R., and Thomas, H. M. (1990). The emerging concept of dual diagnosis: An overview and implications. In D. F. O'Connell (Ed.), *Managing the dually diagnosed patient: Current issues and clinical approaches.* Binghamton, New York: The Haworth Press; 1-54.

Perkins, K. A., Simpson, J. C., and Tsuang, M. T. (1986). Ten-year follow-up of drug abusers with acute or chronic psychosis. *Hospital and Community Psychiatry, 37,* 481-484.

Teague, G. B., Schwab, B., and Drake, R. E. (1990). *Evaluation of services for young adults with severe mental illness and substance use disorders.* Alexandria, VA: National Association of State Mental Health Program Directors.

Todd, J. M. (1980). The mentally-ill alcoholic. *Maryland State Medical Journal, 5,* 21-26.

Wallen, M. C. and Weiner, H. D. (1989). Impediments to effective treatment of the dually diagnosed patient. *Journal of Psychoactive Drugs, 21,* 161-168.

Woody, G. E., McLellan, A. T., Luborsky, L., O'Brien, C. P., Blaine, J., Fox, S., Herman, I., and Beck, A. T. (1984). Severity of psychiatric symptoms as a predictor of benefits from psychotherapy: The Veterans Administration-Penn study. *American Journal of Psychiatry, 141,* 1172-1177.

Suggested Reading

Daley, D.C., Moss, H., and Campbell, F. (1993). *Dual disorders: Counseling clients with mental illness and chemical dependence,* Second Edition. Center City, MN: Hazleden.

Evans, K. and Sullivan, J. M. (1990). *Dual diagnosis: Counseling the mentally ill substance abuser.* New York: Guilford Press.

Harrison, P. A., Martin, J. A., Tuason, V. B., and Hoffmann, N. G. (1985). Conjoint treatment of dual disorders. In A. I. Alterman (Ed.), *Substance abuse and psychopathology.* New York: Plenum Press; 367-390.

Miller, N. S. (Ed.) (1994). *Treating coexisting psychiatric and addictive disorders: A practical guide.* Center City, MN: Hazleden.

Wallen, M. C. and Weiner, H. D. (1989). Impediments to effective treatment of the dually diagnosed patient. *Journal of Psychoactive Drugs, 21,* 161-168.

Chapter 2

Behnke, R. H. (1976). Recognition and management of alcohol withdrawal syndrome. *Hospital Practice, 11,* 79-84.

Bernstein, E. M. and Putnam, F. W. (1986). Development, reliability, and validity of a dissociation scale. *The Journal of Nervous and Mental Disease, 174,* 727-735.

Folstein, M. F., Folstein, S. E., and McHugh, P. R. (1975). "Mini-Mental State": A practical method of grading the cognitive state of patients for the clinician. *Journal of Psychiatric Research, 12,* 189-198.

Garner, D. M. and Garfinkel, P. E. (Eds.) (1985). *Handbook of psychotherapy for anorexia and bulimia.* New York: Guilford Press.

Kreitman, N. (1986). The critical assessment and management of the suicidal patient. In A. Roy (Ed.), *Suicide.* Baltimore, MD: Williams and Wilkins; 181-195.

Patterson, W. M., Dohn, H. H., Bird, J., and Patterson, S. A. (1983). Evaluation of suicidal patients: The SAD PERSONS scale. *Psychosomatics, 24,* 343-349.

Pollack, B. (1942). The validity of the Shipley-Hartford Retreat Test for "Deterioration." *Psychiatric Quarterly, 16,* 119-131.

Tarter, R. E. and Edwards, M. L. (1987). Brief and comprehensive neurological assessment of alcohol and substance abuse. In L. C. Hartlage, M. J. Asken, and J. L. Hornsby (Eds.), *Essentials of neuropsychological assessment.* New York: Springer; 138-162.

Yager, J. (1989). Clinical manifestations of psychiatric disorders. In H. I. Kaplan and B. J. Sadock (Eds.), *Comprehensive textbook of psychiatry /V* (Vol. 1) Baltimore, MD: Williams and Wilkins; 553-582.

Chapter 3

American Psychiatric Association. (1994). *Diagnostic and statistical manual of mental disorders,* fourth edition. Washington, DC: Author.
Bean-Bayog, M. (1986). Psychopathology produced by alcoholism. In R. E. Meyer (Ed.), *Psychopathology and addictive disorders.* New York: Guilford Press; 334-345.
Beck, A. T., Wright, F. D., Newman, C. F., and Liese, B. S. (1993). *Cognitive therapy of substance abuse.* New York: Guilford Press.
Cull, J. G. and Gill, W. S. (1982). *Suicide probability scale—Manual.* Los Angeles, CA: Western Psychological Services.
Fawcett, J., Scheftner, W., Clark, D., Hedeker, D., Gibbons, R., and Coryell, W. (1987). Clinical predictors of suicide in patients with major affective disorders: A controlled prospective study. *American Journal of Psychiatry, 144,* 35-40.
Howland, R. M. (1991). Pharmacotherapy of dysthymia: A review. *Journal of Clinical Psychopharmacology, 11,* 83-92.
Mayfield, D. (1985). Substance abuse in the affective disorders. In A. I. Alterman (Ed.), *Substance abuse and psychopathology.* New York: Plenum Press; 69-89.
Paykel, E. S. (1982). *Handbook of affective disorders.* New York: Guilford Press.
Sternberg, D. E. (1989). Dual diagnosis: Addiction and affective disorders. *The Psychiatric Hospital, 20,* 71-77.
Winokur, G. and Coryell, W. (1991). Familial alcoholism in primary unipolar major depressive disorder. *American Journal of Psychiatry, 148,* 184-188.

Chapter 4

American Psychiatric Association. (1994). *Diagnostic and statistical manual of mental disorders,* fourth edition, Washington, DC.
Bloomfield, H. (1975). *TM: Discovering inner energy and overcoming stress.* New York: Delacorte Press.
Bourne, E. J. (1990). *The anxiety and phobia workbook.* Oakland, CA: New Harbinger Publications.
Brown, T. A., O'Leary, T. A., and Barlow, D. H. (1993). Generalized anxiety disorder. In D. H. Barlow (Ed.), *Clinical handbook of psychological disorders,* second edition. New York: Guilford Press; 137-188.
Chambless, D. L., Cherney, J., Caputo, G. C., and Rhinestein, B. J. (1987). Anxiety disorders and alcoholism: A study with inpatient alcoholics. *Journal of Anxiety Disorders, 1,* 29-40.
Charney, D. (1990). The neurobiology of anxiety: Neurodevelopmental hypothesis. *Psychiatry Letter, 7,* Fair Oaks Hospital.

Craske, M. G. and Barlow, D. H. (1993). Panic disorder and agoraphobia. In D. H. Barlow (Ed.), *Clinical handbook of psychological disorders*, second edition. New York: Guilford Press; 1-47.

Dillbeck, M. C. (1977). The effect of the transcendental meditation technique on anxiety level. *Journal of Clinical Psychology, 33,* 1076-1078.

Eisen, J. L. and Rasmussen, S. A. (1989). Coexisting obsessive compulsive disorder and alcoholism. *Journal of Clinical Psychiatry, 50,* 96-98.

Eppley, K., Abrams, A., and Shear, J. (1989). The differential effects of relaxation techniques on trait anxiety: A meta-analysis. *Journal of Clinical Psychology, 45,* 957-974.

Goggans, F. C., Odgers, R. P., Luscombe, S. M., Foust, R., and Elmore, M. (1990). Chemical dependency and anxiety disorders. *The Psychiatric Hospital, 20,* 79-83.

Goldstein, A. and Stainbach, B. (1987). *Overcoming agoraphobia*. New York: Viking Press.

Ley, R. (1987). Panic disorder: A hyperventilation interpretation. In L. Michelson and L. M. Ascher (Eds.), *Anxiety and stress disorders cognitive-behavioral assessment and treatment*. New York: Guilford Press; 191-212.

McFall, M. E. and Wallersheim, J. P. (1979). Obsessive compulsive neurosis: A cognitive behavioral formulation and approach to treatment. *Cognitive therapy and research, 3,* 333-342.

Meichenbaum, D. and Jarenko, M. E. (1983). *Stress reduction and prevention*. New York: Plenum Press.

Rapee, R. M. and Barlow, D. H. (Eds.) (1991). *Chronic anxiety, generalized anxiety disorder and mixed anxiety-depression*. New York: Guilford Press.

Regier, D. A., Farmer, M. E., Rae, D. S., Locke, B. E., Keith, S. J., Judd, L. L., and Goodwin, F. K. (1990). Comorbidity of mental disorders with alcohol and other drugs: Results from the Epidemiologic Catchment Area (ECA) Study. *Journal of the American Medical Association, 264,* 2511-2595.

Weissman, M. (1988) Anxiety and alcoholism. *Journal of Clinical Psychiatry, 49* (supplement), 17-19.

Suggested Reading

Barlow, D. H. (Ed) (1993). *Clinical handbook of psychological disorders*. New York: Guilford Press.

Barlow, D. H. and Craske, M. G. (1990). *Mastery of anxiety and panic attacks* (audiocassette). Albany, NY: Graywing Publishers.

Benson, H. (1973). *The relaxation response*. New York: William Morrow.

Bourne, E. J. (1990). *The anxiety and phobia workbook*. Oakland, CA: New Harbinger Publications.

Davis, M., Eshelman, E. R., and McKay, M. (1982). *Relaxation and stress reduction workbook*. Oakland, CA: New Harbinger Publications.

Goggans, F. C., Odgers, R. P., Luscombe, S. M., Foust, R., and Elmore, M. (1990). Chemical dependency and anxiety disorders. *The Psychiatric Hospital, 20,* 79-83.

Handly, R. (1985). *Anxiety and panic attacks: Their causes and cure.* New York: Faucett Crest Books.
LaMott, K. (1975). *Escape from stress.* New York: G.P. Putnum.
Steketee, G. and White, K. (1990). *When once is not enough: Help for obsessive compulsives.* Oakland, CA: New Harbinger Publications.
Stroebel, C. F. (1978). *Quieting response training* (audiocassette). New York: Biomonitoring Applications Publication.
Warren, R. W. and Zgourides, G. D. (1991). *Anxiety disorders: A rational emotive approach.* New York: Pergamon Press.

Chapter 5

Evans, K. and Sullivan, J. M. (1990). *Dual diagnosis: Counseling the mentally ill substance abuser.* New York: Guilford Press.
Hanson, M., Kramer, T. H., and Gross, W. (1990). Outpatient treatment of adults with coexisting substance use and mental disorders. *Journal of Substance Abuse Treatment, 7,* 109-116.
Karon, B. P. and Vandenbos, G. R. (1981). *Psychotherapy of schizophrenia: The treatment of choice.* Northvale, NJ: Jason Aronson.
McGlashan, T. N. (1988). Recent North American long-term follow-up studies of schizophrenia. *Schizophrenia Bulletin, 14,* 515-542.
Minkoff, K. (1989). An integrated treatment model for dual diagnosis of psychosis and addiction. *Hospital and Community Psychiatry, 40,* 1031-1036.
Pao, P. N. (1979). *Schizophrenic disorders: Theory and treatment from a psychodynamic perspective.* New York: International University Press.
Radke, S. (1991). *Curriculum for working in groups with individuals dually diagnosed with mental illness and substance abuse.* Baltimore, MD: State Department of Health and Mental Hygiene.
Ridgely, M. S., Osher, F. C., Goldman, H. H., and Talbott, J. A. (1987). *Executive summary—Chronic mentally ill young adults with substance abuse problems: A review of research, treatment, and training issues.* Baltimore, MD: Mental Health Policy Studies, University of Maryland.
Siris, S. G. (1990). Pharmacological treatment of substance-abusing schizophrenic patients. *Schizophrenia Bulletin, 16,* 111-122.

Suggested Reading

Birchwood, M. J., Hallett, S. E., and Preston, M. C. (1989). *Schizophrenia: An integrated approach to research and treatment.* New York: New York University Press.
Hanson, M., Kramer, T. H., and Gross, W. (1990). Outpatient treatment of adults with coexisting substance use and mental disorders. *Journal of Substance Abuse Treatment, 7,* 109-116.
Hyde, A. P. (1982). *Living with schizophrenia: A guide for patients and their families.* Chicago: Contemporary Books.

Torrey, E. F. (1983). *Surviving schizophrenia: A family manual*. New York: Harper and Row.

Chapter 6

American Psychiatric Association. (1990). *Benzodiazepine dependence, toxicity and abuse: A task force report of the American Psychiatric Association*. Washington, DC: American Psychiatric Association.

American Psychiatric Association. (1994). *Diagnostic and statistical manual of mental disorders*, 4th ed. Washington, DC: American Psychiatric Association.

Becker, J. T. and Kaplan, R. F. (1986). Neurophysiological and neuropsychological concomitants of brain dysfunction in alcoholics. In R. E. Meyer (Ed.), *Psychopathology and addictive disorders*. New York: The Guilford Press; 263-292.

Benson, D. F. (1978). Amnesia. *South Medical Journal*, 1221-1228.

Cummings, J. L., Benson, D. F., and LoVerme, S. (1980). Reversible dementia. *Journal of the American Medical Association, 243*, 2434-2439.

Folstein, M. F., Folstein, S. E., and McHugh, P. R. (1975). Mini-mental state: A practical method for grading the cognitive state of patients for the clinician. *Journal of Psychiatric Research, 12*, 189.

Friedrich, R. M., and Kus, R. J. (1991). Cognitive impairments in early sobriety: Nursing interventions. *Archives of Psychiatric Nursing, 5*, 105-112.

Kaufman, D. M. (1985). *Clinical neurology for psychiatrists*. Orlando: Grune and Stratton.

McEvoy, C. L. and Patterson, R. L. (1986). Behavioral treatment of deficit skills in dementia patients. *Gerontologist, 26*, 475-478.

Meek, P. S., Clark, H. W., and Solana, V. L. (1989). Neurocognitive impairment: The unrecognized component of dual diagnosis in substance abuse treatment. *Journal of Psychoactive Drugs, 21*, 153-160.

Shelton, M. D. and Parsons, O. A. (1987). Alcoholic's self-assessment of their neuropsychological functioning in everyday life. *Journal of Clinical Psychology, 43*, 395-403.

Tupper, D. E. (1991). Rehabilitation of cognitive and neuropsychological deficit following stroke. In *Neurobehavioral aspects of cerebrovascular disease*. New York: Oxford University Press; 337-358.

Suggested Reading

Asaad, G. (1995). *Understanding mental disorders due to medical conditions or substance abuse: What every therapist should know*. New York: Brunner/ Mazel.

Berg, R., Franzen, M., and Wedding, D. (1987). *Screening for brain impairment: A manual for mental health practice*. New York: Springer.

Strub, R. L. and Black, F. W. (1988). *Neurobehavioral disorders: A clinical approach*. Philadelphia, PA: F. A. Davis Company.

Chapter 7

Bowers, W. A., Evans, K., and Van Cleve, L. (1996). Treatment of adolescent eating disorders. In M. A. Reineke, F. M. Dattilio, and A. Freeman (Eds.), *Cognitive therapy with children and adolescents: A caseguide for clinical teaching*. New York: Guilford; 227-250.

Bulik, C. M. (1987). Drug and alcohol abuse by bulimic women and their families. *American Journal of Psychiatry, 144*, 1604-1606.

Fairburn, C. G. (1985). Cognitive Behavorial Treatment for Bulimia. In D. M. Garner and P. E. Garfinkel (Eds.), *Handbook of Psychotherapy for Anorexia Nervosa and Bulimia*. New York: The Guilford Press, 160-192.

Garner, D. M. and Bemis, K. M. (1982). A cognitive behavioral approach to anorexia nervosa. *Cognitive Therapy and Research, 6*, 1-27

Garner, D. M. and Garfinkel, P. E. (1985). *Handbook of psychotherapy for anorexia and bulimia*. New York: Guilford Press.

Mitchell, J. E., Hatsukami, D., Eckert, E. D., and Pyle, R. L. (1985). Characteristics of 275 patients with bulimia. *American Journal of Psychiatry, 142*, 482-485.

Wooley, S. C. and Wooley, O. W. (1985). Intensive outpatient and residential treatment for bulimia. In D. M. Garner, and P. E. Garfinkel (Eds.), *Handbook of psychotherapy for anorexia and bulimia*. New York: Guilford Press.

Yeary, J. R. and Heck, C. L. (1989). Dual diagnosis: Eating disorders and psychoactive substance dependence. *Journal of Psychoactive Drugs, 21*, 239-249.

Suggested Reading

Hollis, J. (1985). *Fat is a family affair: Help and hope for those who suffer from eating disorders and those who love them*. Center City, MN: Hazelden.

Katz, J. L. (1990). Eating disorders: A primer for the substance abuse specialist. *Journal of Substance Abuse Treatment, 7*, 143-149.

Siegel, M., Brisman, J., and Weinshel, M. (1988). *Surviving an eating disorder: New perspectives and strategies for family and friends*. New York: Harper and Row.

Chapter 8

American Psychiatric Association. (1994). *Diagnostic and statistical manual of mental disorders*, fourth edition. Washington, DC: American Psychiatric Association.

Barley, W. D. (1986). Behavioral and cognitive treatment of criminal and delinquent behavior. In W. H. Reid, D. Door, J. I. Walker, and J. W. Bonner (Eds.), *Unmasking the psychopath*. New York: W. W. Norton and Company.

Beck, M. T., Freeman, A., and Associates. (1990). *Cognitive therapy of personality disorders*. New York: Guilford.

Cleckley, H. (1964). *The mask of sanity,* 4th ed. St. Louis, MO: Mosby.

Doren, D. M. (1987). *Understanding and treating the psychopath.* New York: John Wiley and Sons.

Gray, K. C. and Hutchison, H. C. (1964). The psychopathic personality: A survey of Canadian psychiatrists opinion. *Canadian Psychiatric Association Journal, 9,* 452-461.

King, M., Novik, L., and Citrenbaum, C. (1984). *Irresistible communication: Creative skills for the health professional.* Philadelphia, PA: WB Saunders Company.

Meloy, J. R. (1988). *The psychopathic mind: Origins, dynamics and treatment.* New York: Jason Aronson.

O'Malley, S. S., Kosten, T. R., and Renner, J. A., Jr. (1990). Dual diagnosis: Substance abuse and personality disorders. *New Directions for Mental Health Services, 47,* 115-137.

Reid, W., Dorn, D., Walker, J. I., and Bonner, J. W. (1986). *Unmasking the psychopath: Antisocial personality and related syndromes.* New York: Norton and Co.

Suggested Reading

Eysenck, H. J. (1977). *Crime and personality,* 3rd ed. London: Routledge and Kegan Paul.

Samenow, S. E. (1984). *Inside the criminal mind.* New York: Times Books.

Chapter 9

American Psychiatric Association. (1994). *Diagnostic and statistical manual of mental disorders,* 4th edition. Washington, DC: American Psychiatric Association.

Beck, A. T., Freeman, A., and Associates. (1990). *Cognitive therapy of personality disorders.* New York: Guilford Press.

Druck, A. B. (1989). *Four therapeutic approaches to the borderline patient: Principles and techniques of the basic dynamic stances.* North Vale, NJ: Jason Aronson.

Gardner, D. L. and Cowdry, R. W. (1989). Pharmacotherapy of borderline personality disorder: A review. *Psychopharmacology Bulletin, 25,* 515-523.

Gorski, T. and Miller, M. (1979). *Counseling for relapse prevention.* Hazel Creste, IL: Alcoholism Systems Associates.

Kabat-Zinn, J. (1994). *Wherever you go, there you are: Mindfulness meditation in everyday life.* New York: Hyperion.

Kernberg, O. (1975). *Borderline conditions and pathological narcissism.* New York: Jason Aronson.

Levine, S. (1979). *A gradual awakening.* New York: Doubleday.

Linehan, M. M. (1993a). *Cognitive behavioral treatment of borderline personality disorder.* New York: Guilford Press.

Linehan, M. M. (1993b). *Skills training manual for treating borderline personality disorder.* New York: Guilford Press.

O'Connell, D. F. and Alexander, C. N. (1994). *Self-recovery: Treating addictions using transcendental meditation and Maharishi Ayurveda.* New York: Harrington Park Press.

Reeve, B. S. (1990, September). *The treatment of chemical dependency in patients with borderline personality disorder.* Presented at Grand Rounds, Sheppard Pratt Hospital, Baltimore, MD.

Yalom, I. D. (1975). *The theory and practice of group psychotherapy*, second edition. New York: Basic Books.

Suggested Reading

Dulit, R. A., Fyer, M. R., Haas, G. L., Sullivan, T., and Frances, A. J. (1990). Substance use in borderline personality disorder. *American Journal of Psychiatry, 147*, 1002-1007.

Kernberg, O., Selzer, M. A., Koenigsberg, H. W., Carr, A. C., and Appelbaum, A. H. (1989). *Psychodynamic psychotherapy of borderline patients.* New York: Basic Books.

Kreisman, J. J. and Straus, H. (1989). *I hate you—don't leave me: Understanding the borderline personality.* New York: Avon Books.

Chapter 10

American Psychiatric Association. (1994). *Diagnostic and statistical manual of mental disorders*, fourth-revised edition. Washington, DC: American Psychiatric Association.

Beck, A. T., Freeman, A., and Associates. (1990). *Cognitive therapy of personality disorders.* New York: Guilford Press.

Deltito, J. and Stam, M. (1989) Pharmacological Treatment of Avoidant Personality Disorder. *Comprehensive Psychiatry, 30*, 498-574.

Sperry, L. (1995). *Handbook of diagnosis and treatment of the DSM-IV personality disorders.* New York: Brunner/Mazel.

Suggested Reading

Blume, S. B. (1989). Dual diagnosis: Psychoactive substance dependence and the personality disorders. *Journal of Psychoactive Drugs, 21*, 139-144.

Frances, A. (1987). *DSM-III Personality disorders: Diagnosis and Treatment* (audiocassette). New York: BMA Audiocassette Publishers.

Millon, T. (1981). *Disorders of personality DSM-III: Axis II.* New York: John Wiley.

Chapter 11

Coleman, E. (1987). Child physical sexual abuse among chemically dependent individuals. *Journal of Chemical Dependency Treatment, 1*, 27-38.

Courtois, C. A. (1988). *Healing the incest wound: Adult survivors in therapy.* New York: Norton.

Evans, S. and Schaefer, S. (1987). Incest and chemically dependent women: Treatment implications. *Journal of Chemical Dependency Treatment, 1,* 141-173.

Figley, C. R. (1985). *Trauma and its wake: The study and treatment of post-traumatic stress disorder.* New York: Brunner/Mazel.

Finkelhor, D. (1984). *Child sexual abuse: New theory and research.* New York: Free Press.

Resick, P. A. and Schnicke, M. K. (1992). Cognitive processing therapy for sexual assault victims. *Journal of Consulting and Clinical Psychology, 60,* 748-756

Root, M. P. P. (1989). Treatment failures: The role of sexual victimization in women's addictive behavior. *American Journal of Orthopsychiatry, 59,* 542-549.

Russell, D. E. H. (1986). *The secret trauma: Incest in the lives of girls and women.* New York: Basic Books.

Shapiro, F. (1995). *Eye movement desensitization and reprocessing: Basic principles, protocols and procedures.* New York: Guilford Press.

Scurfield, R. M. (1985). Post-trauma stress assessment and treatment: Overview and formulations. In C. R. Figley (ed.), *Trauma and its wake: The study and treatment of post-traumatic stress disorder.* New York: Brunner/Mazel.

Steele, B. F. (1986). Notes on the lasting effects of early child abuse throughout the life cycle. *Child Abuse and Neglect, 10,* 283-291.

Weinberg, S. K. (1976). *Incest behavior.* Secaucus, NJ: Citadel Press.

Wyatt, G. E. (1985). The sexual abuse of Afro-American and white women in childhood. *Child Abuse and Neglect, 9,* 507-519.

Suggested Reading

Bollerud, K. (1990). A model for the treatment of trauma-related syndromes among chemically dependent inpatient women. *Journal of Substance Abuse Treatment, 7,* 83-87.

Follingstad, D. R., Neckerman, A. P., and Vormbrock, J. (1988). Reactions to victimization and coping strategies of battered women: The ties that bind. *Clinical Psychology Review, 8,* 373-390.

Gelinas, D. J. (1983). The persisting negative effects of incest. *Psychiatry, 46,* 312-332.

Herman, J. and Schatzow, E. (1984). Time-limited group therapy for women with a history of incest. *International Journal of Group Psychotherapy, 34,* 605-616.

Kovach, J. A. (1986). Incest as a treatment issue for alcoholic women. *Alcoholism Treatment Quarterly, 3,* 1-15.

Mayer, A. (1985). *Sexual abuse: Causes, consequences, and treatment of incestuous and pedophilic acts.* Holmes Beach, FL: Learning Publications, Inc.

Rieker, P. P. and Carmen, E. H. (1986). The Victim-to-patient process: The disconfirmation and transformation of abuse. *American Journal of Orthopsychiatry, 56,* 360-370.

Redlich, F. C. (1986). The use and abuse of power in psychotherapy. *Psychiatric Annals, 16,* 637-639.
Young, E. B. (1990). The role of incest issues in relapse. *Journal of Psychoactive Drugs, 22,* 249-258.

Appendix A

Beck, A. (1976). *Cognitive therapy and the emotional disorders.* New York: International Universities Press.
Beck, A. T., Freeman, A., and Associates. (1990). *Cognitive therapy of personality disorders.* New York: Guilford Press.
Burns, D. (1980). *Feeling good: The new mood therapy.* New York: William Morrow.
Burns, D. (1989). *The feeling good handbook.* New York: William Morrow.
Ellis, A. (1962). *Reason and emotion in psychotherapy.* New York: Lyle Stewart.
Freeman, A. (1987). Cognitive therapy: An overview. In A. Freman and V. Greenwood (Eds.), *Cognitive therapy: Applications in psychiatric and mental settings.* New York: Human Science Press.
Greenberger, D. and Padesky, C. A. (1995). *Mind over mood: A cognitive therapy treatment manual for clients.* New York: Guilford Press
Young, J. E. (1990). *Cognitive therapy for personality disorders: A schema focused approach.* Sarasota, FL: Professional Resource Exchange.

Suggested Reading

Beck, A., Rush, A., Shaw, B., and Emery, G. (1979). *Cognitive therapy of depression.* New York: Guilford Press.
Beck, A. T., Wright, F. D., Newman, C. F., and Liese, B. S. (1993). *Cognitive therapy of substance abuse.* New York: Guilford Press.
Craighead, L. W., Craighead, E. W., Kardin, A. E., and Mahoney, M.J. (Eds.) (1994). *Cognitive and behavioral interventions: An empirical approach to mental health problems.* Boston: Allyn and Bacon.
Freeman, A. and Dattilio, F. M. (1992). *Comprehensive casebook of cognitive therapy.* New York: Plenum Press
McMullin, R. E. (1986). *Handbook of cognitive therapy techniques.* New York: Norton.
O'Connell, D. F. and Patterson, H. O. (1996). Recovery maintenance and relapse prevention with chemically dependent adolescents. In M. A. Reineke, F. M. Dattilio, and A. Freeman (Eds.), *Cognitive therapy with children and adolescents: A casebook for clinical practice.* New York: Guilford Press; 79-102.

Appendix B

Appleton, W. S. (1991). *The fifth psychoactive drug usage guide.* Memphis, TN: Physicians Postgraduate Press.

Ellison, J. M. and Adler, D. A. (1990). A strategy for the pharmacotherapy of personality disorders. *New Directions for Mental Health Services*, *47*, 43-63.

Preston, J., O'Neal, J. H., and Talaga, M.C. (1994). *Handbook of Clinical Psychopharmacology for Therapists*. Oakland, CA: New Harbinger Publications.

Vogel, W. H. (1986). Interactions of drugs of abuse with prescription drugs. In R. E. Meyer (Ed.), *Psychopathology and addictive disorders*. New York: The Guilford Press; 213-237.

Suggested Reading

Zweben, J. E. and Smith, D. E. (1989). Considerations in using psychotropic medication with dual diagnosis patients in recovery. *Journal of Psychoactive Drugs*, *21*, 221-228.

Index

Alcohol, withdrawal *(continued)*
 symptoms, 23,53. *See also*
  Chemical withdrawal
Alcoholic
 depressed, subgroups of, 31-32
 and PTSD, 68
Alcoholics Anonymous (AA), 5,122
 attendance at, 32,71,81,122
 benefit of, 13
 and the borderline personality, 146
Alcoholism
 and agoraphobia, 58-59
 familial basis of, 33
Alcohol-persisting amnestic disorder,
  99-100
All-or-none thinking, 116, 145, 197
Altruism, and the borderline
  personality, 141-142
Alzheimer's disease, 92
Amantadine (Symmetrel), 212
Amitriptyline, 209
 for anorexics, 105
Amnestic disorder, 98
 cognitive disorder, 87
 DSM-IV definition of, 98-99
 substance induced, 87,99-100
Amoxapine (Asendin), 157
Amphetamines, and cognitive
  disorders, 87
Amygdala, and anxiety, 49
Anger
 and borderline personalities, 4
 dependent personality disorder,
  167-168
 histrionic personality disorder, 159
 paranoid personality disorder,
  149,150
 PTSD, 69
 therapist's response, 140
Anhedonia, 78,213
Anorexia nervosa, 102-104. *See also*
  Eating disorders
 belief system, 108
 psychological discussion of, 103,
  106-107

Anorexia nervosa *(continued)*
 testing for, 27
 treatment for, 104-109
Antianxiety agents, 210-211
 for delirium, 90
Anticholinergic effect, 209,212
Anticonvulsant, 210
 personality disorders, 213
Antidepressants, 33,39,56,208-210
 for anorexics, 105
 for dysphoria, 213
 personality disorders, 213
Antiparkinsonian drugs, 212
Antipsychotic drugs, for delirium, 90
Antisocial personality disorder,
  119-123. *See also*
   Psychopaths
 biological factors, 120-121
 DSM-IV, 120
 medications for, 213
 treatment of, 123-130
 treatment plans, 217
Anxiety
 and the borderline personality,
  134,136
 cognitive-behavior therapy with,
  5,13
 dementia and, 95
 and depression, 34,36
 histrionic personality disorder, 159
 impact of stress, 8
 medications for, 213-214
 personality disordered patients,
  148
 physiology of, 49-50
 stress symptom, 187
 types of, 26,50
Anxiety disorders
 and AA, 13
 familial basis of, 50
 isolation in, 24
 theories of, 49
 treatment plans, 215
Apathy, 99
Aphasia, 92

Flushed face
  GAD, 50
  panic disorder, 53,57
Fourth step, 122
Fugue states, 178
Functional impairment, personality
    disorders, 119

GAD. *See* Generalized anxiety
    disorder (GAD)
Gender equality backlash, sexual
    abuse, 174
Gender, of therapist, incestuous
    abuse, 181
Generalized anxiety disorder (GAD),
    26,50-52
Generational blurring, incestuous
    families, 176
Gestalt therapy, agoraphobic and, 60
"Get honest," 179
"Getting over," 124
Girls, incest victims, 173,174
Goldstein and Stainback,
    agoraphobic/panic disorder
    treatment, 59-60
Gradual Awakening, A, 143
Graduated exposure, 59
Grandiosity, narcissistic personality
    disorder, 160,161,162
Gratification, delay of, 122
Grief, narcissistic personality
    disorder, 162
Grieving losses, 186
Group discussion, 96,97
Group therapy, 37,81,83-84
  and agoraphobia, 60
  for anorexics, 106,107
  avoidant personality disorder, 165
  and the borderline personality,
    141-142
  paranoid personality disorder, 150
  PTSD, 68
  schizoid personality disorder, 153
  and social phobics, 66

Guided association, cognitive
    intervention, 201
Guilt
  and depression, 34,35,38
  incestuous abuse, 178,188,189
  PTSD, 67
  survivor, 69
Gulf war, 70-71

Habituation, 51-52
Haldol (haloperidol), 211
Halfway houses, 85
Hallucinations
  auditory, 11,75-76
  and the borderline personality, 137
  delirium, 23-24,89
  medications for, 211-212
  and the schizophrenic patient, 4,
    10
  schizotypal personality disorder,
    155
  transient psychosis, 213
  types of, 24
  and violence, 23
  visual, 75-76,89,90
Hallucinogens, and cognitive
    disorders, 87
Haloperidol (Haldol), 211
Head trauma, 88-89
Headaches, GAD, 50
Heart palpitations, panic disorder, 53
Helplessness, incestuous abuse, 184
Herbal teas, and panic disordered
    addict, 56
Heterocyclic antidepressants, 209
Higher power, 188
High-income families, incestuous
    abuse, 175
Hippocratic exhortation, 4
Histrionic personality disorder,
    157-158
  medications for, 213
  treatment of, 159
Homeless, schizophrenic, 73-74

Psychopath *(continued)*
  emotions of, 122
  fascination with psychopath,
    124-125
  interpersonal relations, 122-123
  treatment of, 123-130
Psychopathology, study of, 1
Psychosis
  impact of stress, 8
  isolation in, 24
  medications for, 211-212
  perceptual disturbance, 21
Psychotherapy
  and AA, 13
  and borderline patient, 135-136,
    146
  for dementia patients, 96
  and depression, 39
  study of, 1
Psychotic disorders, and dementia,
    95
Psychotic episodes, and the
    borderline patient, 136
Psychotropic agents, 206
  and AA, 13,57
  and delirium, 89
  and dual diagnosed patient, 5,12
PTSD. *See* Post-traumatic Stress
    Disorder
Public speaking, and social phobia,
    64
Pulse rate, rapid, GAD, 50
Punching bags, 83
Purging, 109,110,112,115

Questioning the evidence, cognitive
    intervention, 199

Rage
  incestuous abuse, 184
  narcissistic personality disorder,
    161
  PTSD, 69

Rationalization, pedophilia, 191
Reaction formation, OCD, 62
Reactive depression, 26
Reading, 96,97
  assignments, in treatment
    programs, 10
Reality testing, 66,79
  for schizophrenics, 82
  and violence, 23
Reassurance, GAD, 52
Reattribution, cognitive intervention,
    200
Record keeping, for bulimic patient,
    115
Recovery
  key concepts of, 186
  similarities with trauma, 186
Reframing, 69-70
Regressed pedophilia, 190-192
Relapse
  in anorexics, 109
  and borderline personality, 140
  bulimic patients, 117-118
  childhood sexual abuse, 178
  dual disorder patients, 5
  and major depressions, 32
  prevention counseling, 12
Relaxation therapy
  GAD, 51,52
  and panic disordered addict, 56
  PTSD, 72
  and social phobia, 65
Religious cults, 136
Remission, in schizophrenics, 74
Replacement imagery, cognitive
    intervention, 200
Reports
  neuropsychological, 7
  psychiatric, 6-8,10,11
  psychological, 6-8,10,11
Rescue fantasy, 182
Residual phase, schizophrenia, 78
Response prevention, 63
Retardation, 21

Order Your Own Copy of
This Important Book for Your Personal Library!

DUAL DISORDERS
Essentials for Assessment and Treatment

_____ in hardbound at $39.95 (ISBN: 0-7890-0249-3)

_____ in softbound at $19.95 (ISBN: 0-7890-0401-1)

COST OF BOOKS_____

OUTSIDE USA/CANADA/
MEXICO: ADD 20%_____

POSTAGE & HANDLING_____
(US: $3.00 for first book & $1.25
for each additional book)
Outside US: $4.75 for first book
& $1.75 for each additional book)

SUBTOTAL_____

IN CANADA: ADD 7% GST_____

STATE TAX_____
(NY, OH & MN residents, please
add appropriate local sales tax)

FINAL TOTAL_____
(If paying in Canadian funds,
convert using the current
exchange rate. UNESCO
coupons welcome.)

☐ **BILL ME LATER:** ($5 service charge will be added)
(Bill-me option is good on US/Canada/Mexico orders only;
not good to jobbers, wholesalers, or subscription agencies.)

☐ Check here if billing address is different from
shipping address and attach purchase order and
billing address information.

Signature_____

☐ **PAYMENT ENCLOSED: $**_____

☐ **PLEASE CHARGE TO MY CREDIT CARD.**

☐ Visa   ☐ MasterCard   ☐ AmEx   ☐ Discover
☐ Diners Club
Account # _____

Exp. Date _____

Signature _____

Prices in US dollars and subject to change without notice.

NAME _____

INSTITUTION _____

ADDRESS _____

CITY _____

STATE/ZIP _____

COUNTRY _____ COUNTY (NY residents only) _____

TEL _____ FAX _____

E-MAIL_____
May we use your e-mail address for confirmations and other types of information? ☐ Yes   ☐ No

Order From Your Local Bookstore or Directly From
The Haworth Press, Inc.
10 Alice Street, Binghamton, New York 13904-1580 • USA
TELEPHONE: 1-800-HAWORTH (1-800-429-6784) / Outside US/Canada: (607) 722-5857
FAX: 1-800-895-0582 / Outside US/Canada: (607) 772-6362
E-mail: getinfo@haworth.com
PLEASE PHOTOCOPY THIS FORM FOR YOUR PERSONAL USE.

BOF96